Lost Among the Birds

Lost Among the Birds

*Accidentally Finding Myself in
One Very Big Year*

Neil Hayward

BLOOMSBURY

NEW YORK · LONDON · OXFORD · NEW DELHI · SYDNEY

Bloomsbury USA
An imprint of Bloomsbury Publishing Plc

1385 Broadway	50 Bedford Square
New York	London
NY 10018	WC1B 3DP
USA	UK

www.bloomsbury.com

First published 2016

ISBN: HB: 978-1-63286-579-3
         ePub: 978-1-63286-580-9

British Library Cataloguing-in-Publication Data
A catalogue record for this book is available from the British Library

LIBRARY OF CONGRESS CATALOGING-IN-PUBLICATION DATA HAS BEEN APPLIED FOR.

2   4   6   8   10   9   7   5   3

Typeset by RefineCatch Limited, Bungay, Suffolk
Printed and bound in the U.S.A. by Sheridan

To find out more about our authors and books visit www.bloomsbury.com. Here you will
find extracts, author interviews, details of forthcoming events and the option to sign up for
our newsletters.

Bloomsbury books may be purchased for business or promotional use. For information on
bulk purchases please contact Macmillan Corporate and Premium Sales Department at
specialmarkets@macmillan.com.

To Gerri, of course.

"I see that it is by no means useless to travel, if a man wants to see something new."

—Jules Verne, *Around the World in Eighty Days*

CONTENTS

INTRODUCTION

I ONCE HEARD IT'S a good thing for your blood to move around a bit, or, to use the technical term, "circulate." I shift my weight cautiously from one frozen limb to the other, trying to get a good slosh going. My nose and ears feel pricked by a thousand bee stings, and my hands are considering applying for a more internal body position. The morning sun, hidden behind some unseen horizon, seems to have already given up for the day. The ground is concealed beneath a layer of loud crunching snow, and the surrounding woodland strains under the weight of sugarcoated branches. If my nose were doing what it's supposed to do, instead of sending annoying burning sensations to a brain that's long since figured out that, yes, it's cold, it would inform me of the surrounding sweet, lemony scent of eastern white pines and perhaps trigger a recent memory of Christmas, New Year's Eve, and the passing of yet another year. All reasons enough for me to be thankful for living in the cold, brain-numbing north.

Why didn't I come yesterday when the bird was first found? Why do I never seem to be wearing enough clothes for this kind of ridiculousness?

Did I forget to feed the cats? Did I leave my headlights on? The distant caws of American Crows yank me back from my inane mental wanderings and provide an eerie soundtrack to what could easily be the setting for some Nordic crime novel. Except there are too many witnesses toting too many optics: telescopes, binoculars, cameras. Ten other brave, shivering, ill-advised souls also seem to think coming here was a better idea than staying in bed or getting to work on time. As I approach the waiting birding flock, there's a brief exchange of nods and grunts. It's March 28, 2013, and it's been four months since I last saw them, huddled around telescopes at a windy marsh on Cape Cod to watch a rare Little Egret, a ghostly white European heron, chasing after unsuspecting fish. I know more about which birds these folks have seen (and not seen) than I do about their "real" lives. They all share the same haunted look that almost certainly crosses my own iced face—a look of desperation for a bird they all "need," like heroin addicts itching for their next fix.

And that's when the magic happens. I hear the three words beloved by birders: "There it is!" A single bird flaps high above the tree line, crossing the wide forest clearing. The anticipation momentarily arrests my breathing. With a sense of fear—*Will I miss it? Will this be the only view?*—I lift my binoculars, lock onto the robin-size bird, and see the diagnostic flash of white on the underwings. That's it! A Fieldfare! My breathing reboots, and the frozen stillness explodes with a stuttering of cameras and the oohing and aahing of grown men, like children at a fireworks display.

The collective sigh of relief is audible, as is the patting of backs. The brief appearance of this lost European bird has warmed the hearts of this morning's unusual rural gathering and defrosted the previously anxious demeanors. Now sated, we feel permission to talk, to share: "Wow, did you see the pattern on the belly?" "Did you hear it call?" "What now?! Fieldfare? Where?" "Did I really forget to turn my headlights off?" Although I've seen Fieldfares many times in the English winters of my childhood, there's something special about seeing one here in Massachusetts, my new home. I'm happy I'm still not immune to the superlatives, the laughter, and the innocent joy this morning's bird has brought.

I watch the Fieldfare hopping around at the edge of the clearing. Now joined by a group of American Robins, its transatlantic cousins, it is easy to pick out by its gray face, yellow bill, and reddish-brown wings. Rows of black chevrons march their way down from a toffee-colored throat to a bright white belly. A white line above the eye—a supercilium—gives the bird a questioning look, as if it's raising an eyebrow and asking us what all this fuss is about. And maybe it knows. Maybe it remembers taking a wrong turn and flying all the way across the wintry Atlantic, instead of apple picking across the orchards of Europe. Maybe it has noticed there's something odd about the other thrushes, the American Robins, with their brick-red breasts, slate-gray wings, and whiny accents. And maybe it realizes that it's lost, that there are no other Fieldfares here and it may never see another one again. But what it almost certainly doesn't know is that it's also a tick on my precious state list: number 371.

My Massachusetts list is one of the many birding lists I keep: year list, life list, US list, Lower 48 list, North American list, world list. I've always kept lists, not just of birds but also of countries and states. I'm the type of person who will drive one hundred miles from Colorado to the Wyoming border and then turn around—a tick (number 42, no less!) on my "states visited" list more than enough reward for the boring and selfishly gas-guzzling ride. (I once even kept lists of license plate numbers, which in the UK, where I grew up, are technically called registration plates; although it doesn't really matter what they're called—other kids will still mock you relentlessly.) But it's the birding lists that have meant the most. Some people experience serenity by seeing their home team win, others by spending time with a loved one or racing downhill on a mountain bike. For me, it's watching birds— seeing them, identifying them, wondering what they're doing, marveling at their powers of navigation, or simply taking in their exquisite beauty. I love birds.

The group slowly starts to peel away. A quieter sense of reality has replaced the earlier hysteria and the desperate fear of missing the bird. It's as if they're adults again, suddenly embarrassed to find themselves here "just" to see a bird. I look around and can almost hear their thoughts: *"What am I going to tell my boss? Car trouble? Again?" "Maybe I can still make that meeting?" "Shit—what time was I supposed to pick up Tommy?" "Wait! Did you guys really just see a Fieldfare?"* That childlike wonder of being subsumed into the natural world, of witnessing a rare event, has gone. Suddenly, it starts to feel cold again.

Unlike the others, I'm in no particular hurry to leave. I don't have to be at work. I have no meeting to be late for. And I don't have to pick up Tommy. Instead, after mentally folding up my state bird list, I have another list to get back to: the what-the-hell-am-I-going-to-do-with-my-life list. Apparently, it's not enough to see 371 birds in Massachusetts before you're forty (which, for me, is 288 days away, according to one list). Somehow, despite seeing a Resplendent Quetzal, an Ivory Gull, and a Laughing Kookaburra, I've managed to miss all the things normal adults are supposed to do: marriage, kids, career, divorce, owning more than one set of sheets. I feel like that lost Fieldfare, knowing something isn't quite right, wondering where I took the wrong turn, and fearing the future. This is my real-life list, where there are no easy ticks.

I leave the Fieldfare, which is jabbing at a clump of frosted, bloodred, bittersweet berries, and head back through the whiteness, alone, to my car and back to reality. But something is different. Like Lucy stumbling through the warm fur coats in the wardrobe and suddenly spilling out into Narnia, I am about to embark on an adventure that will take me into my own secret world populated with feathery distractions. I will spend the rest of the year birding, desperately finding as many birds as I can, which really means I'll be avoiding real life as much as I can—and I'll be successful in both. It will be a journey that takes me to the cardinal points of the continent: Barrow in the frozen north of Alaska; Newfoundland, poking out to Canada's east; the Dry Tortugas, dangling off the Florida Keys; and tiny Adak, adrift in the volcanic Aleutian chain of the Bering Sea. And a place they call New Jersey.

My quest to find as many birds as possible in one year, known to birders as a "Big Year," isn't driven by prize money or lucrative birdseed endorsements or the desire to make it into the birding record books. It is as unplanned as it is accidental. While many birders dream of doing a Big Year—finding birds across the vast continent of North America—the sensible ones experience this more as an insane nightmare. For many, the costs are prohibitive, the idea of spending months on the road unappealing, and the thought of all those extremes of temperature is, well, extreme. It's the birding equivalent of climbing all the fourteen-thousand-foot peaks, sailing around the world single-handedly, or meeting a significant other's family for the first time. And, as I'd later discover, there is no prize money.

But perhaps most surprisingly, the distraction would allow me to see real life more clearly—like when you look away from the stars to see them better. Incredibly, I'd find a way to work on both lists—the birding one and the real-life one—at the same time.

But I'm getting ahead of myself. Before all those birds, before the 250,000 miles of crisscrossing the continent looking for them all, the 55 rental cars, the 28 states, the 6 provinces, and the 56 airports, before the 15 days on boats and the 195 days away from home, before the exploding volcanoes and the deadly snakes, bears, crocodiles, and a rather menacing squirrel, before all that, there were a pair of hungry cats and a dishwasher waiting to be fed and another truly disastrous year hoping to be forgotten.

Chapter 1

NEW YEAR DESOLATIONS

YOU WOULD BE hard-pressed to find a more univer-
sally annoying date than January 1. January is named
after Janus, a Roman god with the rather unique feature of
having two faces. Being two-faced is generally considered an
unfriendly and objectionable attribute, although if anyone
could pull it off, it would be the Romans. As I think about
it, the two-faced thing is probably more symbolic than physical, since I imagine having an actual second face might be
problematic—when at a movie theater or wearing a hoodie,
for instance—although the extra set of eyes would come in
handy if Janus were a birder.

January 1 forces you, like our friend Janus, to look back and
(unless you're Leonardo da Vinci or Justin Timberlake) despair
at not having done enough with your life while simultaneously
looking forward to a future of poorly planned to-do lists (the
same ones as last year) with now one year less in which to do all
the things on them. Mix all that with a ripe hangover, and you
have the perfect recipe for a truly vindictive date. I followed
the recipe perfectly, I realized, as I cleaned up the glasses,

plates, and cheese debris from the "celebration" of the passing of yet another year. The only consolation was ignorance—I was already nine hours late for a Big Year I didn't even know I was doing. If I'd known, I suspect the dull ticking in my head would have triggered a sizable brain explosion.

I imagine Janus would scrunch up both of his faces if he were to look at this particular juncture of mine. While I've often looked back from a year's end with some regrets (could have worked harder, could have been a nicer person, how have I still not learned to salsa?), I'd be scratching my one-faced head to find a year with more regrets than 2012. Saying that it was not a good year for me would be like saying that 1188 B.C. could have gone better for the Trojans if they hadn't been so excited about that ridiculous and clearly suspicious horse gift. In 2012 I quit my job. I know, it's a cliché these days—high-powered executive quits job to be with family/ start local bakery/design vegan cat cushions—but that doesn't stop it from being a ridiculously bad idea.

I was the managing director of a successful biotechnology company founded in the UK. I'd joined the company during its start-up phase and had been with it for eleven years. As the company grew, the focus of my role changed from science that I understood to people who I only pretended to understand. By the time I moved to New England in 2005 to head up the US operations, I was so heavily involved in management, finance, and human resources that I couldn't remember Avogadro's number or even his area code.

Somewhere along the line, my excitement and passion for the once-struggling start-up was lost. Ironically, it was probably the success that killed it. Corporate investors demanded more results and higher sales targets. Office politics numbed my creativity, the continual focus on money seemed one-dimensional, and I realized I was part of a company that, if I were contemplating joining now, I probably wouldn't. In short, like most people who've ever had a job, I was bored and unhappy and needed a change.

It was easy to see the mistake as I lurched around the house, one hand stuck to my throbbing forehead, the other finding half-empty glasses and pieces of green plastic train from a game I dimly remembered playing. *What was I thinking?* In my naïveté, I'd forgotten that everyone has a midlife crisis. Was I so self-centered to think it was just me? The sensible ones (the normals) keep their heads down, distract themselves with kids and farmers' markets, and live happily ever after. But not me. I had to be different. Instead of learning new recipes for monkfish or discovering a latent liking for kale, I quit. It was May 2012, and I didn't know the first thing about starting a bakery or what the hell a cat cushion was. Do cats even like cushions? Mine are happy sitting in cardboard boxes all day. Maybe I could sell cardboard boxes?

It wasn't entirely true that I didn't have a plan. I did. It just wasn't a very good one. I started a course in architecture, only to discover it would take half a decade and require an ability to draw—and at the end of it, there would be no jobs except serving coffee in coffee shops. Next, I started a biotechnology consulting company. I enjoyed researching and writing reports from home, safely hidden from the unpredictability of people, but soon realized I missed them. I missed the camaraderie, the drama, and the daily exercise (foosball) that were part of my previous job.

And so, while I was finding more trains on the floor, clearing away slices of Camembert, and filling the dishwasher that first morning of 2013, I didn't want to look back. But looking forward was just as bad: the end of my thirties and a fortieth birthday looming at the end of the year. This wasn't at all where I'd expected to be. I had graduated from Oxford and Cambridge, leaving with a Ph.D. in the fruit fly nervous system, and had an executive position in a global multimillion dollar company. Emphasis on the "had."

I was born a generation too late. I should have been born in my parents' geological era, when you were expected to work in one mind-numbing job until you died. When did this new generation start to worry about being happy? It's so much more stressful worrying about being happy than it is sticking your head in the sand and waiting until you're old enough to retire. That's what my dad did, working in a car factory his whole life. He didn't worry that the endless repetitive tasks made no cosmic sense. No, this quest for happiness was proving to be a real pain in the ass.

"Are those train pieces reminding you of your loss last night?" a voice sniggered from the kitchen. Gerri was one of the good things that had happened in 2012, and another reason to expect 2013 to be a truly disastrous year. Our first date was over afternoon coffee and tea. We'd both got lost finding the coffee shop, which confusingly shared a name with another coffee shop in the same town. When we finally arrived at the same place, I discovered that Gerri was a tall, attractive girl with long, ash-blonde hair from a place called Ohio.

The coffee shop was in Salem, Massachusetts, a town known for its historical prejudice toward witches, and more recently for cornering the northeastern market in Halloween costumes and haunted houses. While we were standing in line, exchanging traffic and weather stories, I was haunted by my own flashbacks to another relationship that had ended two years earlier. Anna and I had been together for four years, although the slow falling apart had started almost immediately. In the years since, I'd gone over and over the possible reasons for the failure, looking for any explanation but the real one: my failure to commit.

Once we were seated with our drinks, I listened as Gerri told me of her mutually exclusive interest in giant pandas and the Tudor monarchy of England. I leaned in close to catch her soft-spoken voice above the competing sounds of "Girlfriend in a Coma" by the Smiths, coffee grinding, and clinking cups. As she fiddled nervously with a green-tea tea bag I wondered (a) if the fact that she's not a coffee drinker could be a deal breaker, and (b) if I could stretch this date into a second cup. Then I asked myself why I was even doing this. It's like getting a kitten, knowing in fifteen years' time you'll have a heartbreaking death to deal with. Would breaking up with Gerri be any easier than it had been with my last girlfriend? Or the one before that? Add to this the growing anxiety that I'm also getting older and running out of time, and the answer seemed to be a resounding no. Besides, I already had not one but two actual future kitten deaths to deal with.

And so I started the dishwasher that first day of 2013, hoping to clean away all traces of 2012, wondering what to do, and wondering when Gerri was going to get bored. I had no real job, no plan, and all the potential to ruin a new relationship. And so, I did what I've always done in difficult situations like this: I went birding.

Normally when I go birding, I go to Plum Island, a thin eleven-mile north–south strip of land in northern coastal Massachusetts. One side is relentlessly pounded by the Atlantic Ocean, while the other defines the shores of Plum Island Sound and the Parker River. There are always good birds to see here, even in the dead of winter. But I was feeling overwhelmed and restless. The fifty miles from Boston to Plum Island weren't enough. I needed to get away, and I knew the perfect place.

One of the first aha moments most birders experience is when they discover the magical link between where you are and what birds you can see. Take a trip to the beach or a woodland or a desert, and the birds are totally different. What's really different is the available food supply (the plants, insects, and animals), the microclimate, and the roosting and possible nesting conditions. In fact, so strong is the association between birds and habitat that birders are really birding habitats. Which habitat birders choose (and where that is in the country) dictates the list of species they can expect to see: nuthatches, woodpeckers, and chickadees in a woodland; and herons, egrets, and rails in a marsh. The rare, sought-after birds are found in restricted and remote habitats. And by a quirk of political mapmaking, southeast Arizona has some of the best.

While the meandering Rio Grande does a pretty good job of dividing American and Mexican habitats to the east, the Arizona border does a lousy job farther west. The southern border of Arizona, at a rather arbitrary 31°20′N, failed to keep back the four northernmost mountains of the otherwise thoroughly Mexican Sierra Madre Occidental. There are birds hopping, chirping, and flitting on those peaks that can be found nowhere else in the United States. Add to that the confluence of three other major biogeographical areas, or biomes—the Sonoran Desert, the Chihuahuan Desert, and the Rocky Mountains—all in an area the size of Maryland, and you have one of the country's birding meccas. And one that, at least for me, was far enough away from home.

I landed in Phoenix, Arizona, on January 16. I sat on the rental-car shuttle, surrounded by creaking luggage and a driver trying his best to sound authentic in his twentieth welcome of the day. None of the other tired, steely-faced travelers seemed to notice the show playing on the windows of the bus: Giant saguaro cacti lined the road, their spiky arms raised to the sun. Other succulents jostled alongside, sporting their own defensive armor. A small cluster of skyscrapers rose up above the city, transposing a perfect blue sky into a shimmering copper reflection. I was already giddy with excitement.

I'd come to Arizona to sort out my life. Over the course of ten days, I'd take stock, develop a plan for what I was going to do, and then draw up a lengthy to-do list of how to get it done. At least, that's what I told Gerri. The real reason was a Nutting's Flycatcher, the rarest bird in the country at the time. It had been found the previous fall near Lake Havasu in western Arizona. Though the bird is normally a resident of western Mexico, occasionally a restless individual will wander. I knew the feeling. It was only the sixth recorded sighting ever in the United States, and I'm sure Gerri would agree that, since I was so close to the bird, I should at least try for it.

My relaxing retreat started the next morning with a two thirty A.M. alarm followed by a three-hour drive west to the shores of Lake Havasu. I rolled into Parker, Arizona, as the dusty, sleepy, and still-dark town was waking up. A few miles short of the lake and perched on the banks of the Colorado River, Parker faces Earp, a smaller and dustier town on the California side. Neon lights flickered on and off in the windows of the gas stations lining the main strip. Stoplights, flashing yellow at this time of day, swung in the cold morning breeze.

The glass doors of the Crossroads Cafe, the only coffee joint in town, slammed behind me. A cursory scan of the habitat revealed a couple of middle-aged waitresses working the tables, teetering between brown- and orange-handled coffee pots, the slow hum of overhead fans, and the whine of country music from unseen speakers. Judging from the smell, they were doing a brisk trade in bacon and Windex. I was out of place: I was the youngest and one of the few who still had hair. As I would discover later in the day, this hot, barren, insipid land was quite the retiree vacation spot.

Standing in the takeout line, I mentally switched to breakfast plan B. This wouldn't be the place to ask if they had any of that caffe latte nonsense. Instead, I got a cup of coffee. It had been a while since I'd had one served in a polystyrene cup (presumably to protect your hands from the foul chemical brew contained within), and even longer since it came with change out of a dollar. I nursed the swilling stomach acid carefully on my way back to the car.

The Nutting's Flycatcher had been reported along the Bill Williams River, a few miles upstream from where it spills into the azure waters of Lake Havasu. Shortly after arriving at the southern reaches of the lake, I turned east onto a dirt trail that stretched out before me. Birding takes you to some off-the-road and remote places, and this felt like one of them. In the UK, if you're ever lost, you just walk a mile in any direction (except the sea) and you're bound to find a pub and a cheese sandwich. But in the United States, there are places where, if you're lost, you're really lost. The road roller-coastered east ahead of me, dusty and ungraded. After one steep incline too many, fearful I wouldn't make it back, I abandoned the car on the side of the road and walked the last half mile.

I knew from bird reports posted online exactly where the bird had been seen. I arrived at the now-famous double pylon before seven thirty A.M., my hands clawlike from the desert cold. I faced north, toward a fertile river valley lush with cottonwood trees. A light breeze rustled the branches of the nearer willows. The silence, broken only by the occasional and descending song of a Canyon Wren, added to the impression that I was in the middle of nowhere. A precipitous canyon wall rose up behind me, marking the edge of the desert. To the east, the sun marched up the last intervening rock cliff. As the first rays hit, sending tingles through my hands, the thick tangle of undergrowth in front of me exploded in a rising *wheep!* I'd never heard a Nutting's Flycatcher before, but I knew from the countless recordings I'd studied that this was the bird.

Nutting's Flycatchers can be elusive, hiding in dense foliage and waiting for insects to fly by before darting out in pursuit. I waited patiently as the calls got louder and closer. *Wheep! Wheep!* I was using my ears to triangulate the call, while my eyes were poised for any movement greater than the gentle swaying of the background leaves. And that's when it popped out, a brown missile flying to the edge of the road. It sat there on a bare mesquite branch, tilting its head, surveying me as if it had never seen a Neil Hayward before and needed one for its life list.

While roughly the size of a bluebird, Nutting's Flycatchers lack any of the exaggerated coloration of that iconic bird. It's an aficionado's bird—the enjoyment derived from the unmistakable call and the more subtle points of its plumage: a lemon-yellow belly rising to a pale-gray breast and throat, the otherwise dull brownish-gray upper parts offset by flashes of terra-cotta red along the edges of the closed wing and accentuated by reddish tones on the long tail. I imagined the bird snapping its heavy bill on insects as it flew from hidden perches on sorties for bugs. I watched the bird preen, shaking its wings and tail, and seeming to take pleasure bathing in those first warming rays of the sun. I felt a bond with this lost little traveler and was relieved not to have to share the bird with anyone else.

I watched as it flitted from the zigzag branches of one mesquite tree to another, crossing the road once to explore a willow, before disappearing into the dense vegetation from which it had first emerged. The show was over. I walked back to the car slowly. To my right, a chorus of silky Phainopepla whistles broke out from the vegetation, accompanied by the gentle drumbeat of a Red-naped Sapsucker and the jazzy improvisation of a Crissal Thrasher. The sun was already beating down. I removed my jacket, wondering that I'd ever needed it, and wiped my newly dripping brow. The afternoon typically means a lull in bird activity, so I decided to take in Lake Havasu City's local sights.

Lake Havasu City was the brainchild of Robert P. McCulloch, who correctly predicted that the eastern side of Lake Havasu, an otherwise lackluster reservoir in the middle of the searing Mojave Desert, desperately needed a city, three chainsaw factories, and a bridge imported from London. McCulloch bought the latter from a city that couldn't believe anyone would pay two and a half million dollars for a bland bridge that was sinking into the Thames and was going to be demolished anyway. It cost the entrepreneur a further seven million dollars to dismantle, ship, and reassemble the bridge, brick by numbered brick, in Arizona. Without him, I wouldn't be sucking down an iced latte in the middle of the desert.

In the winter, Lake Havasu, like Parker, is a favorite hangout for retirees. I drove past countless RV parks surrounding the lake offering "$15 a night hookups" (electricity, water, sewage).

Near the bridge, decked out in fluttering British flags, souvenir shops vied for those few tourists who weren't waterskiing, boating, or tucking into their early-bird-special fish-and-chips at faux British pubs. At some point, the biological clocks of these folks had kicked in, telling them to sell their home, buy an RV, and head to the shores of a desert lake whose main claim to fame was a leading role in the largely forgettable movie *Piranha 3D*. Maybe I'd have enjoyed the place better if I'd been here at a different time of year. The lake apparently comes to life during spring break, when thousands of college kids descend on the place, and when, I imagine, apart from the regrets, the hookups are free.

Tim arrived in Phoenix the next day. A grisly, lean fifty-something from Boston, he was a regular birding companion on my Massachusetts trips. The birding was slow in his home patch of Boston's Public Garden, and he couldn't resist a trip out west.

After I picked Tim up from the airport, we sat in our hotel room with maps, lists, and birding field guides spread before us. Tim and I were used to planning routes with military precision and finding target birds. We had competed on the same team in the Super Bowl of Birding in Massachusetts, a daylong competition to spot the most birds.

We traced our route along the crumpled map before us, plotting a course that would take us to the very southeast corner of the desert state. We'd start in Phoenix with the Rosy-faced Lovebird, an escaped species of parrot that's formed a wild breeding population and earned itself a place on the official American Birding Association (ABA) Checklist of birds. From there, we'd head south down Interstate 10, stopping at the Santa Cruz flats, a vast patchwork of irrigated fields, hoping for wintering Mountain Plovers and birds of prey such as Golden Eagles and Ferruginous Hawks. Continuing down I-10, we'd stop in Tucson to check its wetland parks. Farther south still, down Interstate 19, the saguaro cacti of the Sonoran Desert would yield to the majestic towers of the Santa Rita Mountains, the US incursion of the Sierra Madre Occidental. It was these canyons, most famously the Madera and Florida canyons, that would yield some of the rarest birds on our trip. Pushing east, we'd search the golden savanna of the sweeping San Rafael grasslands for the wintering Baird's Sparrow and then skirt the man-made Patagonia Lake, hoping for a Ruddy Ground-Dove. We would end our campaign in the Sulphur Springs Valley, bookended by two sizable bodies of water: Lake Wilcox and Whitewater Draw. In this desert land, where there was water, there would be birds.

Buddy Holly was never part of the plan. Nor was Tony Bennett. But since the Best Western in Green Valley was the only place in town to get a beer, I had little choice. For many, Green Valley, a half hour south of Tucson off Interstate 19, is the gateway to the Santa Rita Mountains. On Tuesdays, as I discovered, it's also the place to be for karaoke, provided you can remember the 1950s. Apparently, any retirees who were in Arizona and weren't hooking up around the shores of Lake Havasu were here in the 19th Hole Bar and Grille at the Best Western singing their hearts out. Tim was sensibly in his room, leaving me to read about sky islands alone while filling my mouth with a Fat Tire amber ale and plugging my ears with my not-sufficiently-fat fingers.

While the crooning continued, and a smell of burnt steak wafted from the kitchen behind the bar, I read about Clinton Hart Merriam, a naturalist from New York. He'd been studying flowers in this part of the country at the turn of the twentieth century and noticed the effect of altitude on the species he was collecting. Each thousand-foot rise in elevation, he noted, was equivalent to a journey north of three hundred miles and a resulting decrease of four degrees in temperature. And since cold air holds less moisture than warm air does, the higher you go, the wetter it gets, as that moisture falls out as precipitation. Merriam came to describe these stacked altitudinal habitats as "life zones." The mountain ranges of southeast Arizona, such as Santa Rita and Huachuca, while separated only by a short distance of low-lying desert scrub, are more truly separated by these different altitudinal habitats. They are sky islands.

We had arrived in Green Valley the day before and had an opportunity to witness this elevational change in life zones by visiting Madera Canyon, one of the most famous birding spots in the country. After a quick hop east over the interstate and passing through irrigated groves of pecans, we found ourselves in low-lying desert scrub. The Sonoran Desert is more prickly woodland than barren desert. Among the dark-green creosote, the locust tree–like mesquite bushes, and jojoba (looking for all the world like little olive trees) stand the iconic saguaro cacti, the tall men of the desert, flexing biceps on their multiple arms. While these cacti are emblematic of the Southwest deserts, they're found only here in southeastern Arizona and Sonora, Mexico. In the summer months, they flower for just twenty-four hours. The white blossom, smelling like overripe melons, is pollinated by birds such as White-winged Doves during the day and by long-nosed bats at night.

The Sonoran Desert is a rich feeding ground for birds. Our progress had been slow as we'd frequently stopped the car to look at Loggerhead Shrikes, monochrome predators hiding behind their black face masks, perching sentinel atop the cacti. Sparrows, such as Rufous-winged and Black-throated, played among the purple Santa Rita prickly pears and ropelike staghorn cholla. We continued up the road, magnetically pulled by the bluish peaks of the Santa Rita Mountains ahead. On each side of us, the spiny, tentacled arms of ocotillos waved in the cool desert breeze.

The transition to the Madrean pine-oak woodland is abrupt, as if the carpet of forest above were afraid to march any farther down the mountain road. This woodland is home to a number of species whose only foothold in the United States is here: birds such as the Elegant Trogon and the Painted Redstart and summer visitors like the Sulphur-bellied Flycatcher. With guesthouses, gift shops, feeding stations (for birds), picnic areas (for people), and short trails, it's a relaxing place to bird. Tim and I had sat in front of Kubo B&B, an alpine gingerbread house, eating our snacks while huge Magnificent Hummingbirds zipped urgently between dripping, sugary feeders. Acorn Woodpeckers, dressed like little clowns, worked the branches above our heads.

The road gave out after another half mile or so, disappearing into a series of trails that led farther still up the mountain, through ponderosa pine forests, before summiting at Mount Wrightson (9,453 feet). I was thankful we didn't need to climb any higher. In the winter many of the high-altitude species drop down to avoid the cold. I'd watched one of them, the sparrowlike Yellow-eyed Junco, hop around the feeders in front of us. Its bright psychedelic yellow eyes punctured by black irises gave the bird a somewhat demonic look. In the spring, this little gremlin would return to the mountaintop.

"Sir?"

I removed my fingers.

"Another beer, sir?"

I looked around the 19th Hole and discovered the music had stopped. I nodded to the barman, hoping it wasn't a temporary lull.

This morning we'd chosen the neighboring Florida Canyon (pronounced flow-REE-da), where the steep elevation gain is made by foot rather than by car. Consequently, it's considerably less popular than nearby Madera Canyon. If it weren't for a pair of Rufous-capped Warblers at the top of the canyon—at the time the only breeding pair this side of the Mexican border—we'd probably have been the only birders there.

From the parking lot, nestled in oak grassland, it had been a strenuous climb past ocotillos and mesquite. I ignored the Rock, Canyon, and Cactus Wrens whose calls were alternately vying for our attention, saving them for our later descent. We knew we had to be at the top as the sun first warmed the canyon, when the warblers would be most active.

We zigzagged up the dry mountain stream, pausing only to catch our breath in the thin air or to push aside overhanging branches of willow from the overgrown trail. We finally emerged into an amphitheater of crumbling rock. This was where the Rufous-capped Warblers had been reported, hopping around along the bed of the washed-out stream, their presence revealed by frequent *tik tik* contact calls as the birds keep in touch with each other.

"Yeah, so I just heard the bird," a voice said.

Evidently, we weren't the first ones on the scene.

"If you stay with me, I'm sure we'll get it again," the voice continued.

As well as identifying birds, birders spend an inordinate amount of time trying to identify one another. *Have we met on some chase before? Is this a migrant (visiting birder) or a resident (local)? Are they an expert, an intermediate, or a beginner? What equipment are they carrying? Can I believe what they're telling me?* A quick and accurate identification is crucial in answering the latter question.

This particular birder was balding, was in his mid- to late fifties, and towered high above us (neither Tim nor I quite reach five feet ten). An expensive pair of binoculars hung from his neck, and a large camera lens from his shoulder. None of this separated him from 90 percent of other birders. I needed to hear more of his deep, resonant call.

"Did you see the Black-capped Gnatcatcher on the way up?" he grunted.

No, we had not! I would have loved to see a Black-capped Gnatcatcher! It was on our target list of rarities (and would remain there long after we left Arizona). We had, however, seen the more common Black-tailed Gnatcatcher.

"We had a Raven on the way up," I countered. A rather pathetic offering, but it reflected our limited birding this morning.

"Raven, you say? Well, I just had a Chihuahuan Raven fly over here," he said. Checkmate.

Chihuahuan Ravens are rare here and difficult to separate from the more common Ravens. Over the course of the next five minutes we were subjected to a list of birds the guy had seen that morning. Remarkably, for every bird we'd seen, he'd seen a rarer version. For our Lesser Goldfinch, he'd seen Lawrence's Goldfinch. Our Ladder-backed Woodpecker was trumped by his Red-breasted Sapsucker. And so, finally confident in my birder identification, I headed on above the amphitheater, hoping to find the bird higher up, and to lose Baldy farther down.

In short order, I was successful in both. I heard the warbler first—a quiet, smacking *tik tik tik* ahead of me. I sat down on the rocky path, after checking for snakes, cacti, and other bitey things, and waited. After a few minutes, a fluorescent yellow throat popped out from the undergrowth. I raised my binoculars and the rest of the bird soon followed. I could see that the throat was connected to a rich chocolate-brown head, broken by a thick white line above the eye. The short olive-brown body terminated in a long tail, often held erect as the bird flitted or jumped from one stem to another. The warbler stayed low, skulking in the weedy undergrowth, presumably in pursuit of breakfast insects. For any new bird I see, I like to take in the plumage details—the colors and shapes—and get a feel for the behavior: how the bird moves and holds itself. After feeling sated, and remembering my birding responsibility, I headed back down to find Tim and to show Baldy what an actual Rufous-capped Warbler looks like.

"Yeah, that's exactly what I saw earlier. Knew they'd be up here," he said.

You're welcome.

Going downhill was harder. With the excitement of the chase behind us, I was more conscious now of looking out for rattlesnakes (none) as well as Black-chinned Sparrows (check), and Rock, Canyon, and Cactus Wrens (check, check, and check). As we stopped briefly to navigate a stone dam, we looked up and spotted a giant Golden Eagle leisurely soaring over the canyon. I was suddenly grateful for my telescope, which I'd lugged all the way up the canyon. I aimed it at the large, planklike wings, and could make out the tawny head, which moved from side to side, scanning the hillside below for lunch.

"And now Betty and Johnny will be performing 'Bird Dog' by the Everly Brothers." But not before I pay my tab, run to my room, and dream of yellow chocolate warblers.

Whitewater Draw, the last stop on our trip, sits at the southern end of the Sulphur Springs Valley, only fifteen or so miles from the Mexican border. This onetime cattle ranch is an important Arizona wintering site for Sandhill Cranes, graceful, long-necked birds that breed in Arctic Canada and Alaska and spend the winter down here, picking at the stubbly cornfields.

As I drove south down the dusty Codman Road, paralleling the busier valley highway to the east, Tim pointed out the Lark Buntings and Yellow-headed Blackbirds vying for spots along the fence posts, the latter screaming their rusty, screeching calls at us as we sped past. The long, roadside grass would occasionally yield to reveal glimpses of shimmering water beyond.

As soon as I opened the car door in the wildlife refuge parking lot, I could hear them: rattling, trumpet calls echoing across the fields. Above us, cranes by the hundreds were gently gliding in toward the water of the draw—gray concords, necks outstretched, their solid wings ending in darkly splayed fingers. They alighted into the shallow pond as if they were made of nothing but paper, and magically the hundreds above us morphed into thousands on the ground. The vast, shallow reaches of this wetland were carpeted by cranes noisily pecking for food, jostling for space, and grooming their neighbors. I noticed many of them were stained rusty ochre, a result of preening with muddy bills from iron-rich pools. In what few spaces remained, bright white Snow Geese sat looking puzzled and claustrophobic.

I could have spent the entire day there, as many birders and non-birders do, mesmerized by these engaging birds. Unfortunately, I couldn't because we were here to find a Ruddy Ground-Dove—a tiny dove that's widespread in Latin America and very rarely seen here. We'd spent two days chasing one at Patagonia Lake. "Chasing" is a technical birding term, which, while sometimes describing an intense physical pursuit of a bird, can often, as with the Patagonia

Lake bird, also mean sitting still and waiting. Both strategies can result in failure. This was to be our third and final try.

After four hours, Tim wanted to leave. There's a certain type of insanity that comes from walking around the same hundred-square-foot area scanning the same bushes, the same trees, and the same patches of grass, looking for a bird you know to be there. It's like dropping a contact lens on the floor, dropping to your knees, and not understanding why you can't find it. As you gradually increase the radius from the presumed drop zone, you start wondering whether it somehow rolled into the next room or bounced back into your eye, or whether you even wear contact lenses in the first place. Meeting a local who'd photographed the bird in this very spot just before we'd arrived also wasn't helping our mood. Tim and I looked like we hadn't slept for a week, which was almost true. We were dripping in sweat and bug-eyed from searching. My stomach, long since done with the morning's paltry muffin, was growling. But I refused to give up hope.

Birders are superstitious. They commonly believe that a bird will show itself in the next five minutes and you'll miss it if you leave. Having another birder give up and leave before you do (the sacrificial lamb) is a popular way of luring the bird out. Telling the bird this is its last chance and then you're going home, never to return again, and you couldn't care less about such an evidently boring bird anyway, can often embarrass the bird into showing itself. I mouthed this final invocation and set off for five more minutes of grass stomping.

Without thinking, I headed in the direction of the pond next to our tiny search area. I don't know why neither of us had noticed that pond, despite four hours of searching. It wasn't hidden, and it was right next to the water pump where the bird had frequently been reported. Maybe there was some unwritten rule telling us the bird couldn't be in such an obvious spot. As I reached the pond, the cranes, which I'd largely ignored all day, continued to stream overhead, their guttural honking sounding like a Frenchman pronouncing his *r*'s. I was wondering how much it would cost (both financially and to my new relationship) to delay my flight home by a day, when my heart stopped as four doves exploded from the grass under my feet. Four—the magic number! (The Ruddy Ground-Dove had been seen hanging out with three scaly and more common Inca Doves.) So this is where the bastards had been hiding all day, I thought, watching the two idiot humans walk through the grass not twenty feet from them!

I followed the birds to a bush at the side of the pond and frantically waved Tim over. Peering into the undergrowth, we could just make out the small, plump birds. In addition to the longer-tailed and scaly Inca Doves, a tiny Ruddy Ground-Dove sat looking alert and embarrassed. The pale brownish-gray head and back framed a pale-gray face from which popped a beady black eye. This subtly plumaged bird was a female; the males are bright reddish-brown. The wings and scapular feathers covering the shoulders were spotted with large, seemingly random dots. I watched the bird wriggle deeper and deeper into the bush before it rather conclusively disappeared out of sight.

I'm normally elated at seeing a new rare bird. The high can last for days as I relive the experience. But this one had sucked the energy and emotions out of me. The joy this time was more of a relief that the chase was over. I was tired and hungry, and it was time to go home.

Gerri was waiting for me as I touched down at Boston's Logan Airport. As I emerged through the same glass doors that had sucked me in more than a week ago, I smacked into the cold wall that is a winter morning in New England. The air smelled of spent cigarettes and burnt coffee. Khiva Cat was in the backseat, going wild with all the new sights.

I was happy to see Gerri and happy to be home. Yet I couldn't help feeling I'd lost more by leaving Arizona behind me than I'd gained by returning. By the time we emerged from the Sumner Tunnel and were hugging the shore of the Charles River along Storrow Drive, all the serenity and calm I'd felt in Arizona had drained out of me. Out there, I'd found a way to turn off the cogs that normally race inside my head, always coming up with something new to worry about (skin cancer, spontaneous internal combustion, mankind losing the recipe for almond croissants). In the desert, with birds to find, there's no space for any of that. To break the silence, I tried to explain to Gerri what it was like seeing the Nutting's Flycatcher, but I must have sounded like a kid returning from the first day of school, at a loss for the right words to properly express the experience.

I had seen 187 bird species in Arizona. The website eBird.org told me that was more than anyone else had seen there so far that year. If only life were that simple—having a target list, a strategy, and then a leaderboard showing your results (preferably with you at the top). I already felt unsettled back home, and hearing about other rare birds didn't help. Like many birders, I had signed up to receive e-mail alerts from across the continent. Anytime a rare bird was found, I'd get an e-mail with instructions on how to find it. It was the ultimate distraction. Nearly a thousand birds have been seen in the United States and Canada. You could almost make a life out of that kind of distraction. Couldn't you?

If there were a scale for bird awesomeness, let's say from one to ten, then the adult male Red-flanked Bluetail would score a stonking ten. The top of the bird (the head, wings, and tail) is a shimmering, iridescent blue. (In young birds the blue is restricted to the tail, which they impatiently flick up and down.) The breast is white, as are the thick eyebrows. The sides, or flanks, are a rich orange-red, like the yolk of a cage-free hen. In anyone's book, it's an "oh wow" bird. They live in the dark forests of northern Siberia all the way west into Scandinavia. Sometimes young birds lose their way during migration and end up on islands in the Bering Sea. This year, one had made it all the way to downtown Vancouver, British Columbia. It was the first chaseable mainland record, and birders descended on the city from far and wide.

I waited until the day after I returned from Arizona.

"You're going away again?" Gerri asked.

I knew that look. I could see her slipping away, wondering what this all meant.

"To Vancouver?" she said.

I knew this wasn't what normal people do. I could get away

with one trip, to take time out to think about my life. But another?

"It's just a short trip," I explained. "Then I'll be back for good. Sweetie."

I almost believed the lie myself. It's easy to lie when you're with someone new. They haven't figured out all your little "tells"—the rise in your voice, the hand to the face.

And so, the airport pickup was reversed five days later—Khiva Cat on the backseat, happy to be out of her prison again (Sally Cat has a more sensible fear of cars), and my bags slightly heavier this time with winter gear. I knew this was wrong—this wasn't how adults solved problems. But I needed that fix again. I needed to get back to the highs of Arizona. In some weird logic, I told myself that seeing a Red-flanked Bluetail would help. After that I would stop and really focus.

"See you soon," I said, waving goodbye.

I could see behind Gerri's bluish-gray eyes that I was already losing her. I picked up my bags, turned, and disappeared between the giant sliding doors.

My bird count at the end of January 2013: 252

Chapter 2

TRASH BIRDS

"R EASON FOR VISITING THE United States?" Apparently having a US passport and living in the United States didn't make it obvious enough, but thankfully the sensible cell in my brain stopped me from saying so.

"I'm returning from a trip to Vancouver." I could barely make out the officer's face, the upper part eclipsed by a dark blue cap and the lower part lost behind a large, wandering mustache. He looked at me and then looked at a screen with some green writing I couldn't make out. And then he looked back at me. His mustache twitched as if suddenly coming to life.

"You came through last night," he noted. "What's the reason for such a short trip?"

"I came to see a bird—a Red-flanked Bluetail. It's the first one ever seen in Canada."

By his expression I could tell that not only had he not, in fact, heard of the Red-flanked Bluetail, but also he didn't seem to think it was a valid reason for crossing a border. His border.

"Don't we have enough birds here?" he countered. "Is there something wrong with our birds?"

To the left and right of me, barriers alternately nodded up and down, squeezing out cars into the United States. I could feel the weight of the traffic stuck behind me and imagined the news headline: ASIAN BIRD WREAKS A BIT OF HAVOC ON BORDER CROSSING.

"It's a very rare bird. They're normally only found in Asia." None of this was helping. Birding may be odd and at times embarrassing, but I don't remember it ever being criminal, which is how I felt as I sat in my rental car, suddenly desperate to go home. "Other people from America have come to see it too," I said feebly.

He turned to face me, as I warranted further scrutiny. I could make out his eyes, piecing dark orbs buried in their sockets. I watched as a questioning eyebrow inched up his brow, caterpillar-like, until it disappeared beneath the rim of his cap.

"And what do you do for a living, sir?" he asked.

Why does everyone seem to care what I do? Is there a wrong answer besides trafficking guns, smuggling narcotics, or being a lawyer? I plumped for the most accurate and hoped for no follow-up questions.

"I'm a consultant. In biotechnology," I said. "I live in Boston."

I could see from the slight tilt of his head that he didn't trust my accent, which admittedly doesn't sound like it's from Boston—or, for that matter, anywhere in the United States. I could imagine him making the quick mental calculations:

flying from Boston to Seattle, then driving up to Canada for one day to see a bird. But it's always the crazy stuff that turns out to be true.

"Okay. Welcome back, sir," he said. "Hope you got your poo-tail bird."

I'd landed in Seattle the previous night during an unusually heavy rainstorm. Interstate 5 northbound was uglier than its normal ugliness, as though the wrath of some angry god were being unleashed upon this narrow coastal strip. My attention was glued to the brake lights of the car in front, alternately blinking on and off as each squall of rain lashed across the road, sending the driver into a mild panic of renewed braking. The wipers on my car were flapping with such a vengeance that I was afraid they'd fly off at any minute, leaving the windshield behind to quickly drown. I looked for the reassuring landmarks of the Space Needle and skyscrapers, but all were lost in the steamy downpour.

The rain was dialed back to a weak drizzle the next morning when I arrived at Queen's Park in southeast Vancouver, a large green rectangle near the banks of the Fraser River. The Red-flanked Bluetail had been reported in the quieter northwest corner of the park, away from the more open and busy tennis courts, soccer field, baseball diamond, and petting zoo. I stepped from the car into a dark cathedral of western red cedars. I craned my neck to make out the high ceiling above, supported by impossibly tall columns of striated and gnarly gray trunks. Few plants grew from the light-starved floor, otherwise carpeted in soft needles and fallen branches. The wet, aromatic scent of cedar was overpowering. I could see why the bird, usually at home in the dark forests of Siberia, had chosen this spot in which to hide.

Once my eyes had adapted to the gloom, I started to notice movement. A small bird, erect like a European Robin, was hopping around on the ground and flitting up to the bare lower branches of the cedars. When it wasn't moving, it was pumping its bluish tail up and down. Through my binoculars I could make out a streak of orange along the sides of its body. It was the bird that I'd traveled 2,500 miles to see, but starved of light, the flat colors lacked all the iridescence I was expecting. Somehow the dark silence and the oppressive weight of the trees above had squeezed out all the personality from this little fellow.

While I've discovered that so many elements affect how I feel when watching a bird—the lighting, colors, behavior, weather, quality of the company—it's often the cryptic, subtle birds that have more to offer: those that take longer to figure out. *Like Gerri, perhaps?* I watched the bird for another ten minutes, trying to feel more before finally giving up. This bird would remain in the park for another two months and be seen by hundreds of visiting birders until it disappeared into the dark silence.

Vancouver was a double whammy for birders at the time, as another rarity, a Brambling, had recently taken up residence. Bramblings are orange-and-black finches from Europe and Asia, and although not as rare as the bluetail (Bramblings are one of the more common Asian birds to end up lost on our shores), it was attracting its own crowd of devotees. It was only a short drive from the bluetail to the Brambling, which was visiting a residential feeder.

As I pulled up to a dense neighborhood of homes I remembered how much I dislike this type of birding—walking around a neighborhood, peeking into peoples' yards with a pair of binoculars. At best, I feel like an out-of-place idiot; at worst, like some kind of sex offender. Neither is a particularly good feeling, and I always hope I can get the bird quickly and leave. By the time the black-and-orange bird flew in, chowed down on some Nyjer seed, and flew out again, it was forty minutes and several twitching curtains into my discomfort zone.

I saw Gerri's name flash on my phone and immediately felt guilty. She was calling to ask how the trip was going. She was friendly and it was a short call, but as with all important relationship conversations, it's the stuff that's not said that's important. I could sense that she was upset that I hadn't already called her. For some reason I have a mental block in communication. I can remember to check in for flights twenty-three hours and fifty-eight minutes before departure, and to update a Listserv, an e-mail list for birders to share messages about local bird sightings, with a bird I've just seen, but I can't remember to tell [insert current girlfriend's name] what I'm doing. I think about telling Gerri that it's hard to multitask— to be absorbed in the bird and to think about her at the same time, like they're different brain-hemisphere activities that are mutually exclusive. But I don't tell her any of this, as I suspect she'd wonder why the birds always seem to come first. Instead I lie and tell her I've only just gotten phone reception.

The truth was I had been thinking of Gerri a lot: on the flight to Seattle while looking down on the cloud cushions below, while driving around Vancouver, and when I couldn't fall asleep at the cheap motel that smelled of damp cardboard and air freshener. But I wasn't thinking of Gerri herself as much as I was thinking of her as an extension of my previous girlfriend. It had been two years since Anna found somewhere else to live. I watched, helpless to know what to do or say as the books, kitchen supplies, and souvenirs were unshuffled and returned to their original owners. I knew something bad was happening, but the pain was so numb that it felt like I was watching it happen to someone else. Now, the numbness was finally wearing off and I was feeling what I should have felt then. Except, of course, it was too late to do anything about it. Anna was gone.

Gerri had taken me to meet her family in Cincinnati at Christmas. In two weeks we would go to Calgary to visit my friends, which had suddenly become *our* friends. We'd been dating for (only) seven months, and I was on the relationship express. It was like last time, when the initial dates suddenly morphed into discussions about growing the relationship and ensuring that we're "moving forward." But when was that decision made, that there was now a relationship and that we'd both agreed this was worth growing? Is this another thing that's just understood? Either way, I'm never told and never seem to know. I'm so indecisive that I hate breaking up, which means I get trapped. It's like sitting in a plane before departure. You can see the flight attendants getting ready to close the doors, and you have a premonition about a stowed bomb or an engine failure or being surrounded by screaming, puking babies, and you think about standing up and running for that door, shouting, "I'm sorry, I need to get off!" But you never do. Instead, you watch as the door slides closed, with a slight hiss of air as the seal is made, and sit back to enjoy a ride you no longer want to take.

And so I had been thinking about Gerri, but however much time I had, I never seemed to have enough for any of it to make sense.

I'd booked my trip to the Pacific Northwest with plenty of leeway in case it took longer to find the Vancouver rarities, but seeing both the Brambling and the bluetail in a single day left me with four days to spare before my return flight. And so when Gerri rather reasonably asked whether I was coming straight home, I told her (without checking) that it was too expensive to change my ticket and that since I was there, I could do some more birding. Besides, there was a pelagic trip that could be fun.

It's often a surprise to non-birders that there are boat trips, called pelagics, catering specifically to birders. If you're not a birder and looking for a fun, relaxing, sightseeing trip, you should never get on one of these boats. These trips frequently go out in bad weather, the loudspeakers that announce birds prevent you from getting any sleep, the food is terrible, and they lack basic espresso facilities. Using your binoculars on the boat is like birding from a moving car, and as you're shaken from wall to wall, it's impossible to use the toilet with any degree of accuracy. But since the American Birding

Association's listing region extends two hundred miles offshore, where there are an annoying number of birds hiding, birders are obligated to venture seaward.

This particular pelagic boat trip departed from Westport, a tiny fishing community 130 miles southwest of Seattle. I met a gaggle of twenty or so birders lined up at the windy dock, ready to board a boat that looked comically too small for twenty birders. As I was thinking about why I'm almost always late for these departures (a combination of not being a morning person and having to find coffee) and thinking I ought to be worried rather than amused by the size of the boat, a friendly face emerged from the crowd—Jim McCoy. Gerri has gradually met birders on our trips around Massachusetts and has often marveled at the kindness of the folks. Maybe caring about birds makes you warmhearted, or it attracts those with an interest in something other than themselves. Whatever the reason, Jim McCoy would be the perfect ambassador for that group. He pumped my hand, happy and surprised to see me on the other side of the country. He towered over me, a woolly hat covering what I knew to be a perfectly bald head. The kindness of his smile matched that of his eyes.

Pelagics are the true chocolate boxes of birding—you never know what you'll get. And while the season plays an important role, there always seem to be mysterious rarities roaming the oceans, as if they haven't read the *National Geographic Field Guide to the Birds of North America* and don't know where they're supposed to be.

After leaving the relative protection of Gray's Harbor, we plowed west over choppy waves into the Pacific Ocean. Even at the captain's enthusiastic pace we couldn't outrun the sun, which rose quickly behind our shoulders, giving color and depth to an angry, black, and foaming sea. Jim and I caught up on local birding gossip while watching large flights of Common Murres, brown-and-white torpedo-shaped birds, whizz past.

The Pacific was cold, despite our hats, gloves, and thermal underwear. There is no Gulf Stream, as in the Atlantic, to heat its coastal American waters. The currents swirl clockwise, as if a plug has been pulled somewhere near Hawaii. The waters in which we sailed had flowed north off the coast of Japan up through the Kuril Islands and were divided by the giant hanging scimitar that is the Russian peninsula of Kamchatka: Turn to the left and you're in the Sea of Okhotsk. Turn to the right and you're cooled by the icy waters of the Bering Sea to the north, sifted through the volcanic Aleutian chain. The coasts of Alaska, British Columbia, and then Washington force the numbing current southward.

The best birding is often found in deep water, where underwater mountains and seemingly bottomless canyons cause upwellings of seabed nutrients, or along the edges of the continental shelf. Our destination was Gray's Canyon, which sits at the edge of that shelf about thirty-five miles offshore. Of course, you can't see any of that underwater topography, and so when we eventually arrived, it was hard to picture either the canyon or the steep cliffs of the shelf below. The sea looked like all the other bits of sea. The whitecapped Mount Olympus on the horizon was the only reminder that land was near and that we were not desperately lost.

It was the boat's first pelagic run of the new year, and I imagined today's birders were excited for their first 2013 seabird sightings. Along with a life list, most birders keep a year list—the birds seen in a calendar year—resetting their bird count back to zero on January 1 and starting all over again. Suddenly House Sparrows, Starlings, Blue Jays, and Cardinals are all new ticks.

"Albatross! Six o'clock!" screamed one of the guides.

Since there aren't any trees, buildings, or rocks to use as markers, pelagic birders rely on the clock system—twelve is straight ahead (bow), six behind (stern), three to the right (starboard), etc. I could almost feel the boat lurch to six o'clock as a wave of birders headed for the stern. I joined them, raising my binoculars as a dark, horizontally stretched profile appeared in front of us.

The cylindrical body was held aloft by long, thin wings, inches from the cresting waves below. I pushed my hips into the wet metal railing to counter the strong pitching of the boat and suppressed a gag reflex as I was suddenly over-powered by the smell of chum, the bloody remains of fish that we were using to attract the birds. As the albatross glided closer, I could make out a dark eyebrow and a paleness to the front of the head, where the long, hooked bill smacked into the face. Apart from flashes of white in the primaries, at the very end of those impossibly long wings, it was entirely brown. This bird, a Black-footed Albatross, like all albatross, is a nomad of the sea, coming to shore only to breed. We saw several more as we wove along the canyon edge before returning to shore.

After saying goodbye to Jim, I made my way back to Seattle, frequently stopping at the tiny, drive-through coffee shacks that are mercifully dotted all over Washington State. I thought how much Gerri would have liked the day. Or rather, how much I would like it if Gerri would have liked it. There was something important in her understanding this madness, in knowing about Ancient Murrelets (four flying left at nine o'clock!) and gray, soccer-ball-shaped Cassin's Auklets (flying off the bow!). I'd spent so much of my time birding alone, even when ostensibly birding in a group, that I wanted to share this with someone else.

"I think we've tried this alley already," Gerri said.

We definitely had: twice. In fact, we'd tried every street, park, and back alley in a two-mile-square radius. I was hoping Gerri hadn't noticed, and we could keep "discovering" new streets to check.

"You heard the man," I said. "They're here. Probably another five minutes and we'll get them."

The man was Terry Poulton, and the bird was a Gray Partridge. The five minutes were in addition to the three hours of not seeing any. Terry had posted to a local Listserv that these birds regularly come to his yard. "Regularly" apparently didn't mean every day.

When normal people go on a skiing vacation, they go skiing, or they hang out with their friends who've gone skiing. Birders can't be trusted to do normal stuff when they go on vacation. Instead they poke around in local woods and marshes, or in today's case the back alleys and trash cans of Calgary.

It was our third day in Calgary, a large, modern city tucked into the foothills of the towering Canadian Rockies. To the east of the downtown skyscrapers, golden prairies (now hidden by snow) unfurled across Alberta, continuing to provinces beyond. Our friends Edward and Georgina had recently bought a condo here. I knew Georgina from the UK, where we'd worked together and had both graduated with a Ph.D. from Cambridge. Her husband, Edward, was one of those rare Canadians who'd fallen out of love with the country. He'd moved to the UK, married Georgina, fallen out of love with the UK, and now spent most of his time working in the Middle East. He'd evidently rediscovered his love for Canada and readopted his homeland. Edward and Georgina had two kids, of the rare, adorable kind: Alicia and Hattie. We arrived with Bill and Jackie, our best friends from Massachusetts.

It was my first time to Calgary. On our four flights from Boston, every Canadian airport layover looked the same: mountains of snow held back by modern, impersonal glass concourses, each efficiently signed with a European-style sans serif. I stuck my face against each of those glass windows, looking for Snowy Owls outside but never spotting any. It's the curse of the birder to never stop birding, however remote the possibility of seeing or hearing a bird. Our eyes and ears are always primed. It's a kind of personal schizophrenia, hearing voices no one else can hear and seeing ghosts among the trees that somehow the normals ignore or can't perceive.

A week before arriving, while Gerri had been looking up restaurants and scoping out places to run (oh yes, as well as not drinking coffee, she runs every day—two things I have no

interest in doing), I was signing up for the Alberta birding
Listserv. That's how I heard about Terry and his remarkable
Gray Partridges. These birds were introduced from Europe.
They were common enough in the agricultural fields around
the English village where I grew up—small, plump, football-
shaped birds with orange faces and cryptic gray-brown bodies.
They were released here in the early 1900s as game birds and
have since spread throughout western Canada and the
northern United States. Although I had seen these birds many
times in Europe, I had never seen them in North America.
The prospect of a new ABA tick is why we were walking
around the suburbs of Calgary and not skiing with our friends.
I thought it would be a quick, fun introduction to birding for
Gerri, and it was slowly becoming neither of those.

Chasing birds, especially difficult, or better still, non-
existent ones, gives you plenty of time to reflect. I imagine it's
akin to that deep focus and expansive thinking you get while
performing a downward-facing dog. Until you've birded, you
have little idea how exhausting looking can be. It's not like
the looking we do all day: checking out what's in the fridge or
watching cats doing stuff on the Internet. It's more of a
searing, burning gaze into all the dark recesses of the habitats
in front of you. In the backstreets of Calgary it's not enough
to look at the interesting stuff—the nodding reindeer in the
front yard, last year's unwise inflatable snowman purchase, or
the occasional running pants jogging in front of you. You
needed to look everywhere, ever vigilant for the slightest
movement. And it's also a lot easier to focus if you're not
hungover.

The previous night we had gone for dinner in Banff, a village nestled in the Canadian Rockies. With a castlelike hotel set amid forested peaks, it reminded me of Scotland but with more American tourists, more caffe lattes, and fewer bagpipes. Gerri had looked thrilled to be there—more thrilled, I noted, than she did when looking for partridges. We'd been skiing all day, and based on our rosy-flushed cheeks, messed-up hair, and hobbling gaits, we were exhausted.

The restaurant was the Swiss chalet–type Grizzly House where you can cook your own food. The menu featured a menagerie of fondue options: Alberta beef, snake, alligator, and snails, all of which looked like a giant fon-*don't* to vegetarians like Gerri and me.

Edward sat next to Georgina, who sat opposite me. It was the first time I'd seen her since I left my job. She's my age, with long, blondish-brown hair, most of which was hidden by the ski-jacket she was still wearing. Georgina's kind, patient face lit up when she talked to Alicia and Hattie, who sat at the end of the table.

Bill and Jackie sat to one side of us, debating whether to cook reindeer or elk. Or both. Tall and muscular, with closely cropped hair, Bill is thoughtful, taking his time to think through ideas and ask questions. Bill and I had worked together in the company's US office and had been friends since I moved here, despite the strains of occasionally disagreeing about decisions at work. When I left the company, Bill got my job, and the world didn't meet its end. Life went on, and meanwhile, I lost the co-workers that made work and life bearable.

The table soon came alive with various slices of meat and vegetables sizzling on hot stone slabs. The lights flickered around us, and we were warmed by a comforting cloud of friendly talk. Georgina updated Bill and me about gossip from the UK office, while Edward made Jackie laugh. Her rich, nutty brown hair hid her shoulders and framed a warm, friendly smile. Like Edward, Jackie was happy not to be talking about a company that took up too much of Bill's time and thoughts. I watched as she glanced back at Bill, who seemed to predict this perfectly, meeting her gaze and communicating some secret. I had gone to Bill and Jackie's wedding five years before and even if he didn't regularly tell me, I could see by those brief glances that they're still in love.

I turned back to join the conversation with Georgina and Bill. Georgina and I used to fight a lot in those early days. We both cared passionately about the direction of the start-up, which, combined with doses of pettiness (mainly me) and being threatened by the ability of the other (entirely me), made for a stormy relationship. As she was telling us about her staff, alternately laughing and rolling her eyes, I suddenly wondered whether she was happy that Edward had bought a condo— even one with sweeping views over downtown Calgary, modern leather furniture, and a doorman. She was raising her kids in an English village while he was commuting between the Middle East and Canada. How does that work, I wondered?

Hearing about the company, about people I knew and had hired, was bittersweet. I was reminded of the industrious and fast-paced world I'd left behind—a world that may have seemed empty and mindless at the time, but one that provided structure and busyness. While listening to Bill tell Georgina about the new office space, I realized I'd found an even greater and lonelier emptiness. And one entirely of my own making.

I made it all the way to dessert before the inevitable happened.

"So, what's your big plan now, Neil?" Edward bellowed from the end of the table. Georgina flashed him an angry look. It was as though we'd all been pretending everything was like it used to be.

I didn't know how to say that I didn't know, that I didn't have a big plan. I had always known what was next: degree, Ph.D., job, house, cats, matching cushions, and, if I was lucky, a relationship. I was scared not so much of telling my friends that I was lost as of hearing myself say it. I also realized that I didn't want to disappoint them by telling them the truth— that there was no grand plan, not even a back-of-the-restaurant-napkin plan.

In reality, I didn't have to say anything, because while I was thinking these thoughts and taking too long to answer, I could see their faces turn blank, as if someone had pressed pause on the evening. Before I uttered a word, I could hear how stupid it sounded.

"I'm doing a lot of birding again," I said. "I'm really enjoying all the time I have for birding."

I didn't expect them to understand. I didn't understand it myself. But it was as close to the truth as I could put into words. I could feel something healing when I was birding, which meant there was more pain to soothe. I didn't know whether it was from my last relationship, or the loss of my job and the identity that went with it, or the confusion over what was going to happen with Gerri. But I knew that I needed this analgesic now and that birding was playing some important role in my life. But saying that would probably sound even more stupid.

"Maybe you should do a Big Year! I'm sure you could beat Owen Wilson!" Jackie said. She and Bill had watched *The Big Year*, a movie in which three birders ostensibly compete to see the most species across the continent. Owen Wilson's character is based on the real-life Sandy Komito, whose 1998 Big Year netted an incredible 748 species.

"Do I look like a freakin' idiot?" I asked Jackie. It was pretty much the same response I'd given to Gerri after she'd read Mark Obmascik's book *The Big Year*. Gerri had asked me then, rather alarmingly, if I'd ever do that. (Actually, I think she'd asked if I'd ever do that *to her*, since being on the road for an entire year is as much inflicted on others as experienced by the birder.) I'd told her not to worry: no, I would never do that.

"And even if I wanted to do that," I said, feeling like I hadn't convinced them yet, "it's not really possible these days." I explained there was something special, something unique about the 1998 Big Year. It was a year in which an unprecedented number of rare birds were seen on Attu, a tiny island at the far western end of the Aleutian chain of Alaska and a favorite haunt for rarity hunters. Post–El Niño storms had blown in birds from nearby Asia that spring, the species and numbers of which many American birders had never before seen—and may never see again. The US Coast Guard abandoned the island shortly after 1998, and the airfield fell into disrepair. The record was safe.

"Well, couldn't you try for at least seven hundred?" said Jackie, trying, I think, to be helpful.

I was not happy with where this was going. As much as I was glad *The Big Year* made birding look fun and undoubtedly attracted more people to the hobby, I was annoyed that it also gave the impression this is all birders do. It's not. Birding is about the birds, being with the birds, not the numbers.

"Only twelve people have ever seen more than seven hundred species," I explained, trying to contain my frustration that this conversation was still going on, "and they would have spent months planning their Big Years."

As the coffees arrived, some smelling sweet with rum, the conversation turned to Bill and Jackie's upcoming trip to New Orleans, and I was left to reflect on failing at something I hadn't even started. I felt worse, as secretly I had been dreaming of a Big Year—of seeing the continent and spending more time with birds. And if I were ever to do one, this would be the year, as next year I would have figured out my life and would (I hoped?) never have the time again. But it was already the end of February. As I looked around the table at the two married couples, the kids suddenly awake and interested in their dad's dessert, I realized that a Big Year was just one of the many things for which I was already too late.

I didn't know whether it was the red wine, the rum in the coffee, or the port when we got back to the condo in Calgary, but it was not making the partridge hunt any easier.

"Maybe we should take a break," Gerri said. "Come back later and feel more refreshed?"

She was bored. Even in the fresh, romantic snow, city trash cans were still city trash cans. If this didn't go well, it was going to be hard to convince her to join me at the sod farms, sewage plants, and trash dumps that form the mainstay of many birding trips. While Gerri and I were eating lunch, an often forgotten concept when I'm birding alone, I imagined our four friends up in the mountains, perhaps meeting for hot chocolate after their brisk morning of skiing.

We'd skied that first full day in Calgary, at Lake Louise. Gerri was a beginner, unsteady on her now suddenly long fiberglass feet. As with all teaching experiences, I had to remind myself that, at one point, skiing wasn't natural and was a mystery to me too. I saw a look of fear on her face, only briefly abated as I pointed out some of the mountain birds. We had watched nutcrackers peck after scraps around the ski lodge, their gray and black plumage showing flashes of white whenever they stretched their wings. Higher up, we had spotted fuzzy Gray Jays under the chairlift, gliding between the treetops.

On the city streets I was starting to feel desperate. We needed to see these damn partridges. I needed to show Gerri what it was like to find the bird, to feel the joy of tracking it down and then of studying it. I wanted to share an experience like this with her. We were driving now, hoping to cover more ground. I was aware the sun would be setting soon, which gave us plenty of time to get back to the condo before the skiers but would end our chance for partridges. As we headed down a back alley, I saw something out of the corner of my eye. It was an almost imperceptible movement of brown against the brown gravel where the snow had recently melted. I slammed on the brakes. "There, Gerri. Behind the trash can!"

It took several seconds for Gerri's eyes to adjust and make out a shape whose color perfectly matched the backdrop. Only when the shape moved was it obvious that it was a bird. And then another shape thawed from the background and started moving. Soon we had five plump partridges jogging in front of us, clearly getting in one another's way. It was a North American tick for me. I watched as Gerri saw the thing she'd devoted her whole day to finding (arguably against her more sensible judgment). With her eyes hidden behind her raised binoculars, I could safely marvel at the smile that played out below. There are few things more satisfying than finding a bird and showing it to someone else, and few things better than when that someone else is someone you care about.

"To fasten, insert the metal fitting into the buckle . . ." We were sitting with Bill and Jackie in an Air Canada plane on the frosted runway at Calgary International Airport. We'd said our goodbyes to Georgina and Edward and the kids. It would be the last time I'd ever see them together as a couple and the last time I'd ever take in those sweeping views from the condo. I hadn't spotted the deep cracks that had started to run through their marriage, but then who ever does? Other people's marriages are a mystery, a secret place where arguments, resentment, happiness and peace simmer together, the ratios changing day by day and best known only to those within.

I stared out the window, ever hopeful for Snowy Owls, as we awaited the go-ahead for takeoff. Gerri sat next to me, enveloped in her warm white jacket, her face still glowing from the sunny day of skiing. When I looked at her, she returned my smile and I felt my hand being lightly squeezed. She told me she was happy, and I remember feeling happy too, happy that she liked being with my friends and excited that she was starting to see the magical birds that remain hidden to most non-birders. But it was a bittersweet kind of happiness, for I didn't know what I wanted. I felt trapped in an accelerating relationship that I wanted to slow down, and I was still hurting from the one that had stopped long ago. I knew that the more time Gerri and I spent together, the greater the pain would be if this didn't work out. It seemed unfair, I thought, that by the time I'd figured that out, it would be too late to prevent either of us from being hurt.

The trees moved slowly from right to left across my window before accelerating in a dark green blur. I could hear the engine in my left ear, like a giant bowling ball hurtling down an empty alley. I held my breath until the moment that feels like magic, like it's never going to happen, when the ground suddenly falls away and you're in the sky. As I looked down on Calgary, which was wrapped inside frozen rivers, I thought back to that awkward conversation at dinner: what was my big plan? Seeing my friends reminded me of how stuck I was, and how I was suddenly on a different trajectory. Were the birds a distraction from that feeling of anxiety or were they more? And did I really regret not doing a Big Year this year?

People (experts) tell you to find yourself—to find what you're good at and do what you enjoy. But that doesn't work if you're moderately good at everything (except perhaps sports, conversation, and working with others) and if you enjoy lots of things. I wish someone else could make that decision for you: you are hereby condemned to teach algebra, fix colons, or make pastries for the rest of your life, with an option for parole at the age of sixty-five. I wish life were as easy as taking a flight, with someone else in charge of getting you to a single and guaranteed destination. But life isn't like that. It's more like being in an airport with people rushing past while you're trying to make out destinations on one of those large, old-fashioned split-flap display boards, the type that makes a pleasant clapping sound as the individual letters and numbers rotate. While you're making up your mind (Istanbul? Kathmandu? Brownsville?), the destinations are dropping off as fast as the planes leave. At some point, time will run out and you'll find there are no options, or at least no options to places you want to go.

My bird count at the end of February 2013: 294

Chapter 3

THE BLUEBIRDS OF UNHAPPINESS

THE POET T. S. ELIOT once wrote that April is the cruelest month. He was born in the United States and immigrated to the UK at the age of twenty-five. I imagine he was talking about the cold April showers that typified his new home. I don't mind April so much. For me, March is the cruelest month. I apparently emigrated in the wrong direction. I left behind a voluptuous March, where the crocuses are already spent, and the green banks are on fire with bright, golden daffodils. I can smell that sweet elixir of spring when I think of daffodils. I picture the greenness of the weeping willows, the manicured lawns, and the promise of a glorious summer filled with cuckoos, long walks, beer gardens, and the sun lingering long into the night. I've lived in the United States for ten years now, and each new March breaks my heart again, reminding me I still don't feel quite at home. Somehow, it's March again in New England, and the daffodil bulbs are fast asleep in their beds. It's my own private wasteland.

Outside I can hear the squawking neighborhood Blue Jays that always seem to be upset about something. I imagine the birds thousands of miles to the south of me that are just starting to think about heading north. They're quietly waiting, like me, for the snows to retreat and the green to return. Their brains are primed, waiting for the signal as the days lengthen. As departure day approaches, the birds become restless and anxious. Behavioral biologists have a fantastic and typically unpronounceable German term for this: *Zugunruhe* (literally "migration anxiety"). And that's exactly how I felt this particular March. I wanted to be anywhere and everywhere except where I currently was.

I'd been following the rare-bird alerts and Listserv updates as we traveled back from Calgary. A handful of Northern Lapwings, driven out of Europe by a particularly bad winter, were still up and down the East Coast, remainders of an incredible invasion of the species. Rare winter geese straying from Greenland included Barnacle and Pink-footed in New York and New Jersey and a Tufted Duck on Long Island. I'd only been back from Calgary for a day and already it was easier to plan the logistics for all these chases than it was to do something about my life. I was suffering from a serious bout of *Zugunruhe*.

I was still thinking of the Gray Partridges, or rather, I was thinking of the smile they'd produced on Gerri's face. It reminded me of a time, several years back, at the Boston Public Garden, when a Barred Owl had recently been discovered. The Public Garden is a small patch of manicured green in which busy downtown workers hurry past the sculptured hedges and colorful flower beds on their way to their next meeting, while lazy tourists are pedaled around in swan boats. It was a Saturday in November, the lake had been drained, the swan boats had migrated south for the winter, and the tourists were presumably wondering why their guidebooks made such a fuss about the place.

It took a while to find the owl, hidden in a willow tree near a monument commemorating the first use of ether. As I stood with my telescope trained on the bird, people came up to ask me what I was looking at. I'm often tempted to say that I work for the military and that I'm scouring the skies for invading Soviet parachutists. Or that I'm looking for alien spacecraft. But this time, "looking at an owl" seemed a pretty cool thing to say too.

Soon a curious line formed behind the magnified view of the bird. The owl obligingly sat there, its head slowly rotating to the left and then the right, like a soft, feathery R2D2. As folks looked through the telescope, it was impossible for them not to be moved by those deep and empty black eyes that seemed to suck in the light like a pair of tiny black holes. People left with a smile and a sense of childish wonder. It was as if they'd suddenly been shown a parallel universe, one that had been there all along but that they'd never seen before. I felt like I had a super-power: being able to pull birds seemingly out of nowhere.

This winter had been a good one for northern owls, which had dispersed south ahead of the arctic winter. And the Canadian capital, Ottawa, was owl central. There were Great Gray Owls, a Northern Hawk Owl and a tiny, secretive Boreal Owl. And I knew each of these would rekindle that smile on Gerri's face and remind her (and me) of my superpower. It wasn't hard to convince her to take another trip across the border.

Ottawa is a seven-and-a-half-hour drive from Boston. We left early on Friday, March 1, on a northwest bearing that took us first through New Hampshire and then Vermont, both mountainous and white. It was already dark when we crossed the border into Canada (Quebec), which seemed to mark the end of the known world: the two-lane highway from the United States suddenly narrowed to a single lane, the streetlights disappeared (presumably to be replaced by the warm glow of universal health care), and we entered some kind of barren and treeless farmland. As if to confirm the abrupt transition, snow began to fall—the kind that causes the tires to lose their confidence and the windshield to become opaque, like a steamy bathroom mirror. I found the one combination of temperature and airflow to keep open a tiny porthole through which I could make out the road ahead. Gerri was asleep and I was scared. I don't remember what the landscape did after that. I just remember peering through that small, unfrozen aperture, my hunched and knotted shoulders aching, listening to the *crunch-crunch* of the tires.

We awoke in Montreal the next morning to be reminded that Montreal was not Ottawa (it was as far as I'd gotten the previous night) and that we had another two hours of driving ahead of us. The city was still buried in the depths of winter as I searched for an early-morning croissant. The streets were empty and silent except for the clanking of a trundling snowplow. Snowflakes seemed to crystallize before our eyes and hang there, sparkling, so tiny they almost lacked the weight to fall. Once the French pastry was successfully delivered to its target organ, we headed to Ottawa for our first owl, the Great Gray Owl.

The owls had been reported on the far side of a wooded creek near the banks of the Ottawa River, which marked the border between Quebec and Ontario. We picked up a trail from a parking lot for the National Capital Greenbelt, which led down to a frozen stream. I felt that combination of excitement at what lay ahead and panic at potentially missing the bird. That pit in the stomach is a common feeling for birders, whose lives are defined by that short distance between emotional extremes of jubilation and "that's it—I'm never doing this again!" Our pace was painfully slow. In places, the snow came above our knees, and curious branches reached out to snag my telescope and tripod. I turned back to look at Gerri, whose face was hidden behind a cloud of foggy breath.

The night before we had explored the old town of Montreal, which, if you half squint and if you're very tired and the lighting is poor, does a remarkably good impression of a Parisian arrondissement. True, it does lack an Eiffel Tower, a distinctive cuisine, and real, drunk French people, and so one might be tempted to say that the Canadians had improved on the whole Paris concept. We found a quiet little pub on the Rue Saint-Paul where the beer was strong and the staff effortlessly slid between English and French. Warmed by a bowl of steaming onion soup, I was pleasantly reminded that this continent is not a single monoculture and that you can leave Boston by car in the morning and arrive in a foreign land with a confusing language and a different set of customs by evening. (I'd learned this to be true after once leaving Boston and driving west to a place called Ohio.)

While walking back to the hotel, we found a steep snowbank into which stairs had been thoughtfully chiseled. We looked at the slope and then the stairs and then back at the slope. We opted for the butt descent, although by the end we weren't so much sitting and sliding as rolling and screaming and sliding. "*Étrangers stupides!*" I could imagine the natives thinking as they held their offended noses away from us in disgust. We didn't care and laughed like children. It had almost been like falling in love again.

Last night's carefree moment seemed like a distant blur now as the present locked sharply into focus, reminding us of the secretive owls that lay ahead. The wind had picked up, stinging our faces as we crossed the frozen creek, teetering like walkers on a tightrope. To our left and right stretched the wavy edges to the woodland, while a large meadow opened up in front of us, punctuated by scattered pine trees. I felt my heart sink a little as I glimpsed the photographers a short distance away on our left. While I've relied on others to find and communicate many of the birds I've seen, it's more satisfying to find your own—to test out your special powers. I didn't need to see or hear other birders' animated shouting and pointing to know that they already had the bird.

Even before I put the scope on it, I could hear Gerri's excited reaction to the owl. The Great Gray Owl is our largest owl (more than thirty inches long), although in reality it's more like a sparrow covered in a massive feather blanket. At least four inches of feathering surrounds the skull, which not only helps to keep the head warm but also provides a large facial disc, in this case etched in black, for sound collection. Owls are one of the few birds that have forward-facing eyes, like us, rather than eyes on opposite sides of their head, like most other birds. This isn't, as you'd be forgiven for thinking, to take advantage of superior binocular vision; in reality, there's not much overlap between the two eyes. It has more to do with hearing, the primary sense for owls. They have such enormous ears that the only place left in the head for the eyes is squashed up at the front. I explained to Gerri that if you were to fold back all those facial feathers and expose the ear holes, you'd see how asymmetric those ears are; one is at two o'clock and the other at seven o'clock, a further adaptation that allows them to better pinpoint movement, such as invisible voles crawling through tunnels under the snow.

Bird photographers and birders (a large number of whom may also photograph birds) both enjoy looking at birds through lenses. But that seems to be where the similarity ends and the acrimony begins. Who would guess that these two fringe groups could be at war? Rather than be concerned with hunters, kitchen windows, and cats killing birds, it's easier to complain behind their backs about how shittingly terrible that other group is. Photographers annoy birders by, allegedly, getting much too close to a bird, thus causing harassment, all for the sake of that "killer" shot. Photographers are also known to use live or fake mice to draw species like owls nearer and to get flight shots. Photographers, of course, have their own gripes against birders, a group who, they believe, are generally nutcases obsessed with their lists and who think that knowing the Latin names of birds somehow makes them superior.

We didn't see any baiting of the Great Gray Owl, but we did at our next stop—a Northern Hawk Owl. There were twenty or so photographers and probably as many small white mice. It must have been a confusing and frightening time for the latter, removed from the cozy pet store a few hours earlier and now liberated, albeit into a freezing depression in the snow. The long-tailed Northern Hawk Owl had no problem spotting white mice against the white snow—they're trained to spot (hear) movement and do most of their hunting during the day. There are many arguments against baiting: creating an association between humans and food is dangerous, especially near roads, where many slow-flying owls perish in collisions; the shop-bought mice can carry salmonella; and using fake mice (often on the end of a string pulled to mimic movement) causes the owl to lubricate their digestive tracts in anticipation of a meal, potentially causing dehydration. It was getting late and I was glad to have a reason to leave the circus act behind.

Our third owl, a Boreal Owl, was a much more covert operation. As is true of all owl sightings, which tend to attract photographers, the birding Listservs prohibited any discussion of owl locations, for fear of harassment and baiting. I'd heard about the Boreal Owl on the blog of birder Alex Lamoreaux and made covert enquiries—"covert" meaning e-mailing the whole Listserv to ask where the bird was and pissing off the entire local birding community, including the list moderator. Only a charming British accent can rescue you from this kind of mess, and fortunately I'd been cultivating one for the past thirty-nine years. And so, on a cold and snowy afternoon, we met the owl's discoverer, Chris Traynor, a tall elven character. He led us to one of the many small conifers dotting an urban Ottawa park. Chris pulled the branches aside, as if he were opening a door, and we entered into a dark but warm interior. Four feet from us, a pair of tiny yellow eyes, somewhat tired and apathetic, surveyed the new visitors. Strictly nocturnal, and living in inaccessible mountain and northern forests, the Boreal Owl is one of our least known owls, and it was a life bird for me. Gerri and I marveled at the tiny (nine-inch) brown owl. A heart-shaped disk framed the edges of the "face," from which the eyes peeked out. It showed considerably less interest in us than we did in it, and soon tucked its head into its neck and closed its eyes. It was already bored of us. Reluctantly, we opened the "door" and left the little gem to sleep.

"It would be great if you could come," she said, staring ahead at the windshield. "I don't want to go on my own."

We were driving back home from Ottawa, and Gerri and I were having two different conversations. Mine was about the owls, whose feathery forms were burned into my memory. I was still admiring them in my mind, walking around them like they were sculptures, taking them in from different angles. For most birders, the experience of watching birds is framed by hours of preparation before and a period of reflection or debriefing afterward. Both help to magnify the enjoyment of a moment that to non-birders can often seem frustratingly short and ephemeral.

But there was a second reason for wanting to talk about the owls. I didn't want to talk about what Gerri wanted to talk about: her trip to the UK, or more specifically, our trip to the UK. Gerri was a high school teacher, and she would be spending her spring break visiting one of her best friends, Beth.

It would be Gerri's first time to the UK. I could see the double whammy approaching long before it hit: Gerri and I were now a couple who had already traveled internationally (albeit to Canada), and I was from the country that she wanted to visit.

I could think of several reasons why I didn't want to go, none of which were worth explaining to Gerri unless I wanted the silent treatment, and I was pretty sure the silent treatment was exactly what I didn't want. What I did want was to slow things down. There was no subplot to the innocent bird trips—it was just about the birds—but visiting Gerri's friends on a non-birding trip would be different. Very different. Not only did a non-birding trip come with no birds, but it also came with implications, promises, and alarm bells.

I didn't want to meet Beth any more than I had wanted to meet Gerri's other friends or her family. Each new addition was one more person to whom I'd have to apologize when things inevitably didn't work out. Although I am old enough not to care what other people think of me, I am conscientious enough to feel guilty for pretty much anything (including apologizing to people who accidentally walk into me). With Beth, I'd be adding another whole continent of guilt. While Gerri, I'm sure, saw the UK trip as an opportunity for the two of us to spend more time together, I saw it as a trap. We were careening toward the tipping point when enough people knew about us that there could be no easy way out. I'd be stuck, and the resultant mess would be entirely my fault.

Instead I told Gerri about a place in New Mexico called Sandia Crest. It's a mountaintop not far from Albuquerque, where in the winter all three species of North American

rosy-finch can be seen. There are three different flavors—
Brown-capped, Gray-crowned, and Black—and they all share a
pink flush like the inside of Turkish delight. Tracking them
down individually during other seasons is difficult because they
nest at high altitude across the Rockies and up into Canada.
For many, the pilgrimage to Sandia Crest is an annual winter
rejuvenation. And it suddenly seemed very important that I be
there too, on that mountaintop, rather than in the UK.

Later, Gerri told me she knew then that I was already
committed to a Big Year, albeit unknowingly. She could see it
in the way I was planning which winter species I needed
(Bohemian Waxwing, Hoary Redpoll, and Harris's Sparrow),
desperate to catch up with them before they left for more
inaccessible summer residences. She'd listen whenever I'd
look up from my phone and say, "There's a Black-tailed
Godwit in Virginia," in a tone that sounded as if I were asking
permission, or approval, to chase. But wisely, she didn't say
anything, as if the weight of a Big Year would crush these
moments of happiness, like the tiny bluetail in Vancouver,
ignorant of the heavy cedar canopy above. I think she recognized the same in our relationship—that I needed that blink-
ered view of living day to day, date to date, otherwise the
enormity of it would have crushed me. I suppose that's why
she didn't scream or shout when I told her that she'd be going
to London on her own. But I could feel her quiet disappointment that I wasn't ready, and that she'd lost again, this time to
some chirping rosy-finches ten thousand feet in the sky.

A week later I started to receive photos of Gerri in front of
Hampton Court, Gerri at the Houses of Parliament, and Gerri

guarding the Tower of London. I noticed that she stood awkwardly, as if she were aware of the loss of the counterbalance that should have been to one side of her, an awareness that her eyes seemed to confirm. Meanwhile, I was standing on the top of that mountain and safely on my own. I looked down on Albuquerque sprawled out below, as all three flavors of Turkish delight buzzed around the feeders.

While I was busy not doing a Big Year and trying not to get into another serious relationship, I was also kidding myself that I wasn't ill.

It's hard to know when it started. It's like finding a lump and ignoring it because you think it will disappear as mysteriously as it appeared. Or seeing that the check-engine light is on and thinking it's some quirk of the car and nothing to be concerned about. We can get awfully upset about missing a flight or running out of dishwasher detergent and yet can so easily accept the serious as the new normal. But if I had to give a date, I'd say it started in 2009, halfway through my relationship with Anna.

I didn't call it depression, because that was something other people got, like tattoos, IRS audits, or inflatable snowman Christmas decorations. It was easier to see there was something wrong with the world—Anna, my coworkers, the Axis of Evil—than it was to think there might be something wrong with me. And if I were ill, why couldn't I have some cool disease that you can wave around and expect some goddamn sympathy. I wasn't stupid. I knew people didn't admit to being mentally ill.

Depression, if we're to call it that, is a cruel disease that robs you of your awareness and the motivation to do something about it. It's like a symbiotic organism has crept into your ear, jumped headfirst into the nearest blood vessel, and worked its way deep in your brain. Once there, it fiddles around with the circuitry so that you're not aware of what's happening, and that's when the slow and inexorable slide begins and the color drains out of your world. That dim sense that something is wrong, that things aren't as they used to be, remains a distant feeling. I sat with it for so long that I'd almost forgotten that I was once someone else.

When I think back to that time, I remember a sense of being "stuck," as if I'd fallen off some conveyor belt that gently pulled us through life, ensuring we'd pass through different processing centers: engagement, marriage, kids, balding, and irrecoverable loss of fashion sense. Those things never happened to me. Instead, I'd go to work, spend most of the day on the verge of tears, and never consider that there might be something odd about that. I'd then come home to Anna and put an enormous amount of effort into avoiding conversations—my other superpower at the time. Conversations were bad. She'd ask how I was, what I wanted to do that weekend, and why we never talked about the future. I couldn't even decide (or care) what I wanted for dinner. Meanwhile, she wanted more, a lot more.

Mostly, depression stole the future from me, which quickly became the lost present and then the lost past. I was absolutely certain that the best years of my life were behind me—studying at Oxford and Cambridge, spending long hours looking at fruit flies for my Ph.D., playing Luke Skywalker in a college pantomime, backpacking around the world—and that my one and only shot at a relationship was unraveling in front of my eyes. It was as if all my awareness were focused on time: how fast it was going and how I was rapidly running out of it. Since I had no hopes for the future anyway, and couldn't imagine one in which anything important happened, I'm not sure why I cared that it was disappearing, but I did. Perhaps it was the realization that it shouldn't be like this. Other people talked of vacations or weekends with an excitement that both pained and perplexed me. I knew that if things did change, if the colors ever did return and I could see the world in something other than the monochrome Stalin grays, then it would be too late to do anything about it. And that would be much, much worse.

I don't remember much of that time at all. It's possible the weary unhappiness stole my memory, or more likely that I wasn't doing anything that was worth remembering. But I do recall one conversation on our Pottery Barn sofa. I'd come home from work, feeling an amazing sense of success for getting through another day—one less to endure. Anna turned off the television, turned to face me, and told me that she couldn't live like this anymore, that it wasn't fun. As I watched her blue eyes slowly dissolve into tears, I thought back to happier days when we'd gone rollerblading, traveled to Peru, and carved Halloween pumpkins. I wasn't happy now, I could conceive of no future, yet I couldn't bear the thought of all those precious memories turning sour. I knew that if I lost her, I'd lose myself too. She was giving me a final chance. I knew that if I told her to wait and that if I could talk about a future in which things would be different, she'd stay on this sofa with me long after it had worn through. But I couldn't open my mouth, and even if I could, there would be no words inside me. I was an empty husk. I believed the lie that things would never get better and so sat there silently looking at my hands while she cried.

The depression took away the highs and lows and left me with a permanent state of numbness, as if my brain needed to be protected. One day I did manage to experience one of those extremes, ironically in a place usually associated with brain-numbing mediocrity: the living room section of IKEA. Anna had moved out, but not far—a few blocks away to a small one-bedroom apartment. She'd asked me to help her buy new furniture. As I stood in the showroom, while she asked my opinion between two sofas, I felt like the bottom had now dropped out of my world. Somehow this experience, unlike the still-hopeful girl crying on the sofa at home, captured the depths of my despair. I looked around at the other shoppers, busy eyeing Pöang armchairs or measuring Hemnes bookcases, unaware there was someone drowning in their midst. The pain I should have felt on that sofa at home, the loss that should have been there for the past two years, suddenly hit me with a choking stranglehold, and then left as suddenly and mysteriously as it had arrived. This brief revelation had fought through the protective shield and shown me the truth: that something important and devastating was happening in my life.

"Neil, are you listening?" she asked. "I was saying that this one might be better. What do you think?"

It's one thing to see the truth and it's another to do something about it. I told her I liked the one on the left, turned to look at the coffee tables behind me, closed my eyes, and waited for my chest to stop thumping.

I blamed the depression on Anna, but after she left, it didn't go away. I watched, helpless and confused, as I was replaced by two cats and then a boyfriend. Nor did it go away after I left my job, the other obvious reason for my unhappiness. So now I was alone and without a job. I was unwittingly starting a new relationship with Gerri that I knew at some point would stall, just like the last one had. I'd never figure out what to do about it while under this veil of unhappiness, and I was tired of seeing other people pass by on that conveyor belt.

The *National Geographic Field Guide to the Birds of North America* (6th edition) tells you that 990 species of bird have been recorded in the ABA region. It also tells you where and when to see many of them. On page 60 it tells you that Himalayan Snowcocks are found on one mountain in Nevada, and on page 168 that Common Ringed Plovers aren't common at all, and to see one you have to be on an island off Alaska and even then only at the right time of year. It tells you that most birds molt all their feathers at least once a year, usually after breeding. But nowhere does it tell you that birds might actually save your life.

Freed from the shackles of my corporate job, I was birding so much more than I had previously. Although I didn't understand why, I had a sense that there was something therapeutic and necessary about the birding. I suspected it had to do with the intense focus and the way it brings you to the present.

When I was birding, I didn't worry about the past and lament all those best years being over, or fear the future, empty and rapidly disappearing. The present was different, like my brain had declutched from the competing anxieties and I was free to coast in neutral. All that time spent in the present was incremental. My head felt warm and fuzzy, giving me a better, truer perspective on my life. I began to see that not only was the depression not normal but also that it didn't need to be like this. It was a revelation that spurred me to seek help. A week after returning home from the rosy-finches in Sandia Crest, I made an appointment to see a psychiatrist for the first time, and I left with a prescription for antidepressants.

The Florida Keys are an archipelago that stretches 127 miles off the southeast coast of Florida. It's as if some giant hand has pulled at the corner of land just below Miami, teasing it into a gentle arc, down and to the left. We were somewhere on that string of coral beads heading toward a blazing sunset. Gerri had returned from the UK with lots of stories, most of which centered on the theme of how much better it would have been if I'd been there. She didn't explicitly blame the rosy-finches or me, but I could tell she wasn't happy. Easter would be her last time off before the summer, and so to appease her, I'd suggested that we spend more time together. I suggested Florida.

It didn't hurt that Florida was hosting three mega rarities at the time: a White-cheeked Pintail on the east coast, a Thick-billed Vireo at Key Biscayne in Miami, and a Western Spindalis at the Key West Botanical Gardens. None of this was a surprise to Gerri. This was her new normal.

We landed in West Palm Beach, emerging from the airport into the dripping Florida heat. Any residual resentment Gerri may have felt for me while she was alone in the UK seemed to burn off rapidly with the sunny skies. On our two-hour drive up the coast toward the pintail, the only hills we saw were the man-made landfill sites that punctuated the flat landscape, each drawing its own collection of vultures and gulls, hungry for the detritus of human civilization. Gerri marveled at the spiky-haired yellow and orange Cattle Egrets feeding on the side of the road, scattering each time a car passed. She laughed at how they reminded her of Sally Cat and Khiva Cat.

There are many amazing things I can say about Pelican Island: it was the first national wildlife refuge in the United States; it was established by an executive order of President Theodore Roosevelt in 1903; and it's a beautiful series of coastal mangrove beds and dense hammocks of hardwood trees. But for the purposes of this story at least, it's where I missed my first bird of the year. The White-cheeked Pintail wasn't there. It's a duck, it sits on water, and I missed it. I should have read the Listserv messages more carefully and known that the bird disappeared for long periods of time (maybe it was dumpster diving with its vulture friends?). I'd gotten so used to seeing birds that it was quite a surprise not to see the White-cheeked Pintail, but it shouldn't have been. Birding is all about missing birds and the stories of the ones that got that away.

If I'd been there on my own, I'd have waited it out. The White-cheeked Pintail is a resident of the Bahamas and Cuba that rarely reaches our shores. Unfortunately, a lot of them are kept here in captivity. Birders are allowed to count only wild birds, and since wild and escaped ducks look identical, it's often hard to separate the two. But this bird had a lot going for it—it wasn't far from the Bahamas, it was here at the right time of year, hanging out with other wintering ducks, and it was remarkably skittish. But while the skittishness added to the bird's countability, it proved to be a very unappealing quality if you were chasing it.

We left the circular pool at Pelican Island to the sleeping Blue-winged Teals and the annoyingly non-white-cheeked pintails and climbed back into the air-conditioning. We retraced our drive south to Miami, where we planned to spend the night. I raced through the traffic on I-95, hoping to beat the closing gates at Bill Baggs Cape Florida State Park, where the Thick-billed Vireo had been seen.

Miami's afternoon gridlock predictably slowed us down, giving us time to remark on the large flock of urban cranes— the city was still evidently in the midst of a building boom. New blocks of luxury condos had appeared since my last visit. I took a detour through downtown to show Gerri the American Airlines Arena, where the Heat play. Gerri is a sports fan, and so I'd learned in advance not only where the Heat played but also what they played, which was something called basketball. After I'd proudly spilled the sum total of my non-baseball sports knowledge, we turned onto the long Rickenbacker Causeway, which took us past the busy port terminal across the bay to our left, and imagined the art deco buildings of South Beach somewhere beyond. If you continue along the Rickenbacker, you'll arrive at a golf course, exclusive tennis courts, and the upscale stores and residences of Key Biscayne. After all that ugly silliness, there's an entrance gate with a rising barrier protecting the remains of a glorious mangrove wilderness beyond: Bill Baggs Cape Florida State Park.

We had more success with the tiny Thick-billed Vireo than we did with the duck. But it took an hour of waiting, and I'm not sure Gerri thought the small brownish bird that she saw was reward enough for all the fuss. For me, the dark eyes and broken yellow spectacles connecting the eyes above the bill were an interesting variation to the fourteen other species of native vireos, and seeing a bird rarely found beyond the confines of the Bahamas or Cuba added to the significance. But Gerri did like how angry it seemed to be—scolding us for interrupting its busy afternoon of napping.

One of the reasons Gerri had been excited to go to Florida was that her friends Charles and Angela, a married couple, were passing through Miami that weekend. We arranged to meet them for drinks in a hotel bar downtown, not far from the Heat's stadium. The sun was setting as we parked, and a flock of parrots screeched overhead, heading for their evening roost. Florida has the largest number of introduced species in the country. Along with the unwanted Burmese pythons and alligators that are flushed down the toilet, there are also abandoned and escaped birds. Some, such as the White-winged Parakeet, Spot-breasted Oriole, and Red-whiskered Bulbul, now have stable populations and are legitimately countable by birders. Taking a walk or drive through Miami can be like going to a zoo.

The hotel was one of those grand, modern affairs, with television screens dotted around the lobby, a coffee shop, a jewelry store, and a small bar with high stools and a shiny metal counter with a rim around the edges like a dissection table. Designer filaments burned orange-red inside bare lightbulbs.

The cocktails were delicious and the food wasn't bad. We sat on stools around a small table, a fake candle fake-flickering in the middle, and I found myself enjoying the conversation. It's not often I enjoy meeting new people. Generally, I hate the mindless small talk, but mostly I hate pretending to be interested when I discover the other person has (a) successfully given birth, (b) redecorated a bathroom, or (c) read a book by Paulo Coelho. Either these people were very nice or these cocktails were spectacular.

If you'd joined us for the evening, added yours to the four sets of drink orders, and reached over my arm to grab a sweet potato fry or two, you wouldn't have learned how Gerri had met her friend Angela. It never came up. As you grow up, you discover that each of us hold secrets—some obvious, most not. It's a revelation when you first discover the fractured, imperfect world of adults. It takes only a bit of imagination then, at whatever age you discover this, to know that the chances aren't great that you're going to be perfect either.

Gerri's life hadn't been perfect. Ten years earlier she'd had an eating disorder and had to spend time in a residential rehabilitation program. That's where she met Angela. I found it odd that they never spoke of those days. Gerri was okay now, but like a recovering alcoholic, she knew the precipice wasn't far away, waiting for the merest stumble.

As we were walking back to the car, shortly after saying goodbye to Charles and Angela and turning off that flickering candle, I hugged Gerri and told her that I really liked her friends. She had put up with so much birding and had agreed to do stuff that wasn't advertised as birding but then suddenly became birding—"oh yeah, we should just check this out for X," where "just check out" invariably meant a three-hour stakeout in the freezing cold/dripping heat/torrential rain, and "X" meant any of those 990 species in the field guide. I realized that she must like me a lot to put up with this, and I knew that I was lucky to have found her. But finding is the easy part. The keeping part had always been the real challenge for me.

It was dark by the time we arrived in Key West. It was Gerri's first time there, and she was surprised by the booming civilization we found at the end of the otherwise desolate Overseas Highway, which for much of its length is bordered by only a few feet before disappearing into the sea. We found a place for a bite to eat and then checked into our motel. While Gerri was asleep, I slipped out of bed, found my laptop, and sat at a small and very rickety table, trying not to make any noise. I checked the bird reports—the pintail had been seen today (damn it!), as had the Western Spindalis (phew!). The spindalis had been present at the Key West Botanical Gardens for much of the winter and the consensus was that it would leave soon. I needed it to hang on for one more day.

The Botanical Gardens didn't open until ten A.M., which gave us time to walk around Key West. This was once the most populous city in Florida, before the Everglades were drained and Miami emerged from the swamp. It was home to

Ernest Hemingway, whose house and museum we were going to visit after the spindalis was safely ticked. We took photos at the famous MILE O sign that marks the southern start of Highway 1, and also apparently where the lunacy begins. The Lonely Planet guidebook says about Key West: "It's as if someone has shaken the United States and all the nuts fell to the bottom."

One of the nuts was in the Key West Botanical Garden. I was three hours into the spindalis hunt and realized this wasn't going to be easy. After missing the pintail and now potentially this, I was reminded of how frustrating birding can be. One moment you're hitting everything, and the next you're swinging and missing. Same strategy, different results. I suggested to Gerri that she go see the Hemingway museum on her own, and to say hi to the six-toed cats for me. Meanwhile I would spend the afternoon walking around the small piece of wooded coral that is the Botanical Gardens, trying to find a spindalis while trying not to lose my mind.

The spindalis had been hanging out near the yoga deck, a quiet area surrounded by thick, spiky vegetation. By the time Gerri returned to pick me up, as the gardens were closing, I was in a state of mental meltdown. I was sunburnt, thirsty, and sick of looking at the same small number of trees and the elderly women doing downward-facing dogs. Meanwhile, I felt no relaxation at all from that damn yoga deck. I couldn't understand how a bird could hide for this long. Somehow I'd missed it, like the pintail the day before. I felt numb from the failure and reflected that at least I wasn't doing a Big Year. I'd have another chance to add these birds to my life list some time in the future, but for a Big Year birder, this would probably have been it.

I left Key West that evening without seeing a spindalis or stroking a six-toed cat. I dropped Gerri off at the Fort Lauderdale airport, since she had to go back home for her teaching job the next day, and then turned around and drove back along that same string of coral islands. I was headed back to the Key West Botanical Garden for more self-flagellation. I was tired and sleepy and wondering why I was here rather than heading home with Gerri. It took all my effort to stay on the bridges. I didn't want to test the safety barriers on the side.

I was at the gardens the next morning as they opened.

"You again?" said the kind old woman who took your money at the entrance gate, permitting you to ruin a perfectly good day driving yourself slowly mad looking for invisible birds.

I was all over that yoga platform again, to no avail. After three hours, I'd found nothing except a Black-whiskered Vireo and a vagrant Chris Floyd, a visiting birder I knew from Massachusetts. I soon discovered that finding Chris Floyd was the critical part. Not long after that, I heard Chris's voice calling farther up the trail.

"Hey, what does that spindalis look like?" he asked.

As it turned out, it looked exactly like the bird Chris had just found.

My bird count at the end of March 2013: 376

Chapter 4

WHEN HUMMINGBIRDS STOP HUMMING

THE MORNING'S ELIXIR OF burned thermos coffee was wearing off as my extremities started to tingle from the Rocky Mountain cold. The long horizontal slot in front of me, a makeshift window in a converted trailer, sucked in the cool morning breeze, which carried with it the fresh and pungent aroma of sage. There was no moon, and the blackness outside was almost complete. A fuzzy horizontal line barely divided the star-speckled black of the sky from the solid black below. As I waited for my eyes to catch up to my other senses, I could feel my heart beating, resonating with the primitive drum beat throbbing somewhere out there in the dark.

April is the month of the dancing chickens. As the snow slowly recedes from the prairies, the sagebrush, and the fields of Colorado, these otherwise secretive grouse appear as if from a yearlong hibernation. They come together to dance, to show off their moves, and to earn the right to breed. It's an ancient ritual, played out across the leks, or dancing grounds, of the West.

Gradually I started to make out fat, round blobs, the only clue to the slow indiscernible advance toward dawn. There were thirty or so grouse tightly packed in an area of a few hundred feet, wobbling in perpetual motion like particles under a microscope, or like Pac-Man trying to avoid collisions with the ghosts. As the drumming got louder and the curtain of light rose on the show, I forgot the cold nibbling at my hands and feet as I watched the mating ritual of the Greater Sage-Grouse.

Getting here had felt like a secret ritual itself. I'd been told to show up in a strip mall parking lot that fronted the main street in Craig, a dusty and sleepy town in northwest Colorado. Sure enough, as my dashboard clock had blinked to four A.M., a small, funereal procession of headlights had slowly turned into the lot, briefly blinding me before being extinguished. Thickly wrapped birders emerged, eerily shadowed by the harsh sodium lighting from a nearby McDonald's. After quick, whispered introductions and a head count (twelve), we shared three vehicles to drive the forty-five minutes into the sagebrush sea. From there, we found our way by flashlight to the converted trailer we used as a blind, from where we could watch the birds unseen.

The strutting male Greater Sage-Grouse are mottled gray and brown except for a pair of yellow eyebrows, or ocular combs, and a startlingly white, feathery boa, like a majestic Elizabethan ruff. Their tails are fanned like a peacock, a half circle of twenty spiky quills. Elongated feathers, or filoplumes, stick up from the back of their bare heads, making them look as if they've just been shocked. Through my telescope I could make out the birds' feathered legs beating the ground and moving them forward in an atavistic dance: 1-2-3-4. On the third beat, the male stretches his neck as if reaching for the sky, pulling the bend of his wings forward and puffing out his breast. On the fourth beat, two greenish-yellow air sacs appear, inflated, from the breast hidden under the white collar, and then suddenly pop: *swish-swish-kerPLUNK*. The relentless dance never stops. The male turns in a new direction and slowly marches forward, ready to inflate and deflate his sacs again: 1-2-3-4, 1-2-3-4. The lek reverberated with the *swish-swish-kerPLUNK* of the male sage-grouse, all moving and popping with the same choreography. The hollow air sacs, an adaptation of the esophagus, sounded like someone blowing across an empty bottle. These are the drumbeats.

The males dance for several hours every morning and sometimes in the evening too, all the way through spring. All the stomping helps keep the lek open for dancing, free from the tall sagebrush that defines the circular edge. The strutting dance delineates a hierarchy in much the same way I imagined as the Middlesex Lounge did back home. The blinged-out alpha male occupies the center, his territory bumping up against that of the upstart young males and those whose best dancing days were behind them. At the edges of the dance floor (which is where I would have been hiding, along with all the other nerd grouse, looking for a big piece of sagebrush to hide behind), the smaller and more cryptically plumaged females congregated, pretending not to look impressed. I watched as one of the hesitant females entered the lek, her nervousness immediately validated by a frenzy of male activity around her. These were the lowest males—the ones who wouldn't breed this year, although that wouldn't stop them from thinking they might get lucky. Skirmishes broke out as the males fought for the right to direct their bulging yellow sacs toward the female. But it was obvious that this girl was headed for the center, toward the alpha male.

If you'd been watching the nervous pronghorn on the horizon beyond, or reaching back inside the converted trailer to top up your coffee or tea or for another one of those delicious Fig Newtons, you would have missed it. After reaching the center, the female leaned forward, stretching her head and neck, and carefully opened her wings. This was the sign for the male she'd chosen. He wasted no time mounting her, carefully balancing on her back as if afraid to fall. And then, as quickly as they came together, they were apart. He returned to the dance, and she winged her way across the fields of sagebrush. After copulating, females leave the lek for the nesting grounds, returning only if their eggs fail or are eaten, a common enough outcome when living among coyotes, ground squirrels, and Black-billed Magpies.

I'd been in Colorado for a week, joining the other chicken tourists rather than joining Gerri back home. Many of the country's grouse occur in Colorado, albeit scattered around the four corners of a state whose vertiginous contours defy easy travel. I'd fallen into a comfortable if not exhausting pattern of driving from one lek to another, arriving in some small town after dark, ready to be up at three A.M. for the next grouse.

Each grouse species is different. They have different habitats, different dance moves, and different music. This morning's Greater Sage-Grouse was the largest and also the slowest. The following day, I would watch the Gunnison Sage-Grouse, a smaller and more energetic version with many more filoplumes exploding from its head. The much smaller prairie-chickens, which prefer the grasslands of the east, are more like windup toys, frequently breaking from their dance steps to dart after nearby males in a zippy grouse version of tag. They don colorful war helmets made from elongated neck feathers, which they raise over their heads. The air sacs (red in Greater Prairie-Chickens, orange in Lesser) produce a kind of hypnotic didgeridoo chant.

The chicken tour has become an important source of revenue to many small and struggling towns away from the metropolis of Denver. People come to Colorado to see the grouse for two reasons: First, they're some of the hardest birds to find, and visiting a lek (to which the birds return year after year) is often the only way to see them well or at all. Second, because they're disappearing. The Greater Sage-Grouse used to be one of the most populous of the western species—more than sixteen million at one time, sharing the plains with bison and Plains Indians. They're obligate sagebrush breeders—they nest in sagebrush and, for many months of the year, they eat only sagebrush. As that habitat has been lost, succumbing to one threat after another (residential development, livestock overgrazing, and our disruption of the natural cycle of rejuvenating wildfires), grouse numbers have plummeted. Today only 1 percent of those historical Greater Sage-Grouse numbers remain. And the other species are arguably doing worse. The critically endangered Gunnison Sage-Grouse was not recognized as a separate species until 2000, by which time around 90 percent of its former habitat had already been lost. Lesser Prairie-Chickens barely hang on in the southeast of the state, straddling the border with Kansas. As the west opens up to a new energy boom of oil and gas—industries with the potential to make landowners rich and with well-funded political lobbies—the chickens may be facing their greatest threat yet.

There are few places you can travel to these days that offer such a clear window to the past. As I sat in one cold blind after another, it was easy to visualize the plains once full of lekking grouse. I was struck by how much these birds had influenced the Native Americans in their dance—that same 1-2-3-4, throwing back a plumed headdress and stomping the ground with their feet. And now they were inspiring a new genera-tion of chicken tourists who sat in cold blinds wide-eyed with wonder and who took selfies in front of the always-funny Butte Motel. It was heartening to feel the intense pride that the communities felt in their chickens when I talked to locals in coffee shops and restaurants, and when I met the mayor of Wray at an after-lek farmhouse breakfast, and when I sat in a rickety old school bus driven by an equally rickety old man who wanted to share his Lesser Prairie-Chickens with visiting birders.

One of the first birds that Americans tried to save from extinction was a grouse: the Heath Hen. It was a subspecies of the Greater Prairie-Chickens, those zippy little windup birds

I'd watched in Wray, Colorado. The Heath Hen lived in sandy pine barrens along the Atlantic seaboard and was once so plentiful that servants allegedly negotiated down the number of days they were fed its cheap meat. (It's even probable that the first Thanksgiving meal featured the abundant Heath Hen rather than turkey.) But by the mid-nineteenth century, they'd disappeared entirely from the mainland. A hunting ban on Martha's Vineyard in Massachusetts served to protect the last known colony. But despite the protection and a burgeoning tourism industry interested in preserving these chicken dancers, the last bird, Booming Ben, died in 1932.

Losing any species diminishes our planet, but few are so inextricably and uniquely linked to this land as the dancing grouse. Watching the Greater Sage-Grouse stomping and popping, as they had done for millennia before, I could feel the urgency of their individual efforts together with that irony peculiar to life: despite the knowledge of one's own ultimate and bloody mortality, we need to dance like there will always be a tomorrow.

While I was busy ticking new birds, I was also taking the new pills. They were shaped like tiny white pucks from a miniature hockey game. I swallowed one every day, which, like x-ing out the days on a calendar, created a new rhythm to my life—slowing it down somehow. And each was linked to a new bird. I took one on each of the cold, dark mornings at the leks, another while waiting for the Key West Botanical Gardens to open, and another just before we didn't see the White-cheeked Pintail (which, if the pills were meant to make me happy, had either spectacularly failed on that day or had very undesirable side effects). I marveled at how such a nondescript geometrical shape was going to change my life. Well, maybe not change—just bring it back.

The psychiatrist, Jonathan, had told me that it might take six weeks before I'd see a difference. But that didn't stop me from waking up each morning in the first few weeks expecting to feel different. It was like awakening from a vivid nightmare in which all your teeth have fallen out and then hastily checking your mouth to make sure they're all still there. Except in this reverse nightmare I was checking to see if my brain was still there, cold and numb. It was.

I'm not sure which I worried about more: that the pills wouldn't work and I'd be stuck in this faded half life forever, definitively out of options, or that they would work and in the process I'd end up losing myself. I worried that the drugs might change me into a different person. I was desperate to rejoin the normals, but despite all the unhappiness, the stuckness and the feeling of being lost, I rather liked myself. True, I'd always lived on the minor-key side of life: I listened to the Smiths, enjoyed dark art-house movies, drew solace from the great Russian writers, and was pathologically suspicious of the perennially happy people or anyone who genuinely enjoyed small talk. I wanted to be happier, but not extravagantly happy. Really, I just wanted to not be unhappy, if that makes sense. I looked at the pills, so tiny in the palm of my hand. Please be enough, I remember thinking.

On top of the daily pill, I was continuing the weekly routine of traveling across the United States and Canada. The birding was like the medication—it was a prescription that I was following, unquestioningly. It was almost as if I were terminally ill and this was my last year. I was rushing around the continent, trying to take in as much as I could before it was too late. I'd bird away from home for a week and then return, only to plan the next trip. I honestly thought each time would be the last. Deep down I knew that the birding was procrastination from sorting out my life, but I was enjoying it and I was afraid to stop. Making my target lists, planning which birding hot spots to hit, and seeing what I could discover gave me a purpose in life. After being with people all day every day in my last job, it was unbelievably refreshing to be on my own. It was the first time in a very long time that I was able to look forward to the future.

While I was buried in a bird book, looking at birds, traveling to see birds, or planning my next trip, Gerri was quietly looking after me. She fed the cats, petted them, and scratched them in their favorite places. She'd text me to ask how I was doing and dutifully look up all the birds I was seeing (a consistent forty-five seconds would elapse between my texts reporting a Snowy Plover or a McCown's Longspur and the "Oh wow!" reply). She'd take me to Logan airport and be there to meet me without being asked. And she was spending more time at my place. There were colorful clothes in my drawers, coat hangers squeezed into my closet, and a whole pharmacy of bathroom products spilling out of cabinets. Whatever I did—whether I spent more time with Gerri or no time—it didn't seem to make any difference. I couldn't slow this down; she was gradually infiltrating my life.

I didn't know what to think about any of this, and so I tried not to.

When Gerri picked me up from Logan after the grouse trip, she didn't flinch when I told her that what I really needed now was to go to Texas before the Yellow Rails left. It was like some ever-shifting goal post. Whatever I did, and wherever I went, was immediately trumped by the next, even bigger thing. The fact that she didn't know what a rail was, let alone a yellow one, nor indeed why it might be leaving, made its own kind of sense.

I saved the bit of news about a more unusual pair of spring migrants until we got home from the airport. My parents were coming to visit later in the month. I was nervous, as in some way meeting my parents would further solidify whatever it was that Gerri and I had. Her reaction was unsurprisingly along the lines of a normal person—she was excited to meet them. I thought back to my own response when Gerri had invited me to spend Christmas with her family in Cincinnati the previous year. It was only the quick mental calculation that I could see a Trumpeter Swan and an Allen's Hummingbird on the drive there that prevented me from screaming and running away like a demented sage-grouse.

By the time I got to the large pile of communal rubber boots, it was no longer a pile, but a picked-over, pathetic group of mismatched shoes. It reminded me of the selection process for soccer and rugby games at school, where I lamented the fact that reading and sarcasm were not competitive sports. I eventually found a left boot that fit, and then a right one. They didn't match, but making a fashion statement wasn't as high a priority as keeping out the water and the snakes.

Anahuac National Wildlife Refuge sits on the margins of Galveston Bay on the Gulf of Mexico, seventy-odd miles southeast of Houston and tucked behind the Bolivar Peninsula. The coastal prairie and marsh stretch as far as the eye can see. To birders, it's famous for the spring rail walks—when the refuge asks for volunteers to count the Yellow Rails. I'd never been before but was intrigued by the idea that you could count Yellow Rails, a species I'd never seen. Counting suggested that there might be more than one. If grouse are tough, rails are even harder. Yellow Rails are barely larger than sparrows and spend their entire life hiding in long, wet grass. The only way to see them is in flight, by flushing them—for which special technical equipment is needed.

Our leader for the rail count was David Sarkozi, a middle-aged man submerged in a pair of waist-high waders. He was armed with a booming voice and a backpack full of bad jokes and puns. While David explained the complicated logistics of the walk (stand in a line and walk forward), I looked around at the motley group of twenty or so newly water-proofed birders. Some, like me, were already trying to spy the Seaside Sparrows that we could hear singing somewhere off in the watery prairie.

Slosh, swish, slosh, swish. Not only were my boots mismatched but also one apparently had a hole in it. Judging by the amount of cold, sloshing water, it probably wasn't large enough to permit entry to any of the snakes I imagined hiding among the cordgrass. We progressed in single file across the perfectly still prairie. In the distance it looked like a field of grass, and only when you looked down could you see the murky water, ankle-deep. David had deployed the high-tech rail-flushing equipment: A length of rope, about seventy-five feet long, was held at each end by a volunteer, with the rest of us lined up behind it. At intervals of every ten feet or so a plastic milk carton was attached to the rope, empty of milk, but full of stones. Yellow Rails don't like to fly; they'd rather run away unseen. The line of birders, together with the noise caused by the stones in the milk cartons, presented a seemingly impenetrable wall, forcing the rails to take flight.

We spent an hour walking back and forth over that prairie, like a minesweeper in a birding game of battleships. We had no idea where the birds were hiding, but every so often a shout would go up from the line, "Rail!" and if you were lucky, you'd see a tiny bird flying away. If you were really lucky, you'd get your binoculars on it and see the white trailing edge to the wing, identifying the bird as the secretive Yellow Rail. I saw seven Yellow Rails that day. Despite trying to sneak up on a couple after they'd landed, we only saw them in flight. The biggest surprise was flushing a single Black Rail, a smaller and even more secretive bird than the Yellow Rail and a candidate for the hardest regularly occurring bird to see in North America.

April 14, the day I saw the rails, marked a turning point for me. It was the last wintering bird I'd see. As the Yellow Rails were preparing for the flight north to their breeding grounds in the Canadian prairies, a whole wave of migrants from South and Central America were pushing north into the United States. Texas lies in the middle of the Central Flyway, a migration superhighway. Birds that are restricted to either east or west of the country are funneled through the state of Texas, making it one of the richest states in terms of birdlife (Texas has a list of more than six hundred species) and one of the best places to see many migrating summer breeders.

After finding a restroom with a heater to dry off my water-logged foot, which was now the texture of wrinkled ginger, I left the winter birds behind and headed to the coast to meet the spring. High Island is a small community of five hundred or so people on the Gulf Coast, less than twenty miles from Anahuac. At a modest height of thirty-eight feet above sea level, raised above the surrounding land by a geological oddity known as a salt dome, it has the highest elevation on the Gulf Coast from Alabama all the way to the Yucatán. With its dense covering of trees, High Island is a natural rest stop for tired and exhausted migrants.

Boy Scout Woods is the place to go if you want to buy stickers, pins, and bird books or to read the whiteboard listing recent bird sightings. There's a wooden set of bleachers from which you can pass the day watching thirsty birds come to a small pool, fed by a constant drip. The rest is a pleasant, though busy, boardwalk from which you can spot colorful birds without too much effort. Although some, such as the Mourning Warbler, the Least Flycatcher, and birds of prey like the Mississippi Kite, hug the Gulf Coast on the flight north, the majority of warblers, thrushes, vireos, and even tiny hummingbirds make the eighteen-hour, six-hundred-mile leap across the Gulf of Mexico in one go.

It was a fairly quiet though colorful day, with bright blue Indigo Buntings, red and black Scarlet Tanagers, golden Prothonotary Warblers, and deep russet Orchard Orioles. It was warm, but a gentle breeze shook the leaves and carried a sweet smell of hibiscus. I sat in the bleachers and watched a bright-red Summer Tanager bathing with a Tennessee Warbler, two birds that in a week or so could be thousands of miles apart. Every year I'm still blown away by migration—that more than 330 of our species split their time between here and South and Central America. The lack of a year-round abundance of food here (especially in the north) means that many birds leave the winter behind and head for the neotropics, especially the stretch from Mexico to Panama, which for those winter months harbors the greatest concentration of birds in the world. The competition for nesting there is so fierce that, come spring, it's worth flying thousands of miles north to find that extra space.

As I sat that afternoon and watched a parade of tired birds come to drink at the drip, birders would come and go. They'd ask what was being seen or talk about the rail walk (Did you hear they had a Black Rail this morning?). I thought of the irony of these reverse migrants—birders heading south, descending on this tiny piece of Texas coast. In High Island alone there are four sanctuaries (all owned and operated by Houston Audubon). As long as the birds keep coming, so too would the wide-eyed people.

Some of the birders were local migrants. I spotted one

wearing the maroon colors of Texas A&M University, reminding me of my first visit to the United States, when I was an undergraduate studying biochemistry in my second year at Oxford University. Although I'd grown up near the city, the wood-paneled lecture halls, musty libraries, and sherry-before, port-after, gown-wearing dinners were a world away from my working-class upbringing. My rooms were in New College (now entering its 634th year of needing a name change) and directly below Edmond Halley's old room. I liked to think of him sitting up there on long, cold nights, looking at the cosmos, predicting the return of a comet (his comet) that he would never live to see. There was a faded blue plaque on the front of the building that informed tourists of these facts. Every morning I'd draw back my curtains to find one or two of them gazing up, surprised to see a real person rattling around in this seventeenth-century museum.

I lived in only half of that room—the safe half. While I was confident in the rickety old staircase, and wasn't too bothered by the paucity of right angles, I drew the line at the cantilevered end of the room, hanging precipitously over a winding alley of flagstones three floors below, one of the many passageways in Oxford that leads to a hidden pub. And so I lived at the front, with a view of the famous spires framed by a window whose mosaic of glass diamonds gently pinged in their lead frames on windy days.

I was happy to discover my new lecturer in bacteriology was a birder, and that she'd birded in the United States, the holy grail of birding for any British birder. Occasionally we'd glimpse one of the wonders of the avian New World when a lost American bird turned up on our shores (I'd recently chased, unsuccessfully, the first European record of Red-breasted Nuthatch). A few more conversations and I had a three-month summer job lined up at Texas A&M University with a birding colleague of hers.

While I waited for that interminably rainy semester to end and for summer to start, I added another book to the pile of organic chemistry, biochemistry, and genetics books that overflowed my desk: the *National Geographic Field Guide to the Birds of North America*. Before going to bed each night, I'd leaf through that book, careful not to break the spine, learning about the exotic and colorful species that lived within. There were whole families of birds I'd never seen in Europe: hummingbirds, tanagers, and myriad flycatchers. By the time I stepped off the plane in Texas, I was ready for all those birds.

I was not, however, ready for any of the people. Since we spoke the same language (sort of), I hadn't given any thought to any differences I might encounter there. But differences there were. I hadn't expected, for one, that Americans would be so damn friendly. It was incredibly annoying and very rude. I couldn't go anywhere without people being overly concerned that I was having a good day. People would never ask that in the UK. They'd simply assume (probably correctly) that you never were having a good day, and that was how it bloody well should be. And as plainspoken as these people were, they could also be ridiculously sensitive. I couldn't ask where the toilet was for fear of embarrassing them. I quickly discovered that toilets are not toilets, but restrooms or bath-rooms, even though that was probably the last place I'd ever think about going for a rest, and none of them ever did have a bath.

But the biggest problem for me was arriving to discover that no one understood me. It wasn't my polished Oxford brogue but the speed. I was a fast talker, and in Texas they're, well, not. As a concession to being understood I slowed down my speech, and by the time I returned home three months later, everyone . . . thought . . . I'd . . . had . . . some . . . kind . . . of . . . brain . . . aneurysm.

In a blasting furnace of heat, in a town with no history, seemingly no future beyond the next football game, and no comprehension of the word *vegetarian*, and with my newly developed speech retardation, I sought out all those birds I'd studied under my covers in that cantilevered room back in Oxford. I savored my first ever Cardinal and watched salmon-colored Scissor-tailed Flycatchers chase one another across the fields, scaly Inca Doves pick at the seeds scattered under the yard feeders, and the fiery sun set over the university buildings while Common Nighthawks *meep-meeped* above.

Many things remained a mystery after I left Texas that first time and boarded the plane for the long flight back home. I didn't understand why I couldn't drink there (although I did), but I could get married and buy a gun (although I was careful to make sure I didn't). I didn't know how it was possible to live in a place where there was no history or architecture. But I had liked the friendliness of the place and the seemingly class-free system was refreshing. And the optimism was conta-gious, so different from the continual moaning back home. (Although, to be fair, if it's not drizzling every day, your teeth aren't a national embarrassment, and you're not forced to consume lumpy mashed potato and pies made out of shepherds, it probably isn't that hard to be optimistic.) It wouldn't have surprised me then if you'd told me that I would someday call this land home.

My parents arrived the evening of the Boston Marathon bombing. Gerri and I picked them up at Logan, after driving past a city that was silent except for the screaming of emergency vehicles. There were police everywhere, on the ground and in the sky, conveying the sense that nothing was safe.

Gerri and I had been grocery shopping at the time. I'd just returned from Texas, it was midafternoon, and we were already running late. We were at the cash registers, and I was wondering if the machine would remember the cans of tomatoes were buy-2-get-1 free, when I overheard someone say something about an explosion at the finish line. Everyone knew about the marathon that day—it takes place on a state holiday, Patriots' Day, which was the reason Gerri was standing next to me scooping up groceries rather than teaching chemistry to teenagers a few a blocks from the race. But nothing bad had ever happened here, and so we assumed it must have been a gas explosion. It's an old city after all.

My parents emerged from Terminal E, looking slightly older and shorter than they had on their last visit two years before. They were easy to pick out at a distance, toting way more luggage than was needed and sporting a profusion of white hair that I was well on my way to inheriting. They'd heard about the bombing on the plane and were relieved to discover we were okay. We were—we didn't know any of the victims, dead or injured, but like everyone else in the city, we had the sense that the innocence had been shattered, the protective bubble of that warm place you call home had been burst. And no longer would a gas explosion be the obvious go-to answer for any future surprise blast.

We took daily trips outside the city, large parts of whose center had been sealed off as a crime scene. We visited The Breakers, the summer house of the Vanderbilts in Newport, Rhode Island. We took them to Lexington, the site of the opening battle of the Revolution, and to the tourist shops of Rockport. Everywhere we went, the landscape was so virile and restless you could almost hear the erupting leaves unfurl. Gerri's school was closed after the bombing and so we saw more of her. My parents liked Gerri. I knew they would. She's quiet, friendly, and attentive. They never once stumbled over her name, managing to erase Anna from their lexicon in a way that I was still struggling to do.

The bombing was never very far from our thoughts that week. There were reminders on the radio and TV and in the suddenly ubiquitous BOSTON STRONG T-shirts. Losing the security and protection of my new city reminded me of how I felt after I'd been burgled. It was the winter after Anna had left. It had been snowing and I'd returned home from another miserable date to find my place a mess. After wondering if there'd been an earthquake and then considering whether I could have knocked things over myself, the unpleasant reality registered. Some of it I could and did replace, but not the photos on the stolen laptop that I'd put off backing up. They were photos of Anna (smiling in London, laughing in Machu Picchu, and riding a bike on Nantucket). Losing the photos months after losing the actual person seemed like a final and definitive bookend to the relationship. Not long afterward I moved out. I couldn't get over that feeling of violation. When I spoke to people after the bombing, I recognized that same feeling in their expressions and voices.

On April 19 the suspects were cornered. There was a manhunt in Watertown, the neighboring city, and we were in lockdown for the day and night. As the helicopters buzzed over the empty streets, we sat at the dining table placing tiny plastic trains on a large map of the United States. Ticket to Ride was our favorite game—you have to connect cities with trains based on destination cards. I connected Vancouver to Montreal (twenty points!), shooed away a giant cat the size of Canada, and thought back to one of the last times I'd played, on New Year's Eve. That was almost four months ago, and since then I hadn't exactly achieved a lot. (Although I had, ironically, visited Vancouver and Montreal and was well on my way to completing many of the other routes laid out in front of us. If only those points meant something in the real world.)

It's easy to ignore the small stuff, like not making a packed lunch in the morning or no longer setting three alarm clocks to get you out of bed. You keep finding excuses, like "I'm taking a break. Next week I'll decide what to do." It's harder to do that when your parents are visiting. It's as if their presence forces you to consider the embarrassed and confused reflection in the mirror that, until then, has been so easy to avoid. And it wasn't a pretty sight. It was a reminder that I didn't have a job and that I wasn't even speaking to the girl-friend they'd met last time.

Somehow, with all the games and the car drives and the discussions of the weather, we never had enough time to talk about the serious stuff. Everything was accepted without question or debate: Anna gone, Gerri here; all of us slowly aging and arrogantly thinking there was no rush to have these conversations, that there would always be a next time. But what if there wasn't? I felt the weight of not talking about Anna and not knowing how to talk about the secret pills I was taking for the secret disease. But we're British, which meant we said nothing.

Between the board games and the day trips, I'd sneak away to check the Listservs and bird blogs, watching the spring migrants appear in other people's reports: Spotted Redshank in Indiana, La Sagra's Flycatcher at Bill Baggs in Miami, and the pesky White-cheeked Pintail still laughing it up at Pelican Island National Wildlife Refuge. Back in High Island, on that salt-dome along the Texas coast, birders were bracing for one of the biggest "fall-outs" in living memory: a warm front was sweeping thousands of unsuspecting migrants north across the Gulf of Mexico, where they were about to run into a south-moving cold front. The resultant rain and heavy winds would drown any birds that fell into the sea. The lucky ones would make it to the coast, where, having used up all their energy supplies battling the storm, they would descend at the first sight of land. For a birder, it's a truly unique spectacle: a multitude of tired species coating the trees and bushes and carpeting the ground. For the birds, of course, it's a near tragedy.

I couldn't keep up with all these new birds. I wasn't doing a Big Year, but, as if living vicariously through a twin in a parallel universe, I'd felt a sense of excitement in knowing it remained a dim possibility. But now it seemed that even my virtual twin had lost the Big Year before starting. It was one thing chasing down the winter visitors and the odd rarity, but now spring had unleashed an inexorable flood of new birds into a country they would call home but for a few brief months. It didn't help that the day before my parents left, the Listservs exploded with the news of a Bahama Woodstar in Pennsylvania—a tiny hummingbird with a forked tail and an iridescent purple gorget. It was the first record since 1981.

I drove my parents back to Logan airport thinking about all the things left unsaid, wishing for more time, yet knowing that wouldn't help. Whatever we wanted to say would, like every time, have to wait until the next time. I could see their eyes tear up with the same thoughts. I felt lonelier than ever, knowing that after I pulled away from Logan, I'd make the decision to drive straight to the hummingbird, even though the morning reports were negative. For once, I really didn't want to go birding.

I arrived in Denver, Pennsylvania, to discover a small town (population 3,332) in the southeast of the state, nestled in the heart of Pennsylvania Dutch Country. I drove through town with the windows down, savoring the sweet smell of honey-suckle. The houses were wooden, many painted white, with broad decks to enjoy the afternoon sun, although no one appeared to be doing that. The place seemed quietly deserted. Amid the oak trees and white pines, magnolias were bursting into bloom.

The hummingbird had been found at a residence owned by an Amish family. While the Amish may have been blissfully unaware of Kim Kardashian, Candy Crush, and Interstate 95, they did have a sense of the hysteria that a tiny bird from the Bahamas would cause to this small community. They'd had the foresight to order a porta-potty for the expected weekend crowds.

I pulled up behind a long line of cars hugging a hedgerow pinpricked with white flowers. It was mid-afternoon, and a light breeze cooled the otherwise cloying air. After I'd left Boston, I decided not to check the Listserv updates, as the hummingbird might be operating under a kind of Heisenberg uncertainty principle. If I waited for the bird to be reported, I might not have had enough time to make it there before dark. And if it was being seen, then my excitement might have caused me to drive off the road. Either way would result in my not seeing the bird. I didn't have to wait long before the uncertainty was resolved by the first birder I met, a middle-aged bearded fellow who was walking back to his car,

"Hasn't been seen now for twenty-five hours," he said, which, judging from his tone, his slumped shoulders, and the way he threw his binoculars in his car, could equally have referred to his sense of humor.

I walked to the edge of the property where a small crowd was held back by a length of kitchen twine secured between a sapling and the first vertical of a picket fence. On the other side, fifty feet away, hung a bright-red hummingbird feeder to which no one seemed to be paying much attention. Hummingbirds have such a rapid metabolism that they need to feed every thirty minutes or so, otherwise they stop humming. If it wasn't being seen regularly, it wasn't here. The bird had been caught yesterday morning and banded, the measurements confirming this to be a truly unusual hummingbird. The shock of that must have scared the poor thing away for good.

I spent an hour staring at that lonely red feeder, feeling like I'd missed the last flight of the day and knowing there would be no more. I could put off Gerri's inquiring text no longer.

"No, not seen today," I replied, as if revealing the ugly truth conclusively ended my hope.

As I watched the common Purple Finches (first of the year for me!), I couldn't help admiring the setup here. The family had made pretzels for visiting birders and had photos of the bird available. And while the restroom facilities had indeed proved helpful, I think most of us would have agreed that the presence of the actual bird would have been decidedly more helpful.

Interstate 95 is an equal-opportunity crash site, working in both directions. It was midnight before I rolled into the driveway back home. I was exhausted and beaten. I'd said goodbye to my parents that morning, driven sixteen hours, and seen nothing but a few pretzel crumbs, some Purple Finches, and the look of haunting desperation on the faces of grown men. Gerri didn't say anything. She didn't need to. I knew how ridiculous this whole day had been. I also knew normal people didn't do this. I was fast approaching forty years old. I'd quit my job and still hadn't figured out how to have a relationship that lasted. I had no right to be doing this. Gerri could see how upset and tired I was as I slumped onto the sofa, quickly followed by four pairs of cat legs that kneaded my stomach up and down before settling on the perfect spot.

For all Gerri's sympathy and careful restraint in not telling me that she'd told me so (all that way for a stupid humming-bird?), I could tell she was relieved to see that I realized now how reckless this new "career" was and that it was time to stop. It had been fun chasing birds around the country and had been a phenomenally successful strategy for ignoring life. But this wasn't a long-term strategy. It was time to grow up.

It was easy, then, to understand the confusion that played across her face as she heard me say those fateful words.

"That's it. I'm doing a Big Year!"

It didn't make any sense to me either. Maybe there's no greater incentive to do something than after fate has conspired to somehow stop you from doing it. The Bahama no-show had been the kick in the proverbial butt that I evidently needed. With it came a realization that all this time I'd been on autopilot—a Big Year autopilot that had tugged at my imagination and my need for adventure and had shown me birds. Lots of birds. I'd missed some, of course, but I'd seen just enough to stay in the game.

It was April 25, 114 days after everyone else who'd ever done a Big Year had typically started. I'd seen 492 birds. I had no idea how many more I could possibly see or where this would end up taking me. But now I suddenly had a goal (sort of), and it was time to stop making excuses and to run away from life full-time. The race was on. This was a Big Year. My Big Year.

My bird count at the end of April 2013: 506

Chapter 5

BIRDING ON THE EDGE

ONCE I'D DECIDED I was doing a Big Year, I thought I should probably find out what a Big Year actually is and, more important, whom I could blame for inventing it. As far as I could tell from extensive research in the annals of Wikipedia, the latter honor should probably go to Roger Tory Peterson. Peterson, who had grown up in New York State the son of Swedish-German immigrants, is perhaps more famous for inventing the first modern-day field guide for birds. By using painted illustrations and helpful arrows pointing toward distinguishing features, he provided the key to unlocking the secrets of bird identification and made birding accessible to the general population.

Perhaps the most dangerous man armed with Peterson's new *A Field Guide to the Birds* was Mr. Peterson himself. His Pandora's box of new and frightening possibilities included one that surely came to him in a moment of sheer delirium: "Wouldn't it be fun to drive across the country and see all those birds?" In 1953 he and his British naturalist friend James Fisher did just that. The experience was eye-popping enough to become the subject of a book and a movie, both called *Wild America*, although the 572 species he saw were relegated to a mere footnote. But with that footnote a new form of self-flagellation was born—the Big Year—and if there are two things birders are good at, it's counting and driving. (Wearing outrageously unfashionable clothing comes in a close third.)

The American Birding Association, founded in 1968, set about establishing rules for the new sport of "listing". The playing field was defined as the continental United States, plus Alaska and Canada, and enclosed by two hundred gut-heaving miles of sea. Many have since fallen under the spell of the game, perhaps none so eloquently as Kenn Kaufman in 1973, whose memoir, *Kingbird Highway*, recounts the 666 species he saw (including an additional 5 across the border in Baja California, Mexico). Kaufman was eighteen years old at the time, with no money, no job, and no driver's license. He survived by the kindness of strangers, an impressive ability to thumb rides, and a cheap supply of cat food. The better-funded Floyd Murdoch, a college teacher born in the old country and Kaufman's competition that year, ultimately beat the latter, setting a new record of 669. That record stood until 1979, when the unthinkable happened: it was bought.

To many in the birding establishment, James M. Vardaman, a forestry consultant and business owner from Jackson, Mississippi, was a rank amateur. He solved the Big Year as he would any other problem he faced in business: he put together a committee of expert birders (including Kaufman) to come up with his Big Year plan. They told him where to go and when, and then Vardaman hired guides to point at the birds once he got there. To make sure he didn't miss anything, he developed the first birding hotline. Birders from around the country were invited to "Call Collect, Ask for Birdman," whenever they found anything Vardaman still needed.

Perhaps more impressive than the 699 species Vardaman was shown (falling one short of his target of 700) were his powers of persuasion. He not only convinced birders to call collect and give the birdman a lead on an additional twenty species he otherwise would have missed, he also convinced his company to grant him a year off work and to fund his boondoggle. His 161,000 miles of travel together with hiring birding guides at every stop wasn't cheap. At $44,507.38, James M. Vardaman & Co. Inc. outspent Kaufman by at least $43,507.38.

It was a dark time for US birding. The Big Year hero had bought his title and some wondered whether he could separate a Willow from an Alder Flycatcher without one of his experts present. And he probably didn't even suffer from an appalling dress sense. It fell to Benton Basham, a peripatetic anesthesiologist from Tennessee and one of the founding members of the ABA, to restore order to the birding world. In 1983, Basham not only took Vardaman's crown but also was the first to break through the 700 barrier, ending the year with 711 species.

The most famous Big Year of all, though, was waged in 1998, which was immortalized in Mark Obmascik's excellent book *The Big Year*, and in the Hollywood movie of the same name. The star was Sandy Komito, a rough-around-the-edges birding machine. While his two competitors that year, Greg

Miller and Al Levantin, would both break 700 species (715 and 711, respectively), Komito ended up smashing the previous record of 721, which he himself had set in 1987. (Komito is the only person to have completed two 700-plus Big Years.) He saw three species new to the ABA region and close to thirty rare Asian species on Attu, the island at the far western end of the Aleutian chain. The US Coast Guard abandoned Attu at the end of the century and decommissioned the runway; there would be no more planes bringing birders to the best spot in the ABA area to score Asian vagrants. Sandy Komito's 1998 record of 748 species was safe.

Although Attu dropped off the birding map, there was still a lot of Alaska left. Birders migrated to the Bering Sea outposts of Gambell (St. Lawrence Island) and St. Paul (the Pribilof Islands). An increasing number of exotics (escaped birds, such as Budgerigars and parakeets) were being added to the ABA list, and with DNA analysis, species were being split into multiple species. In 2010, a decade after the last flight left Attu, birders were once again recolonizing, this time by boat, thanks to enterprising Washington State birder John Puschock. Together with up-to-the-minute electronic data from eBird, as well as state and provincial Listservs, making it easier to hear about rare birds, Sandy's record of 748 was starting to look shaky. In 2011 the birding community collectively held its breath as Colorado birder John Vanderpoel put the record to the test. Going into December of that year, Vanderpoel was sitting on 734 birds. Although he ultimately fell short—ending the year with 743—he showed that Komito's record, in a post-Attu, electronic world, was most definitely in play.

The 700 Club is an exclusive group. After John Vanderpoel's inauguration in 2011, it numbered twelve birders. More people have visited the British Lawnmower Museum, read all of Proust's seven-volume *In Search of Lost Time*, or randomly impaled themselves on a gearstick. And seeing more than seven hundred species in one year generates about as much veneration from the rest of the population, who are either unaware such a thing exists or who sensibly question why anyone in his or her right mind would ever want to do it. Which is a good question: why do people do crazy shit like this? Perhaps it's enough to say that doing a Big Year is no more unusual than life itself. It's there to be lived if only because no one has found a better alternative.

It wasn't long before the curious tendrils of the 700 Club found me, the first being John Vanderpoel on April 17. It was a polite, matter-of-fact missive, along the lines of "Are you doing a Big Year?" At that point, of course, I didn't know what I was doing, and it was easy to tell him so. But it was harder to ignore the implications: the 700 Club was onto me. I imagined them (eleven men and one woman) reclining in an oak-paneled room of the type Phileas Fogg, Jules Verne's fictional traveler, once frequented when he wasn't traveling the world in eighty days. The thick haze of Cuban cigar smoke would occasionally be cut by the tinkling of expensive glasses slowly being drained of port and sherry. The only disturbance would be the butler, bringing in a telephone (the old-fashioned type with a rotary dial) on a silver platter. Sandy Komito, leader of the group, would pick up, "An Eskimo Curlew, you say? In Anchorage?" Bags would be packed, hot-air balloons commandeered, and the chase for the next life bird would commence. They probably didn't need anyone else to share any of that port and sherry, I imagined, especially someone with a funny British accent.

There is no official historian for Big Years, but if there were one, it would be Chris Hitt. And Chris, unlike John, wouldn't take my no for an answer. Chris saw "only" 704 species during his Lower 48 Big Year in 2010, but he created a new club within a club for which he was the sole member: he's the only birder to have seen more than 700 species in the ABA Area without going to Canada or Alaska. Even Sandy Komito's record-breaking 748 featured fewer than 700 species in the Lower 48.

Chris Hitt gave me an important piece of advice that I didn't particularly want to hear: go to Alaska.

My first official trip as a certified and newly minted Big Year birder was back to southeast Arizona to add the newly-arrived wave of summer breeders. The Sonoran Desert was a blossoming riot of primary colors—red ocotillos, pea-green saguaro cacti topped by white floral explosions, and azure blue skies. But the two colors that came to define the desert for me were green and white: the colors of the US Border Patrol. Their vehicles were as ubiquitous as the cooing White-winged Doves and spotted in equally as remote and unusual places.

I passed one of those minty-green-and-white trucks as I headed west along Ruby Road, paralleling the border four and a half miles to the south of me. The agents waved, spied my binoculars, and knew exactly where I was headed: California Gulch. California Gulch has a poor reputation among birders, which is a shame: it's set in the beautiful desert scrub of the Pajarito Mountains and is the only consistent place in the United States to see the stunning Five-striped Sparrow. Unfortunately, it's a bastard to get there. And more of a bastard to get back again. Hence the brow-furrowing effect its name has on birders.

California Gulch is three and a half miles south of Ruby Road, on dusty, rocky roads that cut through dry washes and past abandoned and evocatively named mines such as Austerlitz and Warsaw. NO TRESPASSING signs perch on rusted posts like sentinels defying you to mess with them. If my eyes weren't so glued to reading the landscape of the dangerously abused and abandoned road, I'd have been looking for the ghost towns here, a testament to the nineteenth-century mining boom and bust. In 1873 Oro Blanco, one of the bigger mines, had a population of 225, including a dentist. Today, these towns are reduced to dust. Dentist population: zero.

As I added more distance between myself and the paved road behind, I could feel my stomach churn—there was a constant knocking on the underside of the car, as if the road were reminding me to take it slow. Occasionally that knocking was interrupted by a heavy *whump!* that made me grip the steering wheel harder and pray that something whose name I invariably wouldn't know hadn't fallen off and totally screwed me. The chances were much greater here of getting stuck than finding anyone to help. I reluctantly agreed with the guidebook— you probably do need a 4WD vehicle with high clearance. And if I could get cellphone reception here, which I couldn't, I'm pretty sure Google would have told me that a Ford Focus is neither of those, hence the road noises and the churning stomach.

I was happy to be back under the yawning blue skies of Arizona. Since I'd last been here, in January, life had moved on (spring had happened!), and the familiar places were now teeming with unfamiliar life. It was like going back to an old high school now populated with new faces. I was grateful for my previous winter trip, which meant I could now focus on all the new arrivals, of which there were many. Those evil-looking Yellow-eyed Juncos had left the feeders at Madera Canyon and moved higher up the slope, to be joined by Red-faced Warblers, Greater Pewees, and Elegant Trogons. Lower down, among the oaks, sang the mournful Dusky-capped Flycatchers (a single descending *peeur*), while spiky-crested Northern Beardless-Tyrannulets and migrating golden-faced Hermit Warblers hunted for bugs. In the trees above the picnic area a pair of Gray Hawks had set up nest, taking turns foraging for snakes in the surrounding territory and showing off their stripy black-and-white tails. It was as if some giant being had breathed warm, rejuvenating life into the canyon. All around me I sensed that same primal urgency I'd felt back in the chicken leks of Colorado.

It wasn't just all the new birds. I suppose I was different too. The Big Year had given me a purpose, albeit one only marginally more defined than before. I still hadn't thought about a target number of species except somewhere in the vague ballpark of "as many birds as I can possibly see." But I already had a feeling even that loose goal would exact a heavy mental cost. For a start, it was harder to lose myself in the present. While watching Violet-crowned Hummingbirds in Patagonia or bright yellow Scott's Orioles at Ash Canyon I was starting to worry about all those other empty boxes on my ABA Checklist. The Golden-cheeked Warblers and Black-capped Vireos, the specialties of the Texas Hill Country, were already back. The Colima Warblers were singing at the top of Big Bend, and the boobies, terns, and noddies were beckoning me to the Dry Tortugas. And did I really plan to go all the way to Alaska—a state I'd never visited? I suppose I should have been grateful that I was being pulled into the future, away from the shoe-gazing past.

The sign caught me unaware: CALIFORNIA GULCH, next to what I assumed was a parking area. Instead of worrying about Texas and Florida I reminded myself that I should be worrying about snakes, heat exhaustion, and making it back on this "road" alive. The trail dropped down precipitously from the parking area to what the guidebook enthusiastically but surely erroneously called the "old road." Now that I was out of the car, I could feel the heat for the first time, causing my head to pound as if I'd surfaced too quickly from a dive.

As I descended into the gulch itself, a kettle of Turkey Vultures drifted overhead, teeter-tottering on unsteady wings. To my right and left the walls of the ravine rose up, its steep sides coated in thorny hackberry and mesquite, an ocotillo or two waving in the light, warm breeze. And that's when I started to see the water. Not in the green riparian streambed, which I imagined to be alive with bubbling torrents after the late summer monsoon rains, but under the shade of prickly mesquite trees, in neat plastic gallon bottles. They're distributed by Humane Borders, Samaritan lifesavers for the hot and thirsty immigrants. Those that pass through this gulch are the lucky ones. Already this year forty-nine sets of remains had been recovered, most lying unidentified in body bags at the Pima County Medical Examiner's Office in Tucson. But how many more were out there, I wondered, slowly bleaching under the baking sun? It's a vast and terrifying area. The few hundred miles of linear border are abutted by one hundred thousand square miles of disorienting desert, a nightmare fracturing at the edges into a shimmering haze.

I moved quickly, aware of the heat and the nagging prospect of navigating the craterous roads back to civilization. At the bottom of the fertile gulch, I started to hear the song for which my ears had been straining: the jangly notes of the Five-striped Sparrow. I could hear them on that thorny hillside to my left, over which Mexico loomed. I set up my scope and waited, stealing what little shade I could from a mesquite tree. The calls moved around invisibly on the slope in front of me, but only the movement of a slithering lizard gave up its presence.

Despite the unquestionable beauty of the place, I was eager to leave. I was starting to imagine a band of immigrants hiding on the hillside, their guide, or "coyote," not favorably impressed with a telescope pointed their way. What popped up next wasn't a human though, but a spiffy black, white, and brown bird. The five white stripes giving the sparrow its name were immediately obvious: one line above each eye,

two moustachial stripes, and a bright white chin. Some black
on the face, together with a black spot in the center of the
breast, rounded out a very neatly patterned bird.

As I watched the sparrow throw its head back, issuing a
cascade of notes, I was hit by a snapshot from the past: not of
the lonely sepia-colored dentist in Oro Blanco, but of those
twelve members of the 700 Club, all of whom had stood right
here, gazing at the same hillside, separated only by time. I
wondered how many of them had been nervous about the
drive back or were distracted by thoughts of where they
were heading next (Texas, Florida, California?). They each
had their own personal reasons for doing a Big Year, some
for the glory, others for one last lap of the world, but all, I'm
sure, thought that a life without birds wasn't a life at all—
at least not one worth living. But they weren't the only
ones caught up in the Big Year. Perhaps they, too, had
worried that after all those birds were ticked, and that last
flight home was booked, there might not be anyone to come
home to.

Gerri quit her job. I'd known this would happen for some
time but had filed it under "things to worry about later." This
particular file was becoming alarmingly full, stuffed with
headaches like Alaska (what the hell do I do there?), life
(what do I do after I run out of birds to count?), and my bathroom (will the ever-growing number of cosmetics ever stop?).
This was Gerri's last semester teaching high school chemistry,
after which there'd be no more grading, pH titration, or
school bureaucracy. I understand it's a familiar story for those

in teaching—for those who love the kids but hate the administrative work. I'd seen how unhappy she'd been, how exhausted and frustrated she was when she came home. The only thing that softened that pain was the smiles on those kids' faces (although I'm sure the long holidays didn't hurt either).

We all have something that makes us tick. If you're lucky, that's your job. But I suspect for most of us it's what we look forward to in our free time (climbing, competitive knitting, or dressing our pets in Halloween costumes). It's that mental space we go to while daydreaming. It's as if we're slightly incomplete and we need to find that missing piece to complete us. That happened to me once in Russia. After my Ph.D. I traveled through Central Asia for a year, winding my way along the ancient pomegranate-lined Silk Road while growing a beard and trying out new diseases for size (I'd recommend avoiding amoebic dysentery if you can). Before all that, though, I lived in St. Petersburg for three months, teaching science and learning Russian.

I lived with an old and grumpy babushka at the top of a concrete stairwell covered in graffiti. It was the summer during the white nights—*belye nochi*—when the sun never sets. The large windows of the apartment were hidden behind thick carpeted drapes, as if fearful of a surprise wartime blitz. She fed me fresh food, which I'd seen for sale across the city: mushrooms, onions, tomatoes, and all manner of beets laid out on blankets and bed linens behind which shrunken old women patiently sat. But no salt. My body figured this out somehow, and I'd find myself sneaking into restaurants to upturn a saltcellar, spilling its contents on my palm before lustily licking it up.

In the same way, my body missed and sought out birds—especially when I was stressed at work, firing an employee, or preparing for a difficult meeting. I'd get up early and head to Mount Auburn Cemetery before work or sneak out before the end of the day to beat the rush-hour traffic to Plum Island. It didn't seem to matter what the weather was doing, or even whether there were that many birds; my head felt warm and fuzzy as I entered the slim plane that is the present, too thin to accommodate worries about the past or the future. All my mental energy was consumed by looking and identifying. I was connected to the seasons, the environment, and life in a way that I wasn't when behind a desk or in a windowless meeting room. The birding was my salt, the thing that was missing, that essential amino acid I couldn't get from anywhere else. It gave me life and reminded me that I was part of life.

I was home from Arizona for four days before I headed back to Florida and Texas. I was running out of time.

A Big Year is a long time, you might think, even if you only start taking it seriously in April. But as soon as I sat down to plan it, thumbing through the field guide from geese past ducks, hawks, hummingbirds, and warblers through to sparrows, I realized that time would be my biggest competitor. A Big Year is a complex, strategic problem. Many species are present in only certain parts of North America (some are highly localized, like the Five-striped Sparrows), and many are seasonal (winter visitors, summer breeders, spring or fall migrants). In fact, only about 375 are resident, meaning predictably present in the same place all year long—the rest come and go. For the latter it's a game of whack-a-mole, getting them in the right place at the right time.

I needed to get to the summer migrants before they left the ABA Area. I'd picked up a good number as they funneled north through Texas and Florida in the spring—but there were many that I had missed and would need to track down in their summer breeding grounds. Thankfully, for each, there was at least one well-known hot spot, traded between birders like baseball cards: Kirtland's Warbler (central Michigan), Bicknell's Thrush (New Hampshire), and, in a cruel piece of false advertising, the Connecticut Warbler (the smelly bogs of Minnesota and not nearby Connecticut). This knowledge would save me weeks of scouring boreal forests and bogs. Each species was on a different time schedule. Many, like the Connecticut Warbler, would become extremely difficult to find once they stopped singing and started nesting. Others, such as the Thick-billed Kingbirds of Arizona, had yet to arrive, meaning at least one more trip there for me.

I'd recently started to carry a copy of John Vanderpoel's bird list from his 2011 Big Year. It made for fun and instructive reading and showed the exponential nature of the Big Year. He saw half of his 743 birds in the first ten weeks of the year, and 88 percent in the first six months. After that it got a lot harder. Vanderpoel ended up chasing single species, sometimes in Alaska. It was hard to stop myself from comparing our lists. On May 8, I was at 547. Vanderpoel had been at 566. Although I wasn't intending to follow him to Alaska, perhaps

I could keep up with him long enough to limp over the
700-species barrier?

The trip to Florida (my third of the year) didn't start well.
There'd been a Black-faced Grassquit reported at Bill Baggs
(where Gerri had met the angry Thick-billed Vireo two
months earlier). The grassquit is a small, finchlike bird that
feeds on seeds and, depending on your level of cynicism,
either comes from the Bahamas and the West Indies or from
the local pet store (they're a common cage bird). Wherever it
came from, it was gone by the time I arrived. I could live with
that—I mean, I didn't expect to see every bird. But I did learn
two important lessons: First, if I did want to see every bird, I
needed to hustle quicker. And second, I wasn't the only one
doing a Big Year.

I'd been relying on the eBird website, a vast database of
bird records, to help me find target species. Each bird report
lists the species seen, the location, and the observer. Not only
can you see where the birds are, but you can also work out
what all the other birders are up to. One of those birders was
a certain Hans de Grys, who, I noticed, was seeing an awful
lot of birds. I could tell that he was following the same route
as I was: Arizona-Florida-Texas, except that he was a couple
days ahead, scooping up all the good birds.

I pictured my new arch-nemesis as a tall figure, wrapped in
a black cape, hiding under a menacing wide-brimmed hat (the
kind that would hide his face in shadow). While he wasn't spotting good birds, I imagined him drawing on a long black pipe.
When Gerri found out that he was a high school chemistry

teacher from Seattle, his character lost some of the menace (and probably the pipe) but none of the rivalry. It was no surprise when I discovered that he'd already been to the Dry Tortugas and had seen the Black Noddy. Suddenly, my Big Year had turned into a competition.

The Dry Tortugas are a bunch of islands, or keys, sixty-seven miles west of Key West. Some are little more than sand-bars, and because of the action of the wind and the waves, the exact number depends on which particular year you go. In 2013 there were seven. Fort Jefferson, built to protect the lucrative Mississippi River trade, hovers a few feet above water, a giant hexagon imprisoning much of Garden Key except for a white sandy beach where the ferry docks and a scrubby area of mangroves optimistically called a campsite.

From my perch atop the roof of the fort I had a panoramic view of sparkling aquamarine. Below me to the south sat the ferry, the *Yankee Freedom*, my ride this morning. To the east of the fort, the neighboring Bush Key was covered by mangroves, which themselves were decorated by thousands of seabirds: Sooty Terns, jet-black above, white below, with a deeply forked tail; and Brown Noddies, an all-brown version with a long pointed tail and a frosty white top of the head. Those birds that weren't growing out of the bare mangrove branches like some unusual blossom were wheeling above, like a billowing cloud of dark smoke. This is the lone breeding site for Brown Noddy in the United States and the colony occasionally attracts the very rare Black Noddy. This is the bird my pipe-smoking, cape-wearing arch-nemesis De Grys had already seen. I had four hours before the return ferry, and so far I had found 5,351 Brown Noddies and no Black Noddies. I already hated Mr. de Grys.

It didn't take much imagination for me to picture Fort Jefferson in the 1860s when the ferry brought prisoners, not tourists. The interior of the pentagon was carpeted by grass and faced by open-air cells, which once held the six hundred or so convicts. Its most famous inmate was Dr. Samuel Mudd, who was found guilty of conspiring with John Wilkes Booth in the assassination of Abraham Lincoln. He narrowly avoided execution (by one vote) and ended up in one of the cells below me. While the watery isolation of the prison must have sown despair in him and any others dreaming of escape, I'd like to think they might have gleaned some solace from watching the giant Magnificent Frigatebirds wheeling over-head, their serpentine necks and batlike wings evoking long-dead pterodactyls.

I was grateful for the refreshing breeze captured by the vertical walls of the fort. The pterodactyls were happy too— hanging effortlessly in its wake mere feet from my promon-tory. Below me, a few of the day's travelers were breaking out a picnic lunch on the beach and playing volleyball, unaware of the quixotic race going on above them. As the third hour moved into the fourth and final hour of my vigil, my tele-scope landed on a bird that looked subtly different: it had a longer, finer bill; the white on the head was more strongly demarcated; and in the right light, the jet black lacked a brown hue. I'd found the needle in a haystack! But I knew, as I sat atop the fort, panting with relief, that my year would involve many more of these haystacks.

By the time the ferry departed and the fort was slowly receding into the distance, first flattening to the horizon and then lost completely in the glassy aquamarine, I'd added Masked and Brown Boobies to my list of successful targets. It was a clean sweep and a curious satisfaction—the relief at knowing I wouldn't need to come back. Although I could have spent days gazing out from atop that fort, happily lost on my own desert island, time was a currency of which I would have precious little this year. As I was discovering, the Big Year was more about the empty boxes on my checklist than the checked ones. But for now, I closed my eyes and listened to the soundtrack of the movie playing to a captive and enthralled audience throughout the boat, *The Big Year.* And judging by the laughter, people seemed to think it was rather a funny thing.

The decision to do a Big Year had thrown some invisible switch in my brain, shifting my perception into reverse, like a photographic negative. As well as counting the birds I had yet to see, I also started to count the year backward. And so while May 4 was May 4 to everyone else, to me it was "241 days to go." This was the real number I was chasing: 241 days left of Big Year birds and of playing hooky from real life. I was already worried about that number running out, like coming to the end of a moving walkway, when I would suddenly lurch forward and stumble as the hectic pace of the year would fall away from me. What would be left for me then, I wondered?

I sat on a plane pointed toward Texas, the steaming mangroves of Florida disappearing behind me, and silently cursed Chris Hitt. I cursed him because he was right—I should go to Alaska. There are species in Alaska that are never seen farther south or east, and like a catcher's mitt, the state is poised to snare any overshooting vagrants from Asia. But I knew absolutely nothing of the logistics—when to go, where to go, or how to get around. In my middle seat, bookended by two probing elbows, I opened a copy of *A Birder's Guide to Alaska* by George West, after first inhaling deeply from the binding and gauging the maximum angle before which the spine would crease.

I came to be grateful for these precious moments when I wasn't birding, driving, or sleeping. And, despite the elbows, they were the only times when I could plan my next move. Spring, I read, comes late to Alaska (the end of May), for which I was thankful. The Bering Sea islands of St. Paul (one of the four Pribilof Islands) and St. Lawrence were the best places to find Asian rarities and breeding seabirds. If I wanted to see tundra breeders, like Bluethroats and Arctic Warblers, I'd have to go to Nome, on the west coast, in June. By the time the tray tables needed to be stowed and the seats returned to their upright position, I'd learned enough about Alaska to put together a rudimentary plan: I would try for a week at the end of the month on St. Paul in the Pribilofs.

Birding in Alaska wouldn't be like the two-day trip here in Texas, renting a car and birding on my own. For a start, there weren't many roads and some towns could be reached only by an occasional plane. Additionally, places like St. Paul could be visited only as part of a tour group. And because of the logistics and distances involved, I could end up spending weeks (months?) there, especially if I went back for fall migration. While Gerri had been supportive so far, and even joked about me going to Alaska, I wasn't so sure she'd still be laughing once she discovered the implications of birding there. I closed the Alaska book, admired the puffins sitting on the front cover, and leaned forward to gaze out the window at the shimmering skyscrapers of Austin.

The last time I'd driven across the rugged karst topography of the Texas Hill Country was twenty years ago, half my lifetime. I'd left the lab at Texas A&M for a long weekend and headed to Austin to look for birds, to listen to the bluegrass of the Austin Lounge Lizards, and to convince someone, somewhere, to serve me a beer. Now, heading west onto the limestone Edwards Plateau, I remembered the bluebonnets, black-eyed Susans, and Indian blankets that carpeted the roadsides here in spring, an impressionistic mess of yellows, reds, and blues.

The Black-capped Vireo wasn't singing at Kerr (perhaps it was horrified and culturally embarrassed, like me, by the nearby life-size replica of Stonehenge, a.k.a. Stonehenge II). However, I did manage to flush one from a dense thicket, getting a brief view of its black helmeted head and white spectacles. By the time I got to Lost Maples, a limestone ridge of the Balcones escarpment stocked with the Ashe junipers so beloved by Golden-cheeked Warblers, it was the slow part of the afternoon. Apart from a persistent Acadian Flycatcher singing its olive-colored head off (*peet-sup*), it was deathly quiet.

Unless you're a competitive speed walker (I'm not), walking fast is an entirely useless skill. And if you're a birder, it can be a distinct handicap. It's easy for me to daydream while birding, zip through a place, and miss many of the birds. I have to make a conscious effort to slow down every time and let the birds come to me. After walking up and down the leaf-shaded East Trail for several hours, I reminded myself of this fact and stopped and sat on a rock.

My stomach sounded like it wasn't happy that I hadn't eaten all day. I reached into my shoulder bag and pulled out a bag of mixed nuts, which were fast becoming my breakfast, lunch, and dinner this year. If I missed this bird, I thought, I'd either have to come back again (I wouldn't have time on this two-day trip) or live with a hole on my checklist. Neither were attractive possibilities. As I listened to the swishing leaves of the bigtooth maples brushing across each other, I started to hear another sound—a buzzing one that had been playing in my head this afternoon in anticipation, *bzzz layzee dayzee*. It was a Golden-cheeked Warbler! It took all my will-power to sit still and wait until a tiny head with a shocking yellow face peeked out from the canopy. I could make out the thin black line extending through the eye, giving the bird a pensive look. It hung around long enough to check me out before disappearing back into the leafy canopy. Sometimes, I reflected, you do see more if you slow down. And, I suspected, that probably doesn't apply only to birds.

Big Bend is one of the least visited national parks in the country, and for good reason: it's a seven-and-a-half hour drive from Austin, almost five hundred miles through the deserts of West Texas. What it lacks in visitors and water it makes up for with mountain lions, snakes, and terrifying views. Any birder who's ever seen the Colima Warbler (my third target on this trip) in the United States has been here. Like the Five-striped Sparrow of California Gulch, the Colima Warbler is a Mexican bird, and each year a few trickle across the border to breed. It's a hot five-mile trek starting a mile above sea level and zigzagging another eighteen hundred feet up the steep sides of the Chisos Mountains to the lonely high-elevation oaks, maples, and pinyons where the bird likes to nest.

Even in the chilly cool of the early morning the ascent was hard going. My back ached, my legs were crying out in pain, and my eyes were covered by a slimy film that made it hard to focus. I had arrived late the night before—too late to find a place to stay—and so I had spent the night in Hotel Toyota Camry, frozen by the desert night and searching for the impossible: a comfortable position. As the sun poured into the giant desert bowl from which the Pinnacles Trail snaked, I swore I was never going to sleep in a car again. (It would take less time to break this promise than the earlier ones of not doing a Big Year, not going to Alaska, and not forgetting to text Gerri every day to tell her I was still alive.)

The view was magnificent, but it did little to arrest the thumping in my chest. As I stopped to catch my breath, I looked down on the panoramic vastness of the Chihuahuan Desert below, a full spectrum of browns and grays. But my thoughts were elsewhere. It was hard to imagine there was a place in this country still covered by snow, but there was, and I was suddenly very desperate to go there. This year was starting to feel like my last and final one, and I needed to spread my wings. Alaska had never been part of the plan, but, then again, none of this seemed to be part of any plan. I was making it up as I went along.

It took me about an hour to reach the pinnacles, the crenellated ring that forms the lip to the desert bowl below. The solar furnace was set to maximum, and the dirty red path mercifully stopped its zigzagging and flopped limply over the top, happy to find level ground on which to continue. As I approached the top, I could hear a Colima Warbler singing ahead of me—an insectlike trill fading out at the end. This was number 568. And even though I knew there was a rare Flame-colored Tanager another mile ahead, in the cool forested slopes near an old and long-abandoned horse corral, I sat on the path and listened as the Colima sang and flitted, sang and flitted. I could have spent the whole morning watching that bird, with its bright apricot rump and undertail, and shining white eye-ring. And perhaps I should have done just that, rather than spending the rest of it searching for a tanager that never appeared.

My tour to the Pribilofs was booked for May 20 to 22. If this hadn't been my first-ever trip to Alaska, I wouldn't have been surprised to be spending those days in Anchorage. (Anchorage, of course, is the largest city in Alaska and not anywhere on or near the Pribilofs). The flight to St. Paul had been canceled. Mount Pavlof, one of the country's most irritable volcanoes, was exploding without my permission. Although Mount Pavlof is situated on the Alaskan peninsula far to the south of St. Paul, the enormous quantities of spewed ash were playing havoc with air routes across the Bering Sea. With only three flights a week, and demand quickly backing up, there was a good chance I'd never get to St. Paul. And if I needed more evidence that my luck had turned, a Common Ringed Plover was delighting birders at Plum Island, less than an hour from my home. It was a bird I'd never seen in North America, and one that I would ultimately miss for my Big Year.

My fellow travelers, five men and one woman, were putting on a brave face. We sat around the fireplace of the Coast International Inn, within earshot of Anchorage airport and a steady drone of planes heading everywhere but west. This was all new to me. I was in Alaska and was part of a tour group organized by Wilderness Birding Adventures. Aaron Lang, our tour guide, presented us with an alternative: the Kenai Peninsula, a half-day's drive south of the city. Although it wasn't the Pribilofs, there were birds I needed there. And who knew, maybe Pavlof would shut up soon?

The drive from Anchorage to Homer is one of the most beautiful in the country. The road hugs the coast of Turnagain Arm, a narrow east–west channel of Cook Inlet. I stared at the fearful symmetry of the still water, creating doubles of the giant, blue-tinged mountains of the Chugach National Forest that towered more than five thousand feet above us. A brief stop at a thawing marsh produced Arctic Terns, a Wandering Tattler, and a Red-necked Phalarope (all new birds for the year). And while I prefer to bird alone, the atmosphere in the large van was already starting to become infectious. I immediately liked Aaron, whose vast knowledge of birds was matched only by his unlimited generosity in sharing it. I knew he was disappointed, like the rest of us, not to be on St. Paul, but it never showed. He channeled all that energy into making sure our Plan B felt like Plan A. Standing over six feet tall, he needed to be shoehorned into the driver's seat. I guessed him to be around my age, despite looking much younger, helped no doubt by a much fairer dusting of color to his hair than mine.

While birding often attracts scientists and doctors, our group was top-heavy with lawyers. John and Laurie Cairns, a lawyer and a judge, were from New York. John's accent suggested he'd spent his whole life there, while Laurie hailed from Hawaii. They were old hands at Alaskan birding, and like many couples kept a joint life list. Bill Reeves (another lawyer) and Bob Mustell (chemist) were both from Missouri. I roomed with Bob and enjoyed hearing his birding stories of Adak in the Aleutians, from where he'd just returned (most of the stories could be summed up like this: cold, not many birds). Bill made friends with Guy Pickavance, a Scottish transplant now living in Vancouver. They were constantly joking like a pair of teenagers at the back of the bus. Alex Bloss was from Chicago and the quietest of the bunch. I noticed I was the only one doing a Big Year, suffering from a midlife crisis, and not married. Everyone else was much older (somewhere between sixty and one hundred) and curiously, despite having considerably less life left (I selfishly hoped), seemed so much happier.

While I was waiting for updates on the volcano, we birded around Homer, a cute little town of colorful wooden houses, over which the snow-covered peaks of Kachemak Bay State Park loomed. Homer comes alive in the tourist season, which, judging by the many shutters I saw, was still some way off. The town guards the entrance to the glasslike Kachemak Bay, whose currents concentrate nutrients and attract birds year-round. Aaron had organized a boat trip the next morning from the end of the four-mile-long pier. As we gently steamed across the mirrored surface, Marbled Murrelets, chocolate-brown members of the alcid family roughly the size of American Robins, floated around us on the cold, silty water. All were paired up, like wedding guests. All, that is, except for one: a solitary bird, mottled a shade or two grayer and with larger eyes. It was a Kittlitz's Murrelet, a life bird for all the visiting birders, including me, and the only one I would see all year.

That evening we sat at a long table surrounded by pizza and Alaskan Amber with the sleepless sun still hanging high in the bright white sky. I listened as everyone told their new Kittlitz's Murrelet story. I had another reason to celebrate: Pavlof had decided to stop making a mess of the Bering Sea.

The next morning I said goodbye to the gang in Homer and joined John and Laurie for an early-morning flight to Anchorage. They had confirmed seats to St. Paul. I was on standby, which is how I was feeling about my Big Year, barely managing to stay one step ahead. I sat nervously at the gate, leafing through my lists: I'd seen 598 species. But more important was my list of birds not seen. I counted through those I thought were possible. And then I counted again, thinking I'd made a mistake. Could that be right, I thought? If I saw all my target birds, that would put me at 700. Could I really join the 700 Club after such an unplanned and accidental start? I suddenly felt like a fraud, as if I'd walked out one morning to buy a newspaper and climbed halfway up Everest instead.

They had to call my name twice before I heard it. I was on the flight. I felt like I'd won the lottery. What I'd actually won was a pair of complimentary earplugs and a ride in a twin-prop plane that would take me three hundred miles into the middle of the Bering Sea. And although there was no volcanic ash, there was plenty of fog.

Before I left Anchorage airport, I got a call from Gerri. She'd gotten into Boston College for a master's program in social work. She was excited. BC was her first choice and she was looking forward to her change in career. Her course would start in September, giving her the summer off. I fumbled to hand over my new boarding pass, as the rest of the passengers snaked across the tarmac to the waiting plane.

"Did you hear me?" Gerri said after a moment of silence.

I tried to explain where I was and what I was doing (two bags, a tripod, a boarding pass, not enough hands), but it was too late. Her childish excitement was replaced with disappointment.

"Well, I'll let you go," she said. "I hope you get all your birds!"

She was gone. I thought of all those times she was there to congratulate me on a bird she'd never even heard of, like it was the most important thing in the world. I knew how difficult it was to make a big life decision like leaving your job. I was thrilled for her, and very proud. Both of which I wished I'd told her.

I climbed out of the tiny plane and looked around at a fog-bound and treeless landscape. What the hell was I doing here? I thought. Taking my cue from John and Laurie, who'd been here before, I followed them off the runway into what looked like a giant storeroom, unlit and strewn with debris. I dodged buckets half full of rainwater that sat patiently below an unreliable roof. At the back I emerged through a door into the bright artificial light of the "airport." A space eight feet by twenty feet performed the functions of places typically thousands of times larger: check-in, arrivals, ticket office, baggage claim, everything but security (for which there was none) and a Starbucks.

Beyond the "airport," and still in the same building, was the "hotel." (Almost everything in St. Paul, I was to discover, including "food," "coffee," and "departure date" seemed to require quotation marks.) I looked at a long corridor of rooms stretching out before me, outside which muddy boots and wet socks sat topsy-turvy, hoping to dry, and suddenly felt very alone. This year had pushed me to the ends of the earth, from which there was no easy or quick escape.

Half an hour later, after John, Laurie, and I had "checked in," we joined four other birders who'd already been there for a week. We piled into a white van, our vehicle for the next three days. Our guide and driver was Doug Gochfeld, an exceptional birder from New York. He was in his twenties, and his short, dark hair was slowly overtaking his face. He never went anywhere without his camera or his binoculars and was an expert using both.

Doug was explaining that we'd be heading to dinner first and then birding afterward (even in May it stays light long into the night). He never quite finished what he was telling us because he flipped open his chirping cellphone, and I jerked back as his right foot slammed into the floor. It was the most exciting moment so far, and we'd barely stepped off the plane. As Doug raced, I stared through a dusty window at a pretty town of colorful houses set on a hillside, above which towered the distinctive orange-yellow dome of a Russian Orthodox church, a reminder of this land's earlier roots. Five minutes later, the town had disappeared behind rolling white hills and we pulled up behind a car containing another guide, Scott Schuette. We tumbled out of the van in time to see our first rarity: a huge White-tailed Eagle from northern Siberia. I watched it soar effortlessly over the bluffs of a bay. As it banked, I could make out the whitish tail and a pale, straw-colored head. It was beautiful and I was ecstatic.

St. Paul is famous for its steep cliffs, which have the highest ratio of breeding seabirds to safety barriers anywhere in the country. Every day we'd stop at Reef Cliffs, a few miles south of town, where only a few horizontal feet separated the delicate contents of the van from the pounding Bering Sea three hundred feet below. It was a treat (albeit a terrifying and vertiginous one) to stand on those cliffs, the tundra grasses poking through the hardpacked snow and gaze down on almost all the species of seabirds that are known to breed in the Bering Sea.

The smallest is the Least Auklet—a rather fat, black-and-white bird with white whiskers and bright golden eyes. The Crested Auklet, larger and mostly black with a gray belly, has an orange-red bill and a comical black crest flopping forward from its head, like a feather on a medieval jousting helmet. The superficially similar Parakeet Auklet lacks the crest, and its bill is almost circular, which helps it catch jellyfish. The largest are the Common and Thick-billed Murres, standing tall in communal groups with gleaming white bellies. With their toucan bills, the puffins—Horned and Tufted—nest in holes at the top of the cliff, although most seem to be riding the waves below, diving for food. I couldn't think of a worse and more ridiculous place to breed, but there is a method to this madness. It's the only protection these birds have from the hungry arctic foxes that prowl above.

A map of the island was pinned up at the front of the van. St. Paul is a rectangle, ten miles by four, longer east–west than north–south. The top-right corner contains "Big Lake" and is stretched out to a point beyond. The town sits like a comma at the bottom, sheltering a cove and a harbor and ending at Reef Point. While I could recognize some of the places that had names (like Polovina Hill and Zapadni Point), the rest of it looked all the same to me, hidden under a thick layer of snow—treeless, windswept, and gently rolling. Tour leader Scott Schuette, standing an inch or two higher than me with a thick mop of blond hair and a face buried behind a field of stubble, told me that in a month or two this would all be green hills and wildflowers. By autumn, he said, the flowers would yield to large stands of waist-high celery, known to the locals as putchkie. I didn't believe him. I couldn't imagine any of it. I was wearing all my clothes (I'd even tried to wear the bag I'd brought them in) and I was still cold.

When not filling our stomachs three times a day at the employee cafeteria of the Trident fish cannery (the largest crab facility in the world, and the only place to eat in town), we filled our days piling in and out of the white van and birding every accessible part of the island. I was happy to have John and Laurie, who were my connection to Homer. I missed the camaraderie from that trip. Maybe because I'd joined an existing group here, I never felt much of a bond. It was like starting school halfway through a year, when no one needs to make any more friends. They were an older group, with at least one woman who curiously never left the van.

Although the Bering Sea is one of the best places to find rare birds from Asia, there are never very many of them, and most days we came up empty. Every day, for ten hours, we would walk the marshes and the cliffs, sweep through the lobster pots and anywhere else that birds might shelter from the constant wind. I was grateful for the continual enthusiasm of the guides, who kept us birding despite the often miserable conditions.

By the end of my time there, I'd added eleven new species for the year, including two rarities (as well as the eagle, we also found a Wood Sandpiper—which would be my only one for the year). A Slaty-backed Gull would have been a new bird if the feathers we'd found had still been attached to a living body. It was probably a victim of the many arctic foxes we saw scurrying around the village.

The "departure date" earned its quotation marks. The low ceiling of fog that frequently cancels flights canceled mine. I spent another day on St. Paul, not seeing anything new except for more of the island appearing from beneath the snow. I was grateful for another day where my possibilities were limited to a few miles in each direction. After Alaska, I was headed back to Arizona (Thick-billed Kingbird and Sulphur-bellied Flycatcher) and then Minnesota (Connecticut Warbler and all the other northern migrants I'd missed during spring farther south).

It would be the longest I'd be away from Gerri and would test what little goodwill this Big Year had left. And with a long to-do list of birds, I knew this would just be the start. I'd already asked Aaron about a trip to Gambell and Nome (both were full) and could imagine coming back here to St. Paul in the fall. My year was turning into a search for needles in haystacks—like the Black Noddy in the Dry Tortugas and the rare birds lost in Alaska. And as I traveled farther away and had more time on my own to think, I was beginning to develop an awful suspicion: What if I had one of those rarities at home? Could she fly away, a brief memory on my year list but gone forever from my life?

My bird count at the end of May 2013: 619
John Vanderpoel's bird count at the end of May 2011: 618

Chapter 6

TICKED OFF IN THE BOG

I HAVE FOUND IT inordinately difficult knowing what to do with my life, but once I've started on something, I have no problem following through. After my Ph.D., I accepted my first and only job offer from my first and only interview. If I didn't like it, I thought, I could change my mind. Except, of course, I couldn't, because that would mean giving up. For eleven years I didn't really like my job, and yet not until the end did I think it was possible to leave. I'd wasted my life to stubbornly prove that I wouldn't be beaten rather than do something else, something that I might enjoy. Besides, there was always one more set of stock options to add to my collection, which was slowly making me rich and draining my soul.

Falling in love had been the same. It came easy to me. Breaking up—not so much. No matter how miserable I was in a relationship, I wasn't going to give the universe the benefit of defeating me. I'd still be with Anna today, miserable and wondering how to escape, if she hadn't had the good sense to call it quits. Later on you see that you can survive a breakup, that your world does recover, and that you can meet someone else. But it's never that obvious when you're lost in the troughs, lacking the activation energy to get you over the pain of separation and loss.

I don't know why I agonized so much about giving up, but I did. My dad worked in a car factory his whole life, and I could see how beat up he was when he came home every night, falling asleep as his tired body hit his favorite chair. Maybe he didn't have many options to change his life (no education, no network), or maybe it was a British way of keeping a stiff upper lip and never conceding defeat. But changing your life means first acknowledging that you've made a mistake, and that was something I wasn't particularly good at.

When I left the windy island of St. Paul, I should have flown home. I should have been there to congratulate Gerri on her acceptance to graduate school, to stroke Sally Cat and Khiva Cat, and to fix the broken air-conditioning. But the volcano had erupted all over my plans, and I was behind schedule in a year in which I was already playing catch-up. And so instead of going home and showing my thanks to Gerri for looking after the house and feeding the little monkeys, I was headed to Minnesota for the breeding warblers I'd missed in migration. After Minnesota and Arizona there was a chance I could meet my arch-nemesis.

Hans de Grys had apparently also been keeping tabs on me. While he was watching the Black Noddy in the Dry Tortugas a few days before me, he met Patty O'Neill. Patty is not only a world birding machine (she's seen more than six thousand species) but she's also a friend of mine. When Hans discovered Patty's home was in Massachusetts, he started interrogating her. Patty put the two of us in touch, and after a few surprisingly pleasant e-mails, Hans invited me to Nome, in western Alaska. I'd already crossed off the potential targets in Nome, assuming I wouldn't go. Aaron's tour was full, and without a vehicle (which has to be booked nearly a year in advance during peak birding season) it was almost impossible to get around. Hans, in typically annoying arch-nemesis fashion, had of course planned his Big Year, and thus had booked a vehicle. After reassuring myself that he wasn't inviting me there to quietly remove his competition from the race, I said yes. I was excited to be going back to Alaska, although I'd be away from home for more than three weeks with only one week's worth of packing. I did the olfactory math and it didn't smell good.

Sax-Zim Bog is a mythical place among birders. It's a mixed spruce, tamarack, and northern white cedar bog with patches of alder swamp and hardwood (ash) forest. In summer it's home to many of the breeding birds of the taiga, whose boreal breeding range of inland Canada dips down to this more conveniently accessible location. By my count, there were still twenty-odd summer migrants I had yet to catch up with, and seven of them were in Minnesota.

Sax-Zim bog is forty-five miles northwest of Duluth and 180 miles north of Minneapolis. But the really important number is 359 bazillion, which is the number of mosquitos to every birder. I'd stayed in Duluth the previous night (after driving up from the Minneapolis–St. Paul airport) and stocked up on insect repellent. The cashier at the local Walgreens had asked me where I was heading. When I told her Sax-Zim Bog, she looked at me and presumably thought, "I have no idea what you're saying, so I'll just nod and smile." None of the normals had heard of it, and for good reason—there's nothing really there. Zim seems to have a population of twenty while Sax is a ghost town. In some old maps Sax has the alternative spelling of "Saxe," and in others it has the very alternative spelling of "Wallace."

The Connecticut Warbler was keeping me awake at night. It's the ninja of the birding world, a stealth operative working the ground under thick and impenetrable vegetation. When they're not singing, which is true for the entire breeding season except the first few weeks, they're almost impossible to find. While I'd seen them in Massachusetts in the fall (when they swing much farther east than they do in their spring migration), hoping that I might get lucky again would be a stomach ulcer waiting to happen.

The sun was peeking through the forested horizon, yet to burn off the bluish mist carpeting the soft ground like moss. I drove up and down the gridlike squares of the bog, following Owl Avenue and numbered farm roads. I drove with the windows down, and there were few places where I couldn't hear a cacophony of birds all competing for the available wavelengths. While listening, I was scanning the roadsides for Sharp-tailed Grouse, the only grouse I'd missed in Colorado. When I heard the explosive *chippy-chipper-chippy-chipper*, I slammed on the brakes. Connecticut Warbler! According to the ABA rules, you can count birds that you identify through song only, and a few of my ticks this year, including a Buff-collared Nightjar a few days before in Arizona, were "heard-only." But no birder is really happy with that—although it's not always possible, we always want to see the bird. And seeing this bird meant entering the bog.

The bird was calling from deep within a stand of pine trees. Every inch of vertical space was filled: what the pines left, the tamaracks filled in. I left the road and entered the dark interior, pushing aside branches as if they were fur coats in the wardrobe leading to Narnia. The *chippy-chipper*ing continued somewhere ahead of me, but the dark citric fragrance of black spruce was starting to make me dizzy. Sax-Zim Bog is big enough to get lost in, and as I edged forward, I kept looking over my shoulder, fixing the location of the road behind me long after it had disappeared from sight. I was soon in a thick forest where every direction looked the same.

I stopped as an olive-green bullet shot past me. I thought it landed somewhere ahead of me, which was soon confirmed as the *chippy-chipper* song exploded from that direction. I waited, scanning all the trees, standing perfectly still except for a gradual, downward motion into the bog. Connecticut Warblers are ventriloquial—it's very hard to pinpoint the location of the song. The bird was perhaps twenty feet in front of me, and I couldn't tell if it was on the ground or perched at the top of a tree. Only the barely perceptible movement of something creeping along a branch gave the bird away. I could feel my heart accelerate, swoonlike, as I raised my binoculars and saw one of the most prized and secretive of North American birds.

The Connecticut Warbler is one of our largest warblers: olive-green with a slate-gray hood extending across the breast. The feathers under the tail are so long that the tail itself looks deceptively short, giving the bird a very plump look. But the first thing you'd probably notice about the bird is the pair of ridiculous white monocles, making the warbler look even more surprised to see me than I was to see him. I was swearing under my breath, unable to quite believe the views I had. It's difficult for non-birders to understand the rush of adrenaline and love that you feel when you see a bird you've dreamed about. It's like planning a trip to India. No amount of poring over the guidebooks can quite prepare you for that moment when you walk through the large brass doors in the southern gateway and behold the bone-white marble of the Taj Mahal, its Mughal domes and minarets inverted in the still reflecting pools. That serenity and sense of timelessness is what seeing a Connecticut Warbler feels like to me.

By the time I got back in the car, after successfully retracing my steps, I'd added Mourning Warbler, Yellow-bellied Flycatcher, and Least Flycatcher, as well as another tick about which I was less excited: a deer tick. Feeling an odd itching sensation, I rolled my pant leg up to reveal a feeding frenzy. I quickly discovered the same disgusting feast was simultaneously being hosted on all my other limbs. There were at least twenty of them, which I systematically extracted between thumb and index fingernails, like pulling out splinters. But for the ticks, this was all part of the game. I sped away through the dusty roads of the bog, lobbing the bastards out the window, swerving to confuse their return but to no avail. The boomerang ticks came right back. Maybe that's why Sax was a ghost town?

Two days later I stood in the Minneapolis–St. Paul airport, holding a Caribou coffee and staring at the airport names on a fistful of boarding passes: Minneapolis-Phoenix-Seattle-Anchorage-Nome. I'd recently started to keep track of the miles I was flying. This trip would add another four thousand miles to the forty-eight thousand I'd already flown. I'd added ten new birds in Minnesota, including Henslow's Sparrow, Golden-winged Warbler, and Canada Warbler, and each had come with complimentary ticks of the leg-gnawing variety.

I carried everything in two bags. I never checked luggage, partly because I was scared of losing it, mostly because I was too cheap to pay for it, but logistically because I didn't have time to stare at luggage carousels. I got the closest seat I could to the door and ran from the plane to the car rental counter before it was buried behind a long line. I was always racing against time, maximizing the daylight hours I was spending in the field compared with the time it took to get there.

My telescope and tripod lay contorted in a duffel bag, which fit into the overhead compartment. The legs of the tripod were wrapped with socks, underwear, and T-shirts, the scope body swaddled in sweatshirts. I had a set of thermal underwear, which I took everywhere, as I never knew where I'd find winter. Everything else I wore. My other bag, a back-pack, contained my laptop, field guides, checklist, location notes, targets lists, mixed nuts, and novels. It also contained the orange plastic cylinder of depression pills, which was being lightened by five milligrams each day. By now, according to the psychiatrist Jonathan, I should have been feeling different.

It was Gerri who had first noticed it. For me, it was harder to feel a change that was so gradual, like how you don't notice your own aging when you look at your reflection in the mirror every day. But when I did look closer, I noticed there was something missing. Before, there was fog, of the kind that could ground a plane on the Pribilof Islands, the low ceiling clouding my perception. Now, it was thinner, as if someone had drilled a hole in my head and gently tapped the excess pressure. The new emptiness allowed me to think. In the past, I had to keep myself busy, like a hamster in a wheel. If I stopped, all kinds of worry would feed on that mental freedom. I used to love time on my own, reflecting and enjoying the quiet. But in the past few years I couldn't sit still without fretting, catastrophizing, and re-analyzing all the junctures where I should have turned right rather than left. The depression had robbed me of reading. I would read and then have to reread pages of books as the words vanished off the page into the ether. My mind was elsewhere, and never in a good place.

Did the pills clear the fog? I needed a control experiment—sitting at home doing nothing—as I wasn't just emptying the orange cylinder every day. I was also doing a Big Year, roaming through the United States and Canada, the twin countries of the ABA region, counting birds. I was living life. Maybe that's what cleared my head and allowed me the freedom to think of the future more calmly and to forget the past. I could barely remember now that there was a time when I lived on the verge of tears. It was an almost unimaginable contradiction, like being wrapped up in a Massachusetts winter trying unsuccessfully to recall the sultry heat of the summer nights that you'd give anything to escape. But if it was the pills, and if they really were helping, then I was angry: angry that I hadn't tried them before, and angry that I'd felt so embarrassed and guilty about asking for them, in a way that I wouldn't have been if I'd needed a painkiller, a decongestant, or a personality upgrade.

Nome is one hundred miles south of the Arctic Circle on the coast of western Alaska. It marks the end of the annual Iditarod Trail Sled Dog Race that starts in Anchorage. Nome can be reached only by plane or dog sled. I opted for the plane, which is nine days faster and comes with complimentary peanuts. As we approached the runway, an hour and a half after leaving Anchorage, my head filled the oval opening. Below, the spire of a whitewashed church erupted among the rows of red, blue, and white houses. The town had front-row seats to Norton Sound emptying into the Bering Sea, the edges frosted white with thick pack ice.

Hans de Grys was on the plane, sitting a few rows back. He'd been waiting for me at Gate C4 at Ted Stevens Anchorage International Airport. He didn't look much like an arch-nemesis (no cape, no pipe), although he did tower almost a foot above me. His short dark hair would remain hidden under a black woolen hat for the next three days, the freezing temperatures exposing only a smiling face with scholarly, metal-framed glasses, dark-blue eyes, and a medium-grit goatee. I quickly ran through my checklist, ticking off normal (a relative term for anyone who's decided to do a Big Year), funny, friendly, and knows his birds. He was the same age, had graduated from Yale, was married to a rocket scientist, and had two kids.

The first day we would bird around town. The rental car Hans had booked wouldn't be available until the next day. I checked into the Nome Nugget Inn, which, like all properties in Alaska, blasted the heat at a constant eighty degrees. My room, although primitive, was at the back and had a window overlooking the harbor. I wiped the condensation off with the sleeve of my jacket and looked out on a flotilla of barges waiting for a break in the pack ice to bring their goods ashore. (Three days later, through this dusty window I'd spot my first ever Yellow-billed Loon.)

Hans was checking into his hotel at the other end of town. I took a short walk east down Front Street, paralleling the harbor to my right. It was thirty degrees and the wind was cutting my cheeks. Opposite the Nugget Inn stood the city hall, a large brown wooden structure with a curious gable at the top like a prop from a spaghetti western. This was the finish line for the Iditarod Trail, the rabbit that all those frothing dogs would chase each spring for more than a thousand miles.

Nome's mining heritage was all around me: in the place names (the Dredge Inn, Gold Avenue, and the Gold Coast Cinema, the latter curiously located *inside* a Subway sandwich store), in the gold shops displaying the current price per ounce, and in the metal gold pans decorating the sidewalks. At one time Nome was the largest city in the Alaska Territory. In 1900, at the height of the gold rush, the population of Nome was listed as 12,488. It didn't last long, of course, although the gold never quite petered out. Today the population is less than a third of what it was in its heyday, but there are still boats with dry-suited divers vacuuming the bed of the sound for the shiny stuff.

Once Hans caught up with me, it became clear we weren't going to see much in town apart from a few ravens looking for scraps. I felt comfortable with Hans, as if I already knew him. And in a sense I did—I knew which birds he'd seen, which he'd missed. We'd lived nearly identical lives this year, bouncing back and forth between the same places and the same birds. There was so much I wanted to know about his experiences, but I told myself to slow down—there'd be plenty of time in a land where the sun never sets.

As the ravens wheeled overhead, an SUV pulled up beside us, and a window rolled down. It was the young guy we'd met in the shared taxi (five dollars from the airport to anywhere in town). Abe Borker was in his early thirties, his head and face covered in a mess of blond hair from which a pair of piercing blue eyes peered out. He asked us what we were doing, and in less than two minutes Hans and I were climbing into the backseat of a stranger's car in a way that can only happen with birding.

There are three roads that leave Nome, each about seventy miles long: one heads northwest to the Iñupiat village of Teller, another heads east to the abandoned settlement of

Council, and the third, Kougarok Road, snakes north before
fizzling out into the tundra. We went east on the Council
Road, with Norton Sound on our right and the fifteen-mile-
long Safety Sound to our left. We stopped frequently, scoping
out both sides of the road.

Abe was a research biologist living in Santa Cruz,
California. Despite his age, he'd worked all over the world,
and most recently had guided for Debi Shearwater, the
legendary pelagic tour operator in Northern California. He'd
inherited his love of birding from his father, Joe, a smaller, less
hirsute version of Abe, who sat next to him on the front seat.

Wherever we stopped, there were birds. We found Bar-
tailed Godwits feeding on the shoreline of Safety Sound, their
long legs knee-deep in the snowmelt. I wondered if they'd
just arrived, exhausted from a spring migration that brought
them here from their distant wintering grounds in New
Zealand, with a layover in coastal China. Bar-tailed Godwits
hold the record for the longest nonstop flight: in the fall they
make the 7,145-mile flight back to New Zealand nonstop.
That's nine days with no rest, food, or water! The birds were
probing their long, upturned bills into the mud. The males
were a deep red russet color; the females were plainer and,
like many shorebirds, significantly larger than the males,
possibly because the aerial displays during courtship favor
smaller males.

Nearby, we watched brightly colored Red and Red-necked
Phalaropes picking at the edges of the water for insects and
plankton. Phalaropes, a type of small shorebird, are one of the
few families of birds in which the females are more brightly

colored than the males. Their roles are reversed. After the
eggs are laid, the female abandons the male. He's left to incu-
bate and care for the chicks alone while she's out looking for
other males to repeat the process with.

We followed the Council Road east as it skirted the end of
Safety Sound and turned north inland into the tundra. No
amount of advance reading or hasty scans of the postcards in
the Nome Nugget earlier prepared me for the bizarre tableau
that unfolded in front of us: a train in the tundra. It was
all that was left of the Nome to Vancouver Railroad. Only
thirty-five miles of track were laid before the endeavor, like
many of the gold dredgers, was abandoned. The three loco-
motives, shipped into Nome in 1903, now sat, orange from
rust, pointing toward the distant snow-covered hills, their
wheels half-sunk into the wet and grassy tundra. It was the
last train to nowhere.

I sat on the backseat of the car, gazing out at a frozen
wilderness that I wasn't quite expecting in June while enjoying
the warm and newfound friendships inside. We all looked out
on the Arctic tundra of Nome with the same wide eyes of the
first-time visitor and with firework oohs and aahs. It was
exciting to share the new birds: the Eastern Yellow Wagtails
that flitted around an old cemetery, a distant Emperor Goose
sitting on the shore of Safety Sound, and a pair of Gyrfalcons
that were tending a nest balanced on a metal bridge, feet from
the road. We turned around only because we were tired and
hungry. The sun gave no hint of setting.

I met Hans early the next morning with plans to drive
along the Kougarok Road. We fell into a comfortable routine

of spotting birds and dissecting our Big Years. His was almost up—it was a sabbatical from school, mid-year to mid-year.

"Can't you do a Big Year and a Half?" I asked. I'd enjoyed spending time with him and lamented the fact that that we couldn't continue together for the rest of the year. Birding with Hans made me see how much more fun it could be to bird with someone else. It was going to be a long second half to the year.

Some of the birds we saw were trans-Beringian migrants—like the aptly named Bluethroat and the green, buzzing Arctic Warbler—that fly across the Bering Sea from Russia each spring to breed here, before hightailing back west in the fall. But even the familiar ones weren't that familiar. Birds such as the Red-throated Loon had received a stunning makeover for the breeding season: a crimson throat etched into the silky gray sides of the neck.

All birds molt their feathers. Unlike the similar keratin-containing hair and nails in humans, feathers stop growing when they reach their desired length. Despite daily grooming and waxing to keep them waterproof, they gradually wear down. Most birds replace all their feathers in an annual molt. It's energy consuming and is usually done in the fall after the equally exhausting business of breeding. For some, like the elegant Red-throated Loons, there's another molt in the spring, usually just the body feathers, which allows birds to have a different "breeding" plumage, one stunning enough to attract mates and birdwatchers.

We shared the gravel roads with the fat Willow and Rock Ptarmigans (two uncharacteristically easy grouse ticks) as well as other birders. Not all were as relaxed as we were. A vehicle pulled up behind us one morning on a stretch of lonely tundra. We watched as a tour guide and his four followers piled out of a car that looked much too small for the job. The guide, a bearded guy in his fifties, was lining up his team with military precision. They faced the tundra, overgrown with horizontally spreading dwarf willows. I recognized the song of the Bluethroat as it screamed out of the guide's iPhone. He waited five seconds for a response from a real bird before confirming its absence and then ordered everyone back in the vehicle before speeding off. They looked miserable, and I could only imagine how many times they'd repeat this exercise for the rest of the day. I almost offered to sell tickets to the Hans and Neil tour, which came with more jokes, more nuts, and possibly more Bluethroats.

We met up with Abe on our last day to try for the Bristle-thighed Curlew, a long-billed shorebird that winters in Hawaii and breeds in the remote mountains of western Alaska. It's a seventy-one-mile drive out on the Kougarok Road and then a steep ascent up Coffee Dome, which I was disappointed to discover was not a local caffeine outlet.

The ascent was slow going. The tundra was shaped like bowling balls, and none of us wanted to be stuck up there with a broken ankle. We were ever vigilant for grizzly bears (we never did see any, although we saw lots of musk ox and moose, as well as a pet reindeer named Velvet Eyes who rode around town in the back of a flatbed truck). When we reached the top, I gasped at the panorama of tundra spread out around us, like a patchwork quilt of reds, greens, and yellows. While the other two were excited to see an American Golden-Plover in its black, white, and gold breeding plumage, I brushed away a couple of tears, overcome by the frightening beauty of the place. It was like the times when I'd laid on my back as a kid, looking up at the stars at night—when you appreciate how beautiful this world is, and that it's so much bigger than you are.

It didn't take long before the Bristle-thighed Curlew arrived, flying in accompanied by its liquid *chu-a-wit*. The long trademark bill drooped down at the tip, as if under the magnetic pull of the tundra below. The bird was the same warm buff color as the ones I'd seen on the beach in Homer with Aaron's group, refueling on their way here to the hills of western Alaska. The namesake bristles hung down from the belly in front of the legs. Hans and Abe were smiling and taking congratulatory photos. We felt on top of the world.

I left Nome on June 9. Abe and his father were spending another week there, and Hans was heading to Gambell, on St. Lawrence Island, to finish out his Big Year. (He never did make it. The runway there was fogged in for two days before he eventually gave up and headed back to Seattle. He ended his Big Year on 647, 3 shy of his target.)

I pulled out a manila folder across which the word "Nome" was emblazoned, as the miniature buildings of the city itself fell away rapidly below. While my Big Year may have been unplanned, it wasn't without some kind of structure and neurotic attention to detail. For every trip I would create a separate folder, filled with notes, maps, and lists. On the inside cover was a line of empty check boxes—the target birds I needed at each location. I'd lie if I didn't admit that there was some excitement to checking off those boxes, which is why I'd often create to-do lists where half of the to-dos were already done. I'd added fifteen new birds for the year at Nome, including a Slaty-backed Gull that was a lot more countable than the pile of feathers I'd found on St. Paul. The only bird I'd missed was the Spectacled Eider, a duck that winters in polynyas, openings in the sea ice. That box would remain unchecked unless I went to the north coast of Alaska, where they breed, or to Gambell in the fall, where there was a chance of seeing one fly by.

On each trip I also brought a folder containing year lists—mine and those of the others who'd done a Big Year. I pulled out John Vanderpoel's, which had fast become my benchmark. I noticed that he'd not only come to Nome but also had been to Gambell, where he'd picked up three species that I would miss for the year (Ivory Gull, Great Knot, and Common Ringed Plover). But when I compared the numbers, I was surprised to see that I'd closed the gap. On June 8 he was at 642. I was just one bird behind.

I pointed the nose of the car into the parking lot of the Ramada Grayling Hotel, a blocky two-story affair that I hoped would look less like a communist hotel on the inside than it did from the outside. I killed the engine, took a deep breath, and slowly blew it out. It was a dreary, gray afternoon—a Monday, but not that I would have known it. Three hours earlier I'd stepped off a plane in Detroit, the final airport in a series involving Nome, Anchorage, Seattle, and Dallas. I stared up at the sign outside the hotel and knew I was in the right place: KIRTLAND WARBLER TOURS 7 AM DAILY.

The Kirtland's Warbler is the crack addict of the bird world. Its dangerous obsession with the jack pines of central Michigan, between six and fourteen feet in height, mind you, with a nice understory of interlocking branches and a sandy, burnt soil, had almost killed it. Forest fires create this type of early-growth forestation, and as we've done a better job of preventing these, we've lost much of the habitat and the birds that go with it. (The bird stops being so damn fussy about its habitat in its wintering grounds in the Bahamas, where it's probably thinking, "Hey, this is the Bahamas!") The population crashed around the mid-twentieth century and hit a low of about four hundred birds in the 1970s. The bird was one of the first species to be listed under the Endangered Species Act, which was signed into law by President Richard Nixon in 1973, and with help from the U.S. Fish and Wildlife Service and the Michigan Audubon Society, it was saved from almost certain extinction. Today there are four thousand birds, with some starting to nest in neighboring states and provinces.

The Kirtland's Warbler tour started the following morning in a little back room of the hotel. It was run by Megan, a U.S. Fish and Wildlife volunteer and an enthusiastic blonde in her midtwenties, and featured a short presentation on the plight of this bird (together with free bumper stickers!). I was impressed that a Tuesday morning in the middle of the Lower Peninsula of Michigan could attract more than ten people interested in seeing this bird. Perhaps I shouldn't have been. I'd noticed the street signs adorned with images of the warbler all over the nearby town of Roscommon. It was the same pride I'd seen in the lek towns of Colorado, and it had to be good news for the bird that it was creating a local tourist industry.

I was at the back of a convoy of cars that left the Ramada and headed about five miles east of town. As the residential houses thinned out, the jack pines took over. We left our vehicles at a crossroads, each quadrant filled by jack pines of varying heights. The ground underfoot was sandy, deposited here after the retreat of the glaciers fourteen thousand years ago. I could hear the tantalizing calls of the warblers hidden in the stunted forest: *chip-chip-chip-too-too-weet-weet*. But for being such a bright and colorful bird, they remained hidden. This forest was the perfect height for them—the random forest fires are now replaced by scheduled harvest and regrowth to ensure there's the correct habitat somewhere in this area (after replanting, it takes about eight years before the warblers will start to reuse it).

A short way into the plantation Megan showed us the other major factor that's helped the Kirtland's Warbler come back from the brink of extinction: the cowbird trap. In front of me stood a wooden frame, six feet by six feet and about as high, covered with chicken wire. The ceiling dropped down in the middle, allowing birds to fly in but not out, and giving the structure an M-shaped profile. Inside, about twenty Brown-headed Cowbirds flitted nervously around. If I hadn't known better, I might've thought they were attractive. The males were iridescent black with a brownish hood, the females a more solid pale brown, and both had strong bills marking them as seedeaters. These birds were the bait; their role was to attract others of this social species. A padlocked door provided entry for the staff to recover any captured cowbirds. Megan told us that about four thousand are collected each year. All are destroyed.

Brown-headed Cowbirds were never supposed to be here. It's thought that they moved north as the European pioneers opened up the forests. The success of the Brown-headed Cowbird comes at the expense of others. They lay their eggs in the nests of other birds. And while some species can spot the large eggs and grossly different chicks of the cowbird, clearly unlike their own, the Kirtland's Warbler cannot. The young cowbird chick, much bigger and more aggressive than its foster siblings, takes over the nest, pushing out the eggs and young of the warbler or simply starving them by hogging all the food. Without cowbirds, Kirtland's Warblers have a reproductive success rate of more than three chicks per nest. With cowbird parasitism, it's less than one.

After the successful buildup in anticipation for the star of the show, we walked deeper into the plantation. On both sides of the sandy trail we could hear their *chip-chip-chip-too-too-weet-weet.* I immediately spotted one, teed up on the top of a jack pine, throwing its head back. Although the day was gray, the bird shone, the solid yellow on its breast, chin, and belly almost luminescent. The head was a dark, steel blue, harboring a broken eye-ring—a white crescent above and below the inky eye.

I stood fascinated as the bird proclaimed its territory. The Kirtland's Warbler was one of the lucky ones. The Bachman's

Warbler, a small yellow-and-black warbler of the bottomland swamps of the Southeast, never made it. The last reported sighting was in 1988, and today it's presumed to be extinct. The Kirtland's is destined to remain a "conservation-reliant" species, meaning that without continued human intervention, to create a habitat (that humans destroyed) and to remove cowbirds (that we brought here), it'll probably be lost. But it's doing well enough now that there's discussion of removing it from the endangered species list. I watched the blue and yellow warbler singing its heart out and knew that the world was a better place for its presence.

"But why not? I practically live there already," said the voice on my right.

For once, I was grateful for the long drive (our target, the border between North Carolina and Virginia, was still at least an hour ahead of us). If I have to have difficult conversations, which—like caring about interest rates, eating Brussels sprouts, and knowing how to clean an oven—are apparently necessary parts of being an adult, then facing forward and not making eye contact is the best way to have them. It's not that I don't know how to say what I'm thinking, but rather that I often don't know what I think.

I'd been back home for two days after being away for twenty-three days. I was happy to see Gerri waiting for me at the airport, and even happier to see that the malodorous, stubbly waif that emerged through the sliding doors of Logan didn't repulse her. I always felt awkward when I returned home, like I was living a double life. The triple-decker houses of East Boston rolled by and the skyscrapers of downtown Boston bobbed on the horizon before we disappeared into the Sumner Tunnel and under the harbor. While the sights were familiar, the life was not.

I was leading two very different lives. One had goals and binary checklists to mark my progress, while the other was nebulous: there was no guidebook, no end (except for the ultimate one), and there were people, irrational and uncontrollable. And while there were obvious check boxes—like moving in together—I was a lot more hesitant about ticking those than I was about suggesting driving six hundred miles down to the Great Dismal Swamp (a place that could really benefit from a rebrand) for Swainson's Warbler, my last warbler of the year.

I wasn't annoyed with Gerri for bringing it up. Her arguments made perfect sense: her lease was expiring, her roommates were moving out, and she was paying rent for a place she never saw except when rushing in to collect mail. I was annoyed with myself because I was never the one suggesting this. Isn't that how it's supposed to work? I fooled myself with each relationship, thinking I needed a little more time to feel certain. It had been the same with Anna, who was similarly fed up with keeping clothes in two places, never feeling like she had a home. And yet, I could never explain my twisted logic to her, in the same way that I couldn't to Gerri now: moving in meant there'd be moving out, which was painful. Why couldn't I wait until I was absolutely sure the latter would never happen? But of course, I never could be. I would never wake up one morning and think, *Yes, now I feel sure.* The status quo would continue as status forever.

"Let's wait another couple of months." I said to Gerri. "I'm so tired from the Big Year and we haven't spent enough time together recently. Can't you find a new place that rents month to month?"

I didn't have to turn my head to know this wasn't the answer she wanted to hear. More surprising, perhaps, was that I was sick of hearing it too. It was as if I were programmed to say this, forever trapped with this recording, knowing no good would come of it. Moving in should be fun—mixing our possessions together, going shopping for new stuff. But it never was like that. With Anna, our books stayed on separate bookcases (so there'd be no confusion when she moved out), and there was no photo of her on my desk at work (if people didn't know we were together, they wouldn't see the failure when we weren't).

We sat in silence as a string of Brown Pelicans crossed from Chesapeake Bay on our right to the Atlantic Ocean on our left. The long bridge and tunnel connecting the Delmarva Peninsula with Virginia reminded me of the journey across the keys to Key West, and then my mind was back to my other life. I should go back to Texas, I thought, to that long drive to Big Bend and the hot, stupid climb up the Pinnacles Trail. The Flame-colored Tanager was being seen more regularly, and I needed every bird I could get. But I could also see this for what it was: I was running away again. At least I knew I couldn't keep doing this—if I did, there'd be nothing to run away from.

I was halfway through the year and I'd seen all fifty-one species of breeding warbler, including the Swainson's Warbler at the Great Dismal Swamp. Gerri had heard it first, singing its disgusted *"Ooh, ooh, I stepped in poo!"* song from deep within the thorny tangles of greenbrier vines. It had taken two days for it to eventually show itself and perch long enough for me to capture a photo of its dark body, chocolate-brown cap, and strong bill. On the long drive home we stopped in Philadelphia for breakfast, and somewhere near the Liberty Bell we were rear-ended by a truck, appropriately putting an accident into my accidental Big Year. It was hard to scream at the other driver when Gerri needed my all attention. She was hyperventilating and crying. I watched as my concertinaed car was towed away for two weeks of repairs. But none of that seemed to matter while she was still crying. I realized then how fragile my life was and that my life was more than just me.

In the last few days of the month, Gerri and I were back on the road, this time heading north to Maine. We had an appointment to meet one of the most magical birds of the year: a Red-billed Tropicbird. It had been summering in Maine for the past seven years, well to the north of its Caribbean range. We caught the passenger ferry from Rockland and ninety minutes later were disgorged into the tiny fishing town of Vinalhaven. Brightly colored skiffs bobbed in the harbor, lobster pots crowded the quiet streets, and we felt the summer breeze on our sweating brows. If this had been Nantucket, it would have been crowded and obnoxious. But Vinalhaven, the larger of the two Fox Islands, was a secret from the past.

The next morning we were steaming out of the harbor on a boat captained by John Drury, a tall, quiet man who espouses shoes and small talk and who, for reasons that were never clear, flies a Welsh flag from the mast. John has been keeping track of the tropicbird's arrival and departure dates each year as well as its daily schedule. The bird seems to have reciprocated, knowing exactly when to expect a visit from the captain. The two have developed an uncanny affinity for each another.

As we approached our destination, Seal Island, puffins bobbed around the boat, showing off their bright toucan bills. I almost fell out of the boat when Gerri screamed in my ear, "Tropicbird!" I turned in time to see a huge bright white bird with an impossibly long tail and a bloodred bill. It was flapping enthusiastically, like a windup bird, as it moved along the boat at eye level just out of arm's reach. Soon we were all shouting "Tropicbird"—well, all except for the yogically calm Mr. Tropicbird himself, who was nodding and ready at the helm to follow the bird. It was my 650th bird of the year. I wasn't sure which captivated me more: the elegance of the bird, with its long tail streamers, or Gerri's excitement at finding it. When I thought back to the accident in Philadelphia, and standing on the street holding Gerri, who was shaking in fear, I was overcome by the extremes of this month.

At the end of the month, I calculated there were only two common summering birds left (Black Swift and Vaux's Swift). And while I still had California left, and a few odd rarities that might turn up, I was at the plateau of my Big Year curve. I'd seen 653 birds in the first half of the year. I checked Vanderpoel's numbers—he was on 654 at this point. I was starting to believe that maybe I could join the 700 Club.

One of those 653 birds was the Flame-colored Tanager— the bird I went back to Big Bend for, and re-climbed the

Pinnacles Trail, past the mountain lion signs and the still-singing Colima Warbler. I waited until later that evening when I picked up a cell signal to tell Gerri of my news. When I turned my phone back on, there was a message from her. It appeared that while I was waiting at Boot Spring, near that abandoned horse corral, Gerri was looking for somewhere to live. Or, more accurately, somewhere to leave her stuff while she lived, but not lived, with me. The text told me that she'd found a place and would be moving that weekend.

My bird count at the end of June 2013: 653
John Vanderpoel's bird count at the end of June 2011: 654

Chapter 7

THREE MEN IN A BOAT

THE WOMAN AT THE motel was right: you'd have to be a complete idiot to arrive here without a reservation. It was Friday night and the start of the Fourth of July weekend, the busiest weekend of the year for the small beach towns of the Outer Banks. The skies had long since burned through the spectrum of sunset colors. Without light, the universe was now laid bare above me in all its frightening infinity. After visiting the bathroom, I locked the car door, reclined my seat, rolled my clothes into a pillow, and settled in for a night of extreme discomfort. I drew some solace from the fact that arriving here without a reservation probably wouldn't be the most idiotic thing I'd do this year.

The Outer Banks are a two-hundred-mile long parenthesis that brackets most of the coast of North Carolina. The strip of sandy, barrier islands encloses the Pamlico, Albemarle, and Currituck sounds from the ship-crunching Atlantic Ocean to the east. As I turned south down that thin sandy strip earlier that day, hemmed in by water on both sides, I started to see signs of a less inspirational nature. At first I thought they were celebrating the birdlife here. Green ovals with a bird, facing left with a long forked tail and the words HEY AUDUBON! IDENTIFY THIS BIRD! A closer look revealed the bird to be in the form of a hand, with fingers for the body, the middle one being offensively raised. It wasn't a surprise to me. I'd been prepared for this type of welcome. I'd seen the posts on the local Listserv asking whether it was prudent for birders to visit, after hearing of others being verbally insulted.

It started in 2008, when the Audubon Society, founded in 1905 and one of the oldest organizations in the United States advocating for conservation, started pushing the government to do its job and protect the federally endangered species that live here (sea turtles, plants, and birds). The state of North Carolina had been lax, at best, in doing so. The sudden enforcement of laws, together with the appearance of beach closures and limits on off-road vehicles, were met with frustration and anger, and much of it was directed at birders. Some of the locals and tourists decried a lost way of life: the right to drive on any beach at any speed. The new laws require a beach driver to purchase a permit, sit through a video at a government facility, obey speed limits, and stay off closed beaches.

It's a peculiar type of American libertarianism that feels trodden upon by these types of regulations. The same people weren't raising a hue and cry about not being able to drive on the federal and state roads at any speed they chose or arguing to drive on the wrong side of the road. Whether they had a legal right to or not (and it was a pretty clear not), one thing was certain: birds were being killed. Before the regulations, any Black Skimmers and Gull-billed Terns that were brave enough to nest on the beaches were either crushed, harassed, or had to watch as their eggs or chicks disappeared under the wheels of a recreational vehicle. Now, they're raising their young successfully. Meanwhile, there are still plenty of beaches open for tourists on which to drive, and, once the offensive signs come down, there will be another tourist industry of birders excited to see the newly flourishing wildlife. In any other place, that would be considered a spectacular success.

I could hear the waves crashing against the nearby dock as I tossed and turned inside my tiny aluminum hotel, searching for that elusive comfortable position. Mine was the only car in the lot, although in a few hours it would start filling up with birders for the pelagic trip and day-trippers for the excellent sea fishing. I'd had dinner earlier at Dinky's, a local seafood restaurant. I sat at the bar, as I usually do, alternating between David Mitchell's novel *The Thousand Autumns of Jacob de Zoet* and my field guide. Given all the signs I'd seen, I'd felt a little nervous about revealing my birding intentions. But no one seemed to care, beyond the usual "look at that dweeb sitting on his own reading his books." I was used to people thinking of birders as odd, nerdy, or eccentric, but being unwelcome was new. When did birding become the new fracking?

It was still dark when the third alarm call finally shocked the car into life. I worked a toothbrush around the insides of my mouth, making it foamy with the contents of one of those miniature travel toothpastes, of which I now had quite the collection. I cleared the sleep from my head with a coffee from a nearby store whose lights had just flicked on. It was called Teach's Lair, after Edward Teach, who traded under the more famous business name of Blackbeard the Pirate. He lived, and died, on nearby Ocracoke Island. But what I really needed was a massage to crack my body back into an upright position. I looked at the gruff guy standing behind the counter, wondered if he was a descendent of the salty pirate, and decided this was neither the time nor the place to ask after massages.

The *Stormy Petrel II* bobbed gently beneath me in a dock full of boats. It was still dark, the fifteen or so birders lit by sodium lights and the pale moon overhead. Behind me I could hear the ropes straining loudly, holding on tight to the restless boat. Brian Patteson stood at the bow giving safety directions and instructions on how to be seasick—over the side of the boat, not in the toilet, and (most important) with the wind behind you. Brian has been doing this for almost thirty years. He's the most experienced pelagic captain on the East Coast, and his trips out into the warm waters of the Gulf Stream regularly attract rare seabirds, seldom or never seen from land: petrels, storm-petrels, tropicbirds, and, very rarely, albatross. Brian is about the same height as me, with short blond hair, a bristly goatee, and a quiet, introverted manner. I suspect he's happiest when he's behind the wheel with a pair of binoculars scanning the horizon and converting distant specks into a name, age, and sex.

The Gulf Stream, arcing from southern Florida to northern Europe, passes closest to shore along North Carolina's Outer Banks, which, together with an upwelling from the colder

Labrador Current from the north, makes Hatteras an ideal base for pelagics. But even here at the Gulf Stream's closest point, it's still a two-hour trip to the edge of the current. By the time we'd reached it, the sun was up, and I could taste the saltiness in the air and sense the nervous excitement among the group. We'd already seen shearwaters (Cory's and Great) slicing through the air, the tips of their long, straight wings skating above the sea's surface. We found a single Bridled Tern, black and white like the Sooty Terns of the Dry Tortugas, sitting on a piece of floating flotsam and hunting for the fish attracted by the shade underneath. I leaned over the rail and made out the sharp edges to the current, the warm blue water sliding against the colder green. Clumps of sargassum drifted by, dark green islands of floating algae below which juvenile fish fed and hid.

"Black-capped Petrel! Three o'clock," Brian shouted from the front of the boat. I ran to the starboard side as a large, stiff-winged bird—dark brown above, gleaming white below—arced high above the horizon. Its local name is *diablotín*, or little devil, from its eerie nocturnal mating calls, but those calls are seldom heard these days. Many of its breeding sites in the Caribbean have been lost to predation by rats. And although it's not uncommon in the Gulf Stream, globally it's endangered. Through my binoculars I could make out the thick, stubby bill and dark cap covering the eyes. It arced up and down over the cresting waves at stomach-churning speeds, as if on an invisible roller coaster. If birds really do enjoy flying, which I like to think they do, this one must have been having a blast.

Sea-watching is hard work. There are long periods without birds, the sun is relentless, and my muscles complain from forever bracing against the continually rocking boat. As I watched a small flock of Wilson's Storm-Petrels (like black bats with white rumps) pattering on the surface of the water, I was joined by Kate Sutherland, the chief bird spotter on the boat and a phenomenal multitasker. Kate chatted with everyone on the boat, learned the birds they needed, casually imparted her incredible seabird knowledge, shoveled out stinky chum to attract the birds, and never took her eyes off the horizon. A headset was partially hidden beneath a mess of brown curly hair, keeping her in contact with Brian at the helm.

Although pelagic birds are generally quiet at sea, my ears were strained as I hoped to hear their names over the loud-speakers: European Storm-Petrel, Fea's Petrel, White-tailed Tropicbird (all birds for which I would make multiple trips this year and never once hear their names). But I did pick up nine new species for the year, which, by my calculations, put me ahead of John Vanderpoel for the first time. I thought of how my target this year had ratcheted up from "some birds" to "as many birds as I can see" and then to the more numerical five hundred, six hundred, and now my new target of seven hundred. I stood on the bow, as Brian deftly pointed the boat back toward land. The sun warmed my face and I remembered that other place, where the sun never sets, on the opposite side of this vast continent: the tundra fields of Nome and a car, in which I was sitting next to my newfound birding friend. It was Hans who'd first suggested that I might beat the

Big Year record. I'd laughed at him at the time, in the same way that I'd laughed at Gerri when she said it, and at everyone else who had no idea of what that would take. But now, my eyes blinded by the reflections of the sun, sparkling on the slowly churning waters like a kaleidoscope, I wasn't so sure.

Gerri could tell that I was distracted as soon as I opened the front door. I didn't look like someone who'd just driven home from North Carolina, stealing sleep for a few uncomfortable hours in a parking lot somewhere in southern Delaware. It was in Philly that I heard the news, while I was exchanging the rental car for my own repaired one, unconcertinaed enough for me to drive back home.

I dropped my bags in the hall, walked past the whining cats, and opened my laptop on the kitchen counter.

"Look at this," I said, beckoning Gerri over.

We hunched over the laptop, and I pressed play on a video. The camera was focused on a patch of mud at the edge of a shoreline. A light breeze blew through green cattail reeds at the top of the screen. Gerri recognized the brown, stripy bird immediately—a Least Bittern standing on the mud. She'd seen one in Florida. It edged warily toward the camera, its yellow legs splaying long toes.

"But you've already seen that, right?" she asked.

"Keep watching," I said.

I let the video run. The bittern was now standing in the water, possibly thinking about lunch or what plans it had for the afternoon, and then, with only five seconds left, a large monster appeared from the top-left corner of the screen. It dwarfed the diminutive bittern, its rusty body held aloft by long, pinkish legs that carried the beast quickly to the other side of the screen.

"Whoa! What was what?" Gerri asked.

"That's a Rufous-necked Wood-Rail. They live in coastal mangrove swamps from Mexico to northern South America," I said.

"Cool! Have you seen one before?" she asked.

"No. And neither has anyone else in the United States. It's the first record ever in the ABA region. The video was shot this morning at Bosque del Apache. It's a refuge in New Mexico, between Albuquerque and the Mexican border."

"You should go!" she said, trying to sound enthusiastic.

I booked a flight to Albuquerque for the next morning. Gerri didn't say anything about our vacation to California, which was in three days. But I knew she was thinking about it.

Rarities are the key to a Big Year. Without them, the numbers don't add up. The ABA assigns a code to each bird on its checklist to indicate how common it is. The code is based on the system that Jim Vardaman and his strategy council used in his 1979 attempt to see seven hundred birds. He had seven codes. Today there are six (although one of those is reserved for extinct and extirpated birds). Codes 1 and 2 are for regularly occurring species (1 is common; 2 is less common). Code 3 is for rarities, such as the Rufous-capped Warbler and the Black Noddy, that are typically seen somewhere every year in the ABA region. Code 4 is for less-than-annual rarities, like the Red-flanked Bluetail and Fieldfare, and Code 5 is for the true mega rarities:

birds recorded less than five times ever. I'd seen only one Code
5 this year, the Nutting's Flycatcher near Lake Havasu, Arizona,
back in January. There are 666 Code 1 and 2 birds, which
means that if you want to see more than seven hundred species,
you need at least thirty-four rarities. (By the end of the year, the
ABA would add two new introduced species, Purple Swamphen
and Nutmeg Mannikin to its checklist as well as endorse a
taxonomic split of Sage Sparrow into two species, Sagebrush
Sparrow and Bell's Sparrow, making seven hundred a little
easier to reach.)

Rarity chasing is for the adrenalin junkie. You never know
where or when they'll turn up nor, frustratingly, how long
they'll stay. It's a roller coaster of emotions, and there's a dark
side to the nervous anticipation and high-fiving excitement of
seeing one: the despondency of getting to the bird after it's
flown away. As a kid I'd relied on a recorded phone message,
Birdline, to report all the rarities. These days there's the
Internet. I would receive an e-mail from eBird whenever a
rare bird was reported to that database. The subscription
service North American Rare Bird Alert (NARBA)
performed a similar role. I was also signed up to various
Listservs in states where rarities might be expected (Arizona,
Florida, Texas, etc.). I knew that as I started to run out of
common species, I'd have to start chasing rarities, when a
whole trip would target a single bird.

I arrived at the visitor center at Bosque del Apache the next
day to find a hand-drawn map showing the location of the
Wood-Rail: an arrow labeled "rail" pointed to a spot at the end
of a pond next to another arrow labeled "snag," both opposite a

"boardwalk." What wasn't on the map was the group of high-fiving birders I found jumping up and down on the boardwalk. They'd been waiting for more than an hour and a half, and only when I arrived, did the bird agree to appear. I untelescoped my tripod legs, pointed the scope to the far end of the pond, and focused on the edge of the mud. Walking around in the shade of the cattails was a large chickenlike bird, much bigger than the nearby Green Heron and Virginia Rail. It even walked like a chicken, tail raised as it cautiously explored the edge of the water. For a species that had never been recorded north of Mexico, the bird looked confident in its role as pioneering explorer. Every part was shockingly colorful: reddish-brown neck continuing to the belly, iridescent blue-green upper back, yellow bill, red eyes, and bright bubble-gum-pink legs.

It was the first bird I'd seen this year that wasn't in my guidebooks and had no place on my checklist. Like all the other birders who'd come to see this bird, I was hoping that it would be added to the official checklist and that my provisional plus-one would convert to an actual tick. It's a process that first requires the state committee to officially accept the bird onto its list (in this case the New Mexico Bird Records Committee) and then the ABA Checklist Committee to follow suit. Both groups need to satisfy themselves that the bird is what it appears to be, and not a similar species or a hybrid of two species. The other requirement is more challenging: provenance. The bird needs to have gotten there by its own wings. Many birds are kept in captivity, especially ducks, swans, and geese, and some of them escape. None of them are countable.

During John Vanderpoel's Big Year in 2011, a potential ABA-first Hooded Crane, a bird of East Asia, was seen in four states. While a few are kept in captivity, there were no records of any escapes. Many birders chased that bird believing it to be a genuine vagrant from Siberia. But despite being accepted by two states, the ABA ultimately did not accept the bird, citing uncertainty over its origin. It doesn't appear on the official checklist, but does appear on the pissed-off lists of many now-disgruntled birders. While there was no doubt about the identification of this Wood-Rail, it didn't look like a bird any sane person would keep in a wildfowl collection. Or at least I hoped.

I watched the Wood-Rail for five minutes as it picked at the mud for food before slipping into the cattails and disappearing from view. I stayed another four hours, hoping for more, but with no shade and the mercury breaking one hundred, I was forced to leave with no better views than those of the first few minutes. The bird stayed another ten days, making appearances on local television and national newspapers as well as disappearing for agonizing periods. By the time the pond dried up, forcing the vagrant to find food elsewhere, it had amazed and despaired a great many birders.

I snapped Gerri's photo in front of the bougainvillea vines that blossomed with tiny pinkish-red fireworks. Behind, the octagonal towers of Hearst Castle, decorated in blue and yellow tiles, reached for the dark blue skies above. We'd spent an hour inside the Spanish-revival home of William Randolph Hearst, the newspaper publisher and the inspiration for Orson

Welles' iconic film, *Citizen Kane*. I was impressed with the medieval ceilings, many of which had been harvested and shipped from Europe. But my favorite room was the theater room, its walls lined in bloodred damask with gilded caryatids supporting the ceiling and holding the theater lights. There were large wooden seats for the audience, facing a billowing white screen across which silent films and talkies once played. I imagined the many guests of William Randolph Hearst sitting there spellbound: Charlie Chaplin, Winston Churchill, George Bernard Shaw, and the reclusive Howard Hughes.

In the courtyard, we stood propped against the stone balustrade and looked out on a blanket of golden grass cascading down to the breaking waves of the Pacific Ocean to the west. The air was scented with the fragrance of oleander, lemon bottlebrush, and Irish yew. This was the first day of two different ten-day tours of California. I'd chosen the Big Year tour: to catch up with the more than fifteen species that are hard or impossible to find outside the state. Gerri had chosen the cultural tour. I was the tour leader for both, and so far it was going pretty well. But it was only day one, and I knew that a lot of the so-called cultural tour would inexplicably include a lot of birds.

We'd taken the slow road from the airport in San Francisco: hugging the cliffs and hairpin bends of Highway 1, pausing at photo-op pullouts, slowing for banks of coastal fog, and stopping for coffee near Steinbeck's Cannery Row in Monterey. Green and silver eucalyptus trees, brought over from Australia in the nineteenth century for timber and windbreaks, gently rustled in the breeze as they watched over our slow progress.

We rounded one hairpin bend and emerged though a fog bank to come face to face with a truly giant bird hanging above the cliff in front of us. Gerri was already prepared for this and screamed, "Condor!" The huge bird of prey was flying in profile toward us, followed closely by another, their wings seemingly stretching to the horizon, ending at splayed feathers like outstretched fingers.

California Condors officially became extinct or extirpated in the wild twenty-six years ago. In a controversial sting operation, on Easter Sunday 1987, the last wild bird on the planet was captured. The global population, numbering only twenty-seven birds, was no longer free to soar the mountain thermals, but instead was caged in breeding facilities in San Diego and Los Angeles. Condors once stretched across the country from California to Florida, but that was before they were poisoned to the verge of extinction. They feed on carrion and would ingest lead from spent ammunition buried in the carcasses. That lead paralyzed their digestive system, causing a slow and painful starvation. If the lead didn't kill them, the DDT, an insecticide that was concentrated in the food chain, did. At the right (or wrong) levels, DDT thins eggshells, which collapse, causing total breeding failure. DDT wasn't selective for the condor; it almost wiped out the Peregrine and Bald Eagle too.

I pulled the car over and we watched the two birds glide away from us and disappear into the fog. These birds were descendants of those last twenty-seven birds and the products of the captive breeding programs at the San Diego and Los Angeles zoos. With better protection, a national ban on DDT, and local bans on lead bullets, condors were gradually released back into the wild: in California, Arizona, and Baja California. Today, there are more than two hundred birds. The ABA is still waiting for demonstrable breeding success before it adds the species back to the checklist. The California Condor is currently listed as the uncountable Code 6, or extirpated. (If I'd accidentally waited another year to do my Big Year, I could have counted them, as the ABA added the condor back to the list in 2014.)

When the fog cleared, we made out an adult sitting in a dead tree, high up on the cliff. Above a huge ball of black-and-white feathers sat a perfectly bald red head, lacking feathers like the carrion-scavenging vultures, to which condors are related. We stared at the magnificent bird as it silently surveyed its foggy kingdom below, and we wondered whether it knew how close it had come to complete and final obliteration.

On my bookshelf at home sits a copy of the *National Geographic Field Guide to the Birds of North America*, printed in 1988. It was the book I'd used on that first trip to Texas as a student in 1994. If you're a non-birder, you might be surprised to discover that it's already woefully out of date. Pull back the plastic-wrapped cover, flick through the pages (color plates on the right, text and maps on the left), and you'll start to see why. If you know your birds, you might notice that some of them have been rebranded (Siberian Tit to Gray-headed Chickadee, Water Pipit to American Pipit). And then you might notice that some are missing. Some of those gaps are rarities that were unknown then, like the Shiny Cowbird, a South

American species that has rapidly been expanding its range northward through the Caribbean. But others are from species splits. The evolution of the field guide was why we were on a boat the next day heading for the uninhabited island of Santa Cruz, the largest of the Channel Islands, twenty-eight miles from the dock at Ventura.

The more ornithologists look, the more species they find. Similar-looking populations or subspecies turn out to be separated geographically or reproductively enough to be classified now as bona fide species themselves. Advances in DNA technology have only accelerated these discoveries. While some populations have gone in the other direction (lumping), such as Audubon's and Myrtle Warblers merging as the Yellow-rumped Warbler, the trend is overwhelmingly for splits: dividing one species into two or more.

In 1995 the American Ornithologists' Union (AOU), the group that worries about taxonomy and what is and isn't a species, decided that the Scrub Jay, a blue-and-gray jay primarily of the Southwest, should be three species, not one. Most of the old Scrub Jays got a new name, Western Scrub-Jay, while two far-flung populations were elevated to new species: Florida Scrub-Jay (in central Florida) and Island Scrub-Jay (on Santa Cruz Island). Many birders had already seen the Florida birds, and so enjoyed an "armchair tick" without having to do anything. But Santa Cruz Island was a place few had visited, and far fewer had heard of. As the boat operator was about to discover, there are few things better for business than a new ABA species.

I watched Gerri as she pointed out the school of dolphin jumping happily ahead of the boat, sometimes riding the bow wave, other times nestling along the sides. In front of us, Santa Cruz drew steadily closer. I was still nervous about pulling off this dual-vacation thing and keeping Gerri happy. The plan was to spend the night in Santa Barbara and then head south to Los Angeles. After finding Spotted Doves and Allen's Hummingbirds there, we'd head up into the mountains that enclose the sprawling metropolis, the San Gabriels and San Bernardinos. I knew Gerri liked hiking and hoped she'd enjoy looking for Mountain Quails and White-headed Woodpeckers. After that we'd drop down the other side, to Palm Springs, Joshua Tree National Park, and the Salton Sea, our farthest point south. We'd return north through the Mojave Desert, Yosemite, and back to San Francisco. I'd promised Gerri a couple of days in wine country at the end of the trip.

I was already stressed about missing birds and had my doubts about whether we'd make it to Sonoma Valley. The previous evening, after leaving Hearst Castle, we'd raced to Los Alamos County Park, near Santa Barbara, which is home to the Yellow-billed Magpie, a bird endemic to central California. At least that's what the guidebook says, as did as the dog walker we met.

"Yeah, they're here all the time," he said, seemingly unaware of his own obvious inaccuracy.

Really? I thought. *So, where the hell are they now?* We stayed until the sun slowly slipped below the horizon to prove him and the book wrong. Rather than pushing on to Santa Barbara and a romantic meal, we stayed in Los Alamos, a town with no restaurants, nothing to do, and seemingly no magpies. Our first day had ended with a bird we couldn't count (California Condor), with missing a bird I needed to count, and with medieval-ceiling envy.

We started to hear the jays as soon as we stepped off the boat at Prisoners Harbor. They moved stealthily through the island oaks, calling occasionally—*shreep shreep*—eventually showing themselves to be about the size of a Blue Jay but darker blue and without the crest. They had a brown back and a bright-white chin and throat, were slightly bigger than the mainland Western Scrub-Jay, conveniently supporting Foster's rule: on islands the smaller species evolve larger bodies than their mainland kin because there are fewer predators, while the larger animals become smaller because there's less available food. I'd seen this on St. Paul, where the Gray-crowned Rosy-Finches are almost twice the size of those on Sandia Crest in New Mexico. The famous example here of island dwarfism is the Channel Island Mammoth, which is only about five and a half feet tall. Sadly, apart from the slightly larger jay, I didn't get to witness much more of the island rule: I'd missed the mammoth by thirteen thousand years, and the three hours we did have on the island weren't enough for me to evolve another inch. And so I left the island a stubborn five feet nine inches, but did succeed in growing my year list by one new bird.

I thought the two tandem tours, "Big Year" and "California for Normals," were still going well. Gerri loved the boat trip and exploring the island. On my tour, I did eventually catch up with the Yellow-billed Magpie at Happy Canyon Road—a much happier place than Los Alamos County Park, as it actually had magpies! I also found Tricolored Blackbird in Oxnard and Spotted Dove in Los Angeles. Gerri's tour featured a walking tour of Santa Barbara, some great food, and a romantic cliff-top walk along the Palos Verdes Peninsula, which conveniently also included California Gnatcatcher and Allen's Hummingbird. Both tours coalesced high in the San Gabriel Mountains, which rise up to shield Los Angeles from the Mojave Desert to the east. And at 6,500 feet high, that's where the tour started to go downhill.

Although I liked to complain about it, the truth is I'd become quite good at sleeping in cars. I knew which ones were the best for sleeping (the Ford Fusion being my current favorite), although I soon discovered this wasn't a popular subject when discussing the choice of car with the car rental company. I had a couple of lightweight airplane blankets (pinched from my now-frequent complimentary upgrades to first class), and I'd even bought one of those ridiculous and embarrassing-looking neck pillows once I realized it would make for a better pillow than my folded clothes. I slept in the driver's seat with the seat pushed back and reclined. It was never too hot, but frequently too cold. I'd often wake up shivering, start the car, turn the heat on high, and then turn it off (I worried about carbon monoxide poisoning), before going back to sleep again while the hot air slowly leaked out and the cold air snuck back in. Depending on how cold it was outside, this would be repeated multiple times during the night.

Gerri shared neither my enthusiasm for sleeping in a car nor my cheapness. I discovered this at the top of the San Gabriel Mountains. What I thought might make for a romantic night—twinkling stars, listening to Flammulated

and Northern Saw-whet Owls singing across the coniferous
forests—ended up being an exercise in damage control. I
hadn't expected Gerri to be ill, nor the outside temperature to
be quite so cold. We had to run the car every fifteen minutes
or so to keep from freezing. She wouldn't stop moaning and
shaking. I wasn't sure if it was from fever, cold, or anger, but
it was probably a combination of all three. I worried that she
might cancel the Big Year part of the tour. And then I worried
that she might cancel the whole tour and then the relationship. In the end, she never did say anything. But I knew this
was gold dust that she could save and cash in for any future
argument. And no, we didn't hear any owls.

Things began to look up for us as we descended into the
desert and started to stay in places that had beds and indoor
bathrooms. Gerri loved Joshua Tree National Park with its
prehistoric-looking cactus trees. Palm Springs proved to be a
popular stopover, and the Salton Sea was a surprise hit.

The Salton Sea itself was a colossal mistake. The year was
1905 and the idea was to irrigate the rift valley southeast of
Palm Springs. It was an ancient lakebed and, with some water,
could be fertile enough again for some kind of agriculture.
When the Colorado River tore through the levees of the new
canals, it filled 350 square miles of desert with no natural
outlet except evaporation. California suddenly had a new
largest lake, and one that was 226 feet below sea level (only
five feet higher than the deepest part of Death Valley). It was a
mistake that, for once, benefited wildlife. The lake has hosted
more than four hundred species of birds, including over
80 percent of the wintering population of American White

Pelicans. It has become an important pit stop for species during migration.

The farther south we drove, the higher the mercury rose before eventually topping out at 113 degrees Fahrenheit. We arrived at the Sonny Bono Salton Sea National Wildlife Refuge at the southern part of the sea around mid-afternoon, the perfect time of day to experience the heat and the loneliness of the place. The wildlife refuge was empty of staff, visitors, and seemingly hope. In the five minutes that we ventured from the car, I felt as close to spontaneous human combustion as I've ever felt. But the near inflagration paid off. Alerted by oval fecal pellets on the ground, we found a Barn Owl roosting inside a palm tree. Gerri was ecstatic at seeing the white, heart-shaped face peeking out from its shady hiding place. We found another owl shortly after, a smaller Burrowing Owl, outside the refuge. They live in underground tunnels, like those dug by prairie dogs. This one hopped from one leg to another. We evidently weren't the only ones baking in the heat.

The Salton Sea is dying. It's slowly contracting as the water evaporates faster than it's replaced, and as it does so, it's getting saltier (it's already saltier than the nearby Pacific). Few fish can tolerate such high salinity. Most are dead now except for the introduced tilapia. Agricultural runoff adds to the pollution. In 1992, 150,000 Eared Grebes mysteriously died, possibly the result of toxic metals. It was the largest single die-off of birds ever recorded, second only to that caused by the *Exxon Valdez* oil spill in 1989. In 1996, avian botulism killed 14,000 to 20,000 fish-eating birds, including more than 8,500 American

White Pelicans. Since then the botulism-related bird die-offs have been annual. Botulism causes paralysis. After eating infected fish, the birds can't raise their heads, causing some to drown and others to slowly bake in the sun. (There's now a dedicated rescue center that treats pelicans and other victims of botulism.) Without help, the Salton Sea will follow the Aral Sea in the former Soviet Union and become an ecological disaster with toxic dust clouds.

We drove to one of the raised dikes from where the receding shoreline is now a distant, shimmering mirage. Thankfully I didn't have to get out of the car to see the Yellow-footed Gulls, the reason for our visit, standing on the parched mud. They're an attractive gull, with a charcoal-gray back and yellow legs as well as yellow feet. They breed in the Gulf of California in Mexico and a few like to spend the off-season here. As long as there's fish, I suppose, there will be vacationing gulls.

It was a long drive back north to San Francisco, and much of it was ruined by looking for Mountain Quail. Despite multiple attempts, and many early mornings scrambling over rocky slopes, I managed to miss Mountain Quail everywhere that I looked for them: the San Gabriels, the San Bernardinos, and the Piute Mountains. (I say "I" and not "we" because Gerri did see one. The pain is so raw that you'll have to wait another chapter before I've recovered enough to tell that story.)

Thankfully the other grouse, Chukar, proved to be a lot easier. Chukar is an introduced partridge from the Middle East and Asia. I'd been told about a reliable spot, Galileo Hill, in the middle of the Mojave Desert. We arrived to find a bare, conical hill overlooking the beautifully lush resort of Silver Saddle. It was an oasis in the desert, with tennis courts, a golf course, paddleboats, and koi-filled ponds. Only there was no one there. The buildings were unlocked, but the whole place was eerily empty. Menus lay open on the tables in the restaurant, a TV loudly reported the local weather (hot again) to an empty bar, and cupboards were open, exposing all sorts of potential freebies. It was a zombie apocalypse, presumably followed by an alien abduction.

We explored the rest of the buildings, which continued the similar eerie science-fiction scene. In the last building, in a small office, we heard a voice. It belonged to a woman, and it was speaking into a telephone. We opened the screen door, and based on her expression, our looks must have betrayed our mixed emotions—the excitement of finding a person here, juxtaposed with the disappointment of discovering that there was no zombie apocalypse (or aliens). But she did grant us our wish: to bird around the site (although I'm not sure she knew what a Chukar was and evidently decided it was better not to ask).

We drove halfway up the rocky hill, but the birdlife up there was as dead as it was below. I remembered hearing that when the Chukars aren't walking all over the hill, they'll occasionally come down to enjoy the shade of the resort trees. It was hot, and if I were a Chukar, that's exactly where I would be, and that's exactly where we found them—a couple of silhouettes hiding under one of the leafy umbrellas. I slammed on the brakes, which startled the birds into a run.

I caught a quick glimpse of the black bars on the flanks and the yellowish throat outlined in black, before they swapped legs for wings and disappeared up the side of the hill.

After 2,520 miles, nine days of birding, twenty-two new Big Year species, butt views of a mountain lion and black bear, and learning that Sonny Bono was not the lead singer of U2, we made it to the wine country part of the tour. We stayed in a real hotel in Santa Rosa, wore nice clothes, and generally did things that normal people do. This was Gerri's day, her reward for putting up with the Big Year part of the tour.

We were visiting the Francis Ford Coppola Winery—as much a museum for his movies and Oscars as a working vineyard. There were black-and-white photos from the *Godfather* movie set, including one in which a young and dimpled Diane Keaton smiles to the camera while something causes Al Pacino, sitting in front, to burst out into maniacal laughter. There was Don Corleone's desk and chair, in which Marlon Brando had once sat and brooded. A collection of long buildings, like French châteaus but topped with improbable pyramidal roofs, framed a rectangular courtyard, into which was sunk a deep blue and inviting pool.

It was an advertisement for happiness and relaxation—people laughing, holding hands, and knocking back large balloon glasses of wine under the warm California sun. But my mind was elsewhere—with the Mountain Quail I'd repeatedly missed and would have to leave behind, and now a report of a Slate-throated Restart (Code 4) in Huachuca

Canyon, Arizona. Gerri looked at the pool gathering and then at me, and I could tell that she wasn't happy.

I don't like having public arguments (who does?), but if you don't make time to talk, then that's what invariably happens. We were right back to the argument we'd had in the car on the way to the Great Dismal Swamp, as if we'd suddenly rediscovered it, buried down the back of the sofa, realized it was on pause, and foolishly hit the play button. Except this time the numbers looked worse: we'd been dating for exactly a year now, she'd just moved into a new place that was costing her one thousand dollars a month, and she hadn't spent a single night there.

I knew I was reaching the tipping point and was starting to lose her. Gerri was a catch. She was beautiful and fun, and had so much to give. It wouldn't be difficult for her to find someone else, someone who was more demonstrative than me, who wouldn't abandon her for birds or drag her around the country in pursuit of them. Like everyone, she wanted to be in a relationship where she came first.

I suppose I was still scared, scared of her moving in, and then being stuck if it didn't work out. I wanted to hang on to the status quo in which failure meant having less to lose. Every time I felt closer to her, I would manufacture irresolvable differences to keep us apart: she drinks tea, I drink coffee; she runs, I walk; she doesn't really drink, I drink beer, wine, gin, and anything else I can find; she likes birds, I love birds. I knew those differences were magnified excuses designed to protect me and hold me back, to scare me from anything different. And I knew that if I couldn't reconcile those differences, I'd get exactly what I ostensibly wanted: to spend the rest of my life with myself.

A week later I was back in California, alone.

"Are you Neil Hayward? You're late!"

I so wanted to make a good first impression with Debi Shearwater. Getting lost on the way to the boat while looking for coffee resulted in the lateness. Not having the right cash for the trip resulted in an extra reason for her to be unimpressed. Debi had been running pelagic trips out of California for more than thirty years. She stood on the dock, wrapped in warm layers of clothing, and looked ready to take on the Pacific, her straw-colored hair tamed under a cap and her eyes framed by oval glasses. Behind her a boat full of birders bobbed in the harbor. After she'd finished shouting at me for being late, she spent the rest of the day making me laugh and smile. Behind that efficient, can-do personality was a kind soul with a deep love and respect for the ocean. Debi is an expert on seabirds, whales, oceanic life, and North American birders. If you're one of the latter, chances are that you've been on a Shearwater Journeys boat with Debi.

After the safety talk (no smoking, no standing on the benches, no bow-hogging, and no being a pain in the ass) we set off. Half Moon Bay is a quick thirty-minute hop west over forested hills from the San Francisco airport, which I'd flown into the previous night. After navigating the coastal fog I'd rolled into town around two A.M. The coastline was laid bare before me, like a musical bass clef unfurling against the thin strip of beach. Since I'd be getting up in four hours, I elected to stay at the dock in Hotel Corolla. It charges pretty much the same as Hotel Mazda, but the "bed" was slightly more comfortable. What was not more comfortable was the harbor foghorn, which went off every fifteen seconds. I never found a way to turn that feature off.

I didn't recognize Jay at first, but he recognized me. We were coming out of the harbor, just starting to see Rhinoceros Auklets scared off the water in the path of the advancing boat. Patches of fog rolled in, sealing us off from the world in a bubble from which the horizon and the sky were frequently hidden. I'd heard of Jay Lehman from Chris Hitt. Jay was a retired chemist from Cincinnati and 2013 was his Big Year too.

Meeting Jay was like reconnecting with an old friend. We shared so many acquaintances (Western Spindalis, Fieldfare, Red-flanked Bluetail), and we'd been to all the same places (California Gulch, the Dry Tortugas, Sax-Zim Bog). For the past year we'd been like ships crossing in the night. Jay was enthusiastic, in a quiet way, and he came alive when talking to me about his Big Year, able to share his experiences with one of the few people who understood what it all meant. Like Hans, he knew that there was never enough time for all the birding, traveling, and planning. Jay had a huge amount of birding experience and had seen his eight hundredth ABA life bird (Short-tailed Albatross) this year. He'd even been to Attu, by boat, re-creating the trip he'd taken by plane twenty-five years before.

Ashy Storm-Petrels started to appear alongside the boat— long-tailed and grayer versions of the storm-petrels that I'd seen off Hatteras. Debi explained to us that they were seriously endangered: half of them breed on the Farallon Islands, thirty miles west of the Golden Gate Bridge. The Eurasian mouse, accidentally introduced in the nineteenth century by visiting seal-hunting boats, is destroying the seabird colony. The Farallons now have the highest density of rodents of any island in the world. The mice attract Burrowing Owls, which then develop a taste for the meatier storm-petrels. Debi tells us that there are plans to air-drop rodenticide on the islands, a technique that has been successful in New Zealand, as well as on Anacapa, one of the Channel Islands that Gerri and I had passed on the way to Santa Cruz and its scrub-jays.

"Do you know who that is?" Jay nodded toward the small cabin of the boat, where an older guy stood hunched over his digital camera. He was wearing a dark-blue rain jacket and a cap, and the lower part of his face was hidden behind white hair. There was something familiar about him, yet I couldn't quite place him.

"That's Sandy Komito," said Jay.

Sandy Komito—the guy in whose footsteps I was following, whose 1998 Big Year record set the benchmark for all future Big Years. I was in awe and a little starstuck. I was prepared to see the delicately patterned Buller's Shearwaters, but not a birding legend. What could I possibly have to say to Sandy?

Sandy was sitting in the cabin alone when I walked in, stumbling from side to side with the pitching of the boat. I wondered if I should acknowledge him. Maybe he's fed up with being identified, I thought. Maybe he's sick of the endless question "Are you the guy in the movie?" In the end, I didn't have to worry about what I'd say, as he did it for me.

"Are you Neil Hayward?" he asked.

I spoke to Sandy for an hour, occasionally distracted by shout-outs of passing seabirds—"Fork-tailed Storm-Petrel!" and "Sabine's Gull!"—but otherwise utterly enthralled. The guy had seen it all, as his eighty years, beaten-up Attu hat, and endless stories attested. He'd recently moved to Florida but retained a thick Bronx accent. He laughed constantly and could recall names of people and birds and dates with remarkable speed and accuracy. He was a born storyteller and immediately put me at ease.

Sandy had seen *The Big Year* movie, of course, and he wasn't a fan. For a start, he told me, there was no competition between the three birders: birding is such a personal endeavor that the only person you're ever competing against is yourself. He'd heard about my own Big Year and offered some advice: chase the rarities.

"You can always go back for the common stuff," he said. "If you're in the middle of a trip to Minnesota that you've planned for months and a rarity turns up in Texas, you go to Texas."

I knew he was right. You have only one chance at some of those rarities, and if you wait too long, you'll miss it. I thought back to the White-cheeked Pintail I'd missed in Florida, and the rarities at the start of the year that I hadn't chased— Citrine Wagtail, Gray Heron, and Spotted Redshank. Well, I still had five months left to apply that principle, I thought. And if I were ever insane enough to do a Big Year again, then I'd follow his advice (and probably get up earlier on January 1).

I asked Sandy about the ever-evolving ABA Checklist—nine new splits and five new exotic species added since his Big Year. The rules of the Big Year, as they are, mean that if you saw those birds in your Big Year, you couldn't count them because they weren't on the official list at the time. He didn't seem to care—he had one number, 748, and he didn't spend any time lamenting the fact that some of the uncountable birds he'd seen in 1998 would end up being countable in 2013.

Sandy told me he was too old to do another Big Year. I'm not sure that I believed him. Even at eighty-two he didn't seem to have slowed down much. He regularly sees more than five hundred species every year and is now working on photographing every species recorded in the ABA region (by tracking down many of the rarities to their native countries in Central America, Europe, and East Asia). On this trip Ashy Storm-Petrel was a new bird for "Mr. Camera." I watched as he scribbled notes into a battered old notebook and imagined him doing the same on the windy slopes of Attu, at the Dry Tortugas, and in the thousands of other places his wild obsession had taken him.

As our conversation drew to a close, Sandy wished me luck. He said he hoped he'd live long enough to see someone break his record.

Sandy has been portrayed as an egotistical, hard-nosed figure who cares about birds first and people a distant second. He'd made his money as a roofing contractor in New Jersey, a job that suited and honed his aggressive and confident sales persona. But in the short time I spent with him, I found him to be courteous, engaging, and considerate. And while he may never do another Big Year, it's clear that he's still madly in love with birds. His eyes lit up like a child's on Christmas morning when talking about them.

I joined Jay for the rest of the trip. We fell into a steady banter about places we'd been. Jay told me about the Black-faced Grassquit in Miami that he'd seen and I'd missed. I told him about the Rufous-necked Wood-Rail, which he had yet to see. (The bird would ultimately leave before he could get there.) Listening to Jay, I realized I'd found what I'd lost in Hans—a potential Big Year colleague. And while my mind was still working through all the new ideas and stories I'd heard from the rock star Sandy, it would be the quiet, unassuming Jay, hidden behind a gray mustache and wire-framed spectacles, who would change the rest of the year for me. I would realize for a second time that birding can be more fun when shared.

My bird count at the end of July 2013: 696 (+1 provisional)
John Vanderpoel's bird count at the end of July 2011: 690

Chapter 8

WINNING THE BOOBY PRIZE

I JOKED ABOUT HIMALAYAN Snowcocks when I first contemplated doing a Big Year in April.

"Yeah, okay, whatever. I guess I am doing a Big Year," I said to Gerri. "But I'm definitely not—I repeat, *not*—going to Nevada to see the damn Snowcocks. I'm not a complete idiot."

Four months later I was in Nevada to see the damn Snowcocks.

Himalayan Snowcocks, as their name might suggest, were never supposed to be in Nevada. To understand the weirdness, we need to travel back to the mustachioed and bell-bottomed days of the 1960s. It was probably another slow day at the Nevada Fish and Game Commission, where the combination of boredom, drunkenness, or being sky high led one young upstart to propose two bold and psychedelic thoughts, the first being: "Dude, you know what? Our very own Ruby Mountains look a bit like them world-famous Himalayas."

Presumably our young chap had never been to the Himalayas, or he might have noticed the general lack of yaks, yetis, Buddhist monasteries, and anything over twelve thousand feet from his Nevada workplace. But let's forgive him this oversight and let him continue to the second question, one that nobody had dared ask before.

"Why can't we have our own Snowcocks?"

Why not indeed, one might ask! Snowcocks are large partridges, like Chukars, and it wasn't hard to follow the logic that a few exotic game birds would undoubtedly add some extra spice to an otherwise dull 1960s Nevada. Presumably a few bets were exchanged and a phone call placed to the president of Pakistan. The latter agreed and Pakistan started trapping birds (at a cost of fifty dollars per bird) and shipping them our way. Sadly most of them died, and it was left to a local breeding program to provide the majority of the two thousand birds that were released between 1965 and 1979. The birds loved their new home (except for all the guns) and have been here ever since, making them not only the most ridiculous of the introduced species to North America but also annoyingly one of the most inaccessible. They live above the tree line in the high elevations of the Ruby Mountains.

I picked up the rental car in Salt Lake City, the nearest major airport, and headed west into the Great Basin, an area of two hundred thousand square miles that encompasses most of Nevada, half of Utah, and parts of Wyoming, Idaho, Oregon, and California. Salt Lake City (northeast) and Reno (west) are the major cities in an otherwise vast and empty arena. It's an endorheic basin, like the Salton Sea, which means that all the water, whether from precipitation or springs, drains into internal lakes and never reaches the sea.

The searing temperatures burn off the water and leave behind a crusty residue of salt.

I pulled over on the side of the highway, unable to quite believe the view. On both sides of the arrow-straight road was blinding whiteness. It stretched to a horizon bounded by distant, heat-shimmering hills. I got out of the car and was careful to brace myself for the *whoomping* suction of the passing juggernauts. I could taste the salt in the air, which immediately took me back to the rolling swell of a recent pelagic. I reached down to touch the ground—sand, delicately patterned with wind-blown ripples, like a gentle sea paused. The sand was encrusted with white salt. This was the Bonneville Flats of Utah, the most unearthly place on earth I'd ever visited.

I stopped in the small town of Elko for coffee at Cowboy Joe's before heading up to the Ruby Mountains. As the caffeine molecules latched onto their hungry receptors, jolting my tired brain back into gear, I read a notice for the National Cowboy Poetry Gathering, held in Elko every year. It was the most recent reinvention of a city that had tried its hand at railroad center, ranching, and gold mining. The writer Hunter S. Thompson evidently wasn't much impressed. "The federal government owns 90% of this land," he noted, "and most of it is useless for anything except weapons testing and poison-gas experiments." Still, at least the place had a cool name. Legend has it that Charles Crocker, a railroad executive from New York, had a penchant for animal names and came up with "Elko."

The Snowcocks are most reliably seen at sunrise, when they're most active and vocal. I was hoping that they'd put on an evening show too, saving me from an early ascent the following morning. From the trailhead at 8,750 feet it's a slow, steep climb (1,000 feet in one and a half miles) of switchbacks through Rocky Mountain and whitebark pine that will soon come to define the tree line above. I ignored the melodious MacGillivray's Warblers singing from the streambeds and the whistling White-crowned Sparrows as I pushed on along the hot trail. My calves cried out in pain. After an hour, the trail topped out onto an alpine meadow, spotted with bright colors like a pointillist painting: bloodred Indian paintbrush, yellow mule's-ear daisies, and violet-blue fleabane. Above, mountain ridges fused into a cirque, a towering half-bowl of serrated peaks, standing sentry to the aquamarine blue of Lake Lamoille below. I stood in awe. The vibrant colors and floral smells were a welcome juxtaposition to the caustic landscape of the nearby salt flats. And if birds really are a lens through which to see and marvel at the world around us, I had much for which to thank the Snowcocks.

I'd carried my scope and tripod up the switchbacks, alternating shoulders to ensure each received equal bruising. But I was grateful for it. The birds like to perch on the crest of the cirque, perhaps a half mile distant. As I swept the scope across the sharp, serrated edges, I spotted a Snowcock. I'd been here for only five minutes and I already had the bird! I couldn't believe my luck and obvious skill. Many birders come here and miss the birds. It was distant, but I could make out the heavy body, extended neck, and pointed head. I watched it for five minutes as it sat perfectly still, surveying its territory below. After another five minutes I started to worry. Was it sleeping? I wondered. Or dead? After a few more minutes of hard squinting, I decided it was a Himalayan Snowrock, a distant geological cousin of the Snowcock, which, as yet, is uncountable on the ABA Checklist of birds.

I stood on the side of the lightly wooded slope, scoping the cirque back and forth without success until the carved granite slopes burned with yellow, orange, and then a deep blue as the sun slipped below the zigzaggy horizon. Apart from a few Clark's Nutcrackers, a huge Golden Eagle, and a shaggy white mountain goat doing a fine Spiderman impression, there was nothing new. I made my way down to the parking lot, which would also now, annoyingly, be my accommodation for the night.

There are twenty-four exotics, or non-native species, on the ABA Checklist. Some, like the Snowcocks here, the Chukars on Galileo Hill, and the Gray Partridges I'd shown Gerri in Calgary, were released as game birds. Others were escaped cage birds, like the many species of colorful parrot that now fill the skies and palm trees of urban Miami, the exotics capital of the United States. Others are descendants of birds our forefathers brought over, for the often simple reason that they wanted to surround themselves with something that reminded them of home.

Our most familiar bird perhaps, the House Sparrow, was the first successful introduction. It wasn't an easy immigration. The first attempt in 1851 by the Brooklyn Institute in New York failed when all eight pairs died. A year later, they weren't taking any chances and shipped one hundred birds from England, releasing them the following spring in Greenwood Cemetery, Brooklyn, and even hired a man

specifically to look out for them. (I wonder if the job description asked for previous experience throwing pieces of bread
and chasing after hawks?) This time, the House or "English"
Sparrows did rather well. Today there are 150 million birds in
forty-eight states.

If you were one of the high school kids who suffered under
the sweet sorrows of parting, of ladies that doth protest too
much, and slept, perchance to dream, through the classes of
Shakespeare, you can also blame the bard for the electric
squeaks of the European Starling. Well, maybe you should
more accurately direct your annoyance at Eugene Schieffelin,
chairman of the American Acclimatization Society. Schieffelin
was a fan of the playwright and allegedly resolved to introduce every one of the more than sixty birds mentioned in
Shakespeare's plays to the United States. While many were
unsuccessful, like Bullfinches, Song Thrushes, and Skylarks,
the Starlings released into Central Park in 1890 and 1891 were
a huge success. By the early years of the new century Starlings
had reached the Mississippi River, and by the twenty-first
century there were more than two hundred million stretching
from Alaska to Mexico.

In 1900 Congress passed the Lacey Act, banning the impor-
tation of non-native birds and wildlife that might threaten the
environment, people, and industry. But by then it was too late.
Schieffelin had opened a Pandora's box of ills on the new
world. "Starlings," the Ohio naturalist George Laycock later
wrote, "do nothing in moderation." His was an understate-
ment. They cause crop damage (currently costing about eight
hundred million dollars per year); they spread tick-borne

diseases, such as Lyme disease, and carry the parasite responsible for toxoplasmosis; their droppings contain fungal spores
that cause histoplasmosis; and they oust cavity-nesting birds
such as bluebirds and woodpeckers. And long after death lay on
Schieffelin like an untimely frost, giant flocks, or murmura-
tions, of his released harpies were the bane of pilots. In 1960, an
Eastern Air Lines flight out of Boston was downed in Winthrop
Bay, killing sixty-two of the seventy-two passengers on board.
Investigators found starlings had been sucked into three of the
four turboprop engines, causing the aircraft to stall.

The ABA has tightened the rules on listing introduced or
exotic species. In the past, the requirement was persistence in
the wild for five years. Then it became ten years. The current
ruling is for a minimum of fifteen years, as well as various
parameters measuring population stability. But that may still
be too short, as many of these introductions seem to go
through a boom-and-bust cycle. In the 1890s Crested Mynas
were introduced from Indochina into the Vancouver area,
where they flourished, reaching a high of twenty thousand
birds by the 1920s. But then the Starlings from New York
reached the West Coast and proved to be a major disruption to
the Myna party. Numbers of the latter dropped through
competition, until by 2004 there was only a pair left. By the
end of the year they were extirpated as a breeding species in
the ABA Area. One of them was hit by a car, and the other,
perhaps mourning its lost mate, kept vigil at the scene of the
accident, until it too befell the same fate.

Beep, beep, beep. My alarm jolted me awake. It was my
fourth alarm, after resetting the four A.M. one for four fifteen

A.M., four thirty A.M., and then four forty-five A.M. It was forty-five degrees outside (and inside), and I was shivering, despite having gone to bed in all my clothes as well as my coat, hat, and gloves. Like many times this year, I didn't want to get up, but I knew I would regret it if I didn't. If these birds showed themselves only at first light, then I had only one chance. I grabbed my scope and binoculars and headed up the trail, using my flashlight to give form to the rocks, tree roots, and toads that lined the nocturnal path. I was half afraid of what might lie beyond. My mind conjured ghostly images of eyes, teeth, and claws. I kept a steady hand on the flashlight's natural curiosity, preventing it from straying too far into unwelcome territory.

I was already worrying that I was going to be late. As fast as I scrambled up the trail, the sky moved through the gray color palette with frightening speed. I was barely halfway up, and I was already out of breath, my heart banging inside my chest. And that's when I remembered there was an easier way to do this: by helicopter. You can buzz over the mountaintops, scaring up the birds. But somehow that didn't feel right—like it was cheating in some way. (Although I'm sure the additional $925 probably also accounted for the negative opinion.)

By the time I reached the meadow, I could already see the colors on the flowers. It was too late, I feared. I stood at the edges of the still lake and gazed upward, looking for movement among the snow rocks and hoping to hear the eerie curlewlike calls of the Snowcocks. But it was quiet and still, and I was suddenly struck by the irony of looking for another deliberately released exotic.

However hard I try to remember to use the right terms (*faucet*, *sidewalk*, *restroom*, and to pronounce *water* with a *d* not a *t*, and *croissant* with an *r* not a *w*), my accent still betrays me. Accents can be plastic, adaptable to new landscapes like hairdos to decades, but mine seems to be stuck in an eddy somewhere in the Atlantic, never quite sure where it belongs, but decidedly closer to England. I try not to get upset when people ask where I'm from and for how long I'm visiting. There is no badge showing that I'm a citizen like them, or that I passed the civics test and know that there are 435 members in the House of Representatives, that the Constitution was penned in 1787, and that Benjamin Franklin started the first free libraries.

Most of us accept our nationality as we accept our names and our eye color, never once thinking that the randomness of birth could ever have been different. To choose a nationality is a funny thing. At the end of it all, you're released into the world as a new creature, ostensibly the same as all the others who never had to make that choice, but having passed through a reengineering process of endless paperwork and interviews to get there. The ceremony itself, the final hoop for me, was held in a vast conference center in the Seaport District of South Boston. It was a warm, summer afternoon, sailboats bobbed in the harbor outside, and I stood with more than a thousand others listening to a recorded message of Barack Obama thanking us for wanting to join his team. I surprised myself by choking up on the heartfelt welcome. I brushed the tears from my eyes and walked out into the bright sunshine, alone and American.

But the truth is I've always felt like an exotic, an introduced species out of place, both here and back home. I've suffered from crippling shyness since I was a kid. My whole face would turn beet red when spoken to or called on to speak in class. I never understood the need for small talk, and still fear it, worried that I'll have nothing to say. I have no problem talking about ideas, but never know how to talk about the weather or ask after people's families. I found my cure in high school in acting. I was Henry Higgins in a production of *Pygmalion*. From there, I found myself in other plays and other characters. There was a reassuring confidence in having a script and knowing what to say next.

I suppose that's how I coped with being a managing director of a company—by being someone else. I played a confident character, one whose voice never wavered and who had answers for everything. But it's a tiring business being someone else, pretending to care about things you don't and keeping the real passions hidden. In the end, that's why I had to stop. It wasn't me. Although I wasn't quite sure what "me" was, I knew exactly what it wasn't.

Movement on the cirque! I saw it through my binoculars. By now the sun was warming my face and I could remove my gloves. I pointed the scope in that direction, and after a few anxious moments, up popped a Snowcock. It was alive, non-geological, and ABA-tickable! And then up popped another. I was surprised by their size—they were almost as large and heavy as yesterday's Golden Eagle. The head and neck were a silvery white color, with dark bands arcing down from the face. The fat, stocky body was dark brown and moved quickly for such a size.

I spent the next hour transfixed by the world of the fat Snowcocks as they scampered over the ridge like curious chickens, occasionally calling, throwing back their heads to the hard blue skies above. They gave the impression that they owned the place. Maybe that whole Himalaya/Ruby Mountains bet wasn't so outrageous after all, I thought. And I was still hoping that my own UK to US one wasn't either.

Every birder has one: a nemesis bird. No matter how hard you try, you always seem to miss it. Either you arrive just after the bird's left, or you're the sacrificial lamb, leaving a group of birders who immediately have crippling views of the bird while you're in the car driving away.

This year my nemesis bird was Mountain Quail. It's common (ABA Code 1), although its very secretive behavior and preference for inaccessible and thickly vegetated slopes can make it tough to find. But like most nemesis birds, no one else has a problem seeing them. In fact, it helps if you're with someone who's never seen one before. That's what happened in July in Arrastre Creek in the San Bernardino Mountains of California. Gerri and I had split up for fifteen minutes, which was long enough for her to both hear and see a Mountain Quail. It disappeared before I could relocate it, which made for a fun rest of the day.

I'd gone looking for the bird again after my first trip with Debi Shearwater. I'd been in touch with Bob Barnes, a birder in Kern County, California, who had a reliable spot in the Piute Mountains. He sees them every time he goes up and almost guaranteed that we'd get them. We had a great day seeing California Thrashers and Pinyon Jays, as well as breath-taking scenery. Bob was the perfect host, providing a wealth of knowledge on local birds and habitats. It would be hard to imagine a better day of birding. Although, if pressed I'd have to say that it might possibly have been better if we'd seen a damn Mountain Quail.

I was back on Debi Shearwater's boat again in August, this time out of Monterey. There was no Sandy, nor Jay, with whom I was now communicating almost daily about progress (Jay was stuck in Ohio, his Big Year on hold as he was embroiled in a dispute with a neighboring homeowners' association over stormwater runoff. It would cost him many birds, and he'd be playing catch-up for the rest of the year). The ocean was flat with not a breath of wind. The only activity was the breaching of Blue Whales, breaking the surface for a lungful of air before sinking back to their cold and dark world. The rare petrels for which we hoped, like the Cook's Petrel that Sandy Komito had seen a week before, were nowhere to be found, presumably sitting on the surface waiting for the roller coaster winds to restart.

As we headed back to shore, Debi asked about my trip with Bob Barnes. She was surprised that we'd missed the birds. And then she did what everyone else has done when I tell them about my embarrassing Mountain Quail problem: she told me about her favorite spot. I humored her, knowing that I'd never see them.

"When did you last see them there?" I asked.

"Oh, about twenty years ago," she said. "But other people see them there all the time. I think."

Debi found a scrap piece of paper and wrote her directions to the Holy Quail. I had nothing to lose. I was planning to try Bob Barnes's Piute Mountain spot the next day, and Debi's suggestion turned out to be a lot closer. If I was going to miss the bird anyway, I might as well miss it two hours away rather than five hours away.

I followed Debi's handwriting to Tassajara Road in the Los Padres Mountains south of Salinas. I arrived an hour or so before sunset. My plan was to drive up the unpaved mountain roads before dark, reconnoiter the area, find somewhere to park, and sleep, and then repeat first thing in the morning, when grouse are typically most active. It was a beautiful drive, past open meadows, heavily wooded hillsides, and a busy campsite, but my attention was focused on the sides of the road. When birders are looking for a specific bird, it's helpful to have a search image for which to continually scan. In this case, a fat chicken either in the road or, probably, on the side of the road. The surrounding vegetation was too thick to see much, and my only hope was to surprise one as it encountered and momentarily pondered the open space of the road. As I turned one hairpin bend, my search image and reality fused in one frightening and unbelievable moment. I slammed on the brakes and watched in disbelief as a quail ran across the road in front of me, trailing a pair of long thin plumes pinned to the crown.

While birding is often a slow, patient sport, there are occasionally moments like this, when time seems to stand still. You're suddenly aware that the timeline is stretched, like a rubber band, opening vast chasms between the now-audible tick of distant seconds. You know that you need to make a decision. This moment of clarity won't last forever, and you can choose only one of the parallel universe outcomes. In this case, I debated between getting out of the car and chasing the quail or reaching for either my binoculars or my camera in case there were more quail. In the end I waited too long. The taut rubber band of time snapped back violently into its old, familiar place, and I'd made no decision. Immediately, a second quail hopped up to replace the first one and followed its friend across the dusty road. Then a third. I could see the parallel white lines on the chestnut-colored flanks with my naked eyes, as a fourth and then a fifth quail appeared and disappeared. By the time my right hand had groped, octopuslike, and found my camera and removed the lens cap, the eighth and final quail had followed its flock up an impossibly steep and thickly vegetated slope.

I got out of the car and walked around the crime scene. It was one of the many moments in birding when you wish you could replay what had just happened, knowing the surprise that was coming, and just sit back and enjoy. But birding rarely works like that, and I'm secretly glad for all those heart-pumping moments. Birding may not be like surfing, or rock climbing, but that doesn't mean it lacks the adrenalin rushes. I kicked the dusty road, looking back at the view the surprised quails would have had of me. With the setting sun burning the surrounding mountainous folds, it made for a good commercial for the Ford Fusion. And then I noticed the tiny hieroglyphics etched into the sand—footprints from the quail. I smiled and sent a silent message of thanks to my nemesis god.

★

While I was chasing my nemesis goddess around the hills and mountains of California, on the other side of the country something quieter but more momentous happened: Gerri moved in. It was less of a moving in than a moving out of her stuff from an apartment that she'd still never slept in. It could hardly have been less ceremonious. I returned home to find some cheap furniture clogging up my basement, a stack of books ready to be added to the end of the bookshelves, and a collection of soft toy pandas now "decorating" the bed. Nothing was really different but everything had changed.

I was spending a lot of time on planes—sixty-six thousand miles before our vacation to California. And when I wasn't reading or writing or seeking out delicious sleep, I had time to think. After the wine country end to our dual tour of California, Gerri went home, and I went to Arizona to chase a Slate-throated Redstart. On that flight to Phoenix, I thought a lot about what she'd said, but mostly I couldn't get her tears out of my head. In the end, moving in felt like the right thing to do.

It felt different than the last time—when Anna had pushed me to move in, and the time before that with Katie, whose lease was expiring the month I moved to the United States, and we thought it would be a good idea. (It wasn't.) This time the only pressure I felt was my own, the certainty that otherwise I'd lose Gerri. I now realized how important she was. Whether it was the excitement of the birding, or the daily lifting of the depression, I could now see for the first time how lucky I was to have Gerri. Among the turmoil of the past year, she had been the one unvarying constant. While there were so many unknowns this year and thereafter, I knew that

I didn't want to lose her. I told her when I got back from Arizona. We were in the kitchen, the radio was on, Khiva Cat was restlessly prowling back and forth across the counter, complaining about something, while Sally was distracted by a chewed-up ball of wastepaper on the floor. Gerri started to cry and hugged me tight.

Life is scary. It's scarier when you've been hurt before, and when you start to think that it's cyclical, that you'll always end up with the same results. Before you find the right one, every relationship by definition has to fail. Mix in the depression, where it feels like there is no future, only past failures, and it's hard to move forward; it's like your feet are stuck in blocks of concrete. But this time, I was ready, and I could imagine just enough of the future to want to fight for it.

Birding is a little like baseball. One minute you're hitting everything out of the park, even the Mountain Quails, and the next you're swinging and missing. My slump started in August, right after Gerri moved in (although I'm convinced there was no direct link). It started in San Diego. I was in town for a three-day pelagic trip that would net all the fall seabirds together with excellent prospects for rarities. The Mountain Quail was number 699 for the year. I was about to break the 700 barrier. Perhaps it was fitting that such a milestone would happen on a boat.

I stood on the quay and watched the lights of the incoming aircraft grow brighter, as if magnetized by those of the runway nearby. It was a calm night, the waters of the bay gently moaning with straining ropes and flapping flags. I'd been in the boathouse stocking up on Dramamine for the next day's trip. I replayed the rather bizarre and recent conversation in my mind.

"What time do I need to be here for the birding trip?" I asked, handing over a couple packets of the seasickness pills to a young guy who was restocking fishing tackle. He looked as if he'd rather be at sea than serving behind the counter of this makeshift store.

"Which trip is that?" he asked.

"The one on the *Grande*. It's the fifty-six-hour pelagic trip," I said.

"The what now?" he asked.

I explained again, this time with a slight tingle running down my spine.

"Hey, Steve. You know about a birding trip on the *Grande*?" he said, turning around to a guy hidden in a back office.

"Sure," came the reply. "It was canceled a month ago. Not enough interest. The *Grande*'s on a fishing trip instead."

I considered opening the packets of Dramamine and stuffing them into my face. Perhaps that would take away the sudden feeling of sickness. For once I was in the wrong place at the wrong time. I thought about the rare Blue-footed Booby at a lake in New Mexico and, closer to home, the Curlew Sandpiper at Plum Island, both of which I'd flown over to be here, on the wrong side of the country, for a pelagic trip without a boat.

I paced up and down the moonlit pier in San Diego and vented to Gerri on the phone. It wasn't the first time, and, as long as I kept birding, it wouldn't be the last time. If you're going to chase things that fly, then missing birds was always going to be part of the deal. I had to think fast and plan my escape. Perhaps I could still salvage the two rarities I'd missed.

When birders chase birds, they perform a kind of mental algorithm. They compute the type of bird, the season, the location, and the reputation of the birder who found it, and make a decision whether to chase or not. The single biggest factor is whether the bird is moving through or stopping. Many birders will wait for a positive report the second day before committing to a long-distance chase. They know that shorebirds, like the Curlew Sandpiper, can cover vast feeding areas, and that their food moves with the tide. You need to be there at the right time of day, ideally at the same type of tide as when it was first found. My mental algorithm would rate a shorebird possible in the first three days, and then a good chance of missing thereafter. But, like almost all rarities, you never how long the bird has already been there.

Some rarities spend the summer or winter and will stay for months, like the wintering Nutting's Flycatcher in Arizona. But for the rest of the year, birds don't hang around for long, although they're in less of a rush in the fall to get to their wintering grounds than they are in the spring, when they have nesting territories to fight for and defend. Blue-footed Boobies are seabirds, members of the gannet family. They breed in the Gulf of California, in Mexico, alongside the Yellow-footed Gulls. And as with the latter, they like to disperse after the breeding season and just hang out. When these birds have been seen north of the border, they've historically stayed for months. They'll favor a location to sit and roost and feed locally. This bird was sitting on an island in the middle of a small lake in New Mexico, surrounded by desert. It didn't have a lot of other options.

I performed my mental algorithm and prioritized the more common but more flighty Curlew Sandpiper. The booby could wait. I bought a ticket home to Boston. Unfortunately, Curlew Sandpipers can also use Expedia. When I landed at Logan the following morning, I received a text message from my birding friend Margo Goetschkes, who was on Plum Island at the right tide where there were no Curlew Sandpipers. I confirmed her assessment myself by spending the rest of the day on a decidedly Curlew Sandpiper–less Plum Island. I was worn-out. I wondered if this had anything to do with the 700 barrier. I was still one bird away. You never defeat the goddess Nemesis. You just upgrade one problem bird for another.

I sat at home for the next two days brooding over the Curlew Sandpiper (it never came back) and the reports of the Blue-footed Booby in New Mexico (delighting visiting birders daily). I looked at flights for the latter, but they all seemed too expensive and would involve too much driving. I'd never felt so lethargic and tired, and I'm sure I wasn't much fun to be with, moping at home, stuck on 699. Gerri had officially moved in, and this probably wasn't the reassuring start for which she was hoping. In the end, she ordered me to go for the stupid booby, and I found a cheap flight to Dallas. I'd land at midnight with a seven-hour drive ahead of me.

I woke up with a start as the landing gear screeched on the hot, dry tarmac of Dallas–Fort Worth International Airport. For once, I wasn't excited. I just wanted to get the whole 700 thing over, like you do those last few months of your twenties, when thirty hovers menacingly in front of you. There was none of the nervous worry about whether the bird would be there or not. It was seen as I was stepping on the plane. It was in a small lake surrounded by desert, and it was probably settling in for months. The drive and tick felt more like a job.

We taxied toward the gate, accompanied by a pinging chorus of newly loaded text messages and e-mails. As further news of the American Airlines–US Airways merger appeared on tiny screens, and Sox fans read the box score of the 4–2 win over the Blue Jays, I stared in disbelief at the news on my phone: the booby had been taken into rehab. It was emaciated from not eating. I didn't need to check whether birds in rehab centers were countable (they're not). I shuffled off the plane, zombie-like. At the check-in desk I asked the young airline representative if I could get back on and go home.

"Oh. Did something happen? Did you not want to be here?" she asked, concerned.

Even if it wasn't midnight, and even if I wasn't tired, I don't think I could have found a way to explain what had happened.

"I just need to get back home," I offered. "When is the next flight back?"

"You're in luck," she said. "This plane goes back in an hour."

The good news was that she didn't charge me for changing my return ticket. The bad news was that one hour ended up being two hours, and then three, until the departure time solidified some time around four forty-five A.M. I'd reached my low point. I was still stuck on 699, I hadn't slept properly in months, I was starting to smell, and I was sick of airports, cars, and watching my bank balance drop while unclear exactly what it was that I was getting in return. Although I had questioned the sanity of this Big Year every day, now I wanted it over. I wanted bird number 700 so much. I wanted to be released from the mad counting.

There's a fine line between healthy interest and obsession, and the Big Year wasn't the first time that I'd crossed it. There would always be some lightbulb moment when a perfectly innocuous activity would be revealed as a numerical or mathematical puzzle around which my mind would feast. As a kid, I'd loved postage stamps. I loved the tiny designs, handling them delicately between tweezers, and mounting them under the translucent glassine paper. But most of all I liked the mental images that the exotic place names would conjure up: Siam, Indo-Chine, and the Belgian Congo. It was a lesson in history—countries changed their names (Southern Rhodesia became Zimbabwe), their rulers (to think, there used to be kings before our queen), and currencies (if I'd been born a few years earlier, I'd have seen shillings and known that there were twelve pennies to a shilling and twenty shillings to a pound).

I was happy in that world. My collection was the limit to my knowledge. Until, that is, a secondhand book sale at the local village hall, where I stumbled across a copy of *Stanley Gibbons Stamps of the World, 1977*. It was more than two inches thick, and I think the seller was touting it more as a doorstop (albeit an unsightly orange one) or a cure for insomnia than expecting anyone to buy it for the tiny black-and-white pictures inside. When I opened that book, I saw a whole new world of possibilities: new countries, new stamps, and new gaps in my collection. Whereas before I'd marveled over the stamps I had, now I dreamed about all those I didn't. I drew up checklists and found stamp markets and mailing catalogs for the gaps. I was quietly obsessed.

It was the same with baseball. I knew about the sport before I moved here. On business trips to the United States, I'd be relaxing at a bar, reading a book, and look up to see a TV screen showing some player running headfirst into a wall, or thanking the heavens for a very earthly lesson in projectile ballistics. It didn't make a whole lot of sense, and looked like a more boring version of cricket, if that were possible. I didn't think much more about it until one evening, after I'd moved here, when I noticed the numbers: pitch count, earned run average (ERA), batting average, on-base percentage (OBP). I was hooked and soon knew the batting average of every Red Sox player, the ERA of the pitchers, how to calculate on-base plus slugging—and what I'd be doing most every night at seven ten P.M. Baseball became my friend. On almost any night, a game was being played somewhere. That's when I met Anna, and our dates were secretly determined by a three-by-two-inch Red Sox schedule magnetized to my fridge in my tiny Back Bay studio apartment.

Birding was different. It took longer for the obsession to take over, and that time was spent quietly falling in love with the birds. Most birders have a "spark bird." They spend their life in ignorance of the birds, like the Muggles in Harry Potter who can't see the magic, until one day they see something that jolts them from their carefully ordered world. It might be a stunning Painted Bunting (red, blue, and green!) whose beauty shocks them, or the realization that there are different species with names they've never heard of: Siskin, Redpoll, Crossbill, Grosbeak. Whatever it is, after that, life is never quite the same. After that, there are no "seagulls" (rather Herring, Bonaparte's, Laughing, Ring-billed, Iceland, Glaucous Gulls, etc.), and there are hundreds of new names, different plumages, and ages: in short, an infinity of flying life forms.

While I'm not entirely sure what my spark bird was (I think it was probably a Green Woodpecker), I do know exactly where it was: in my parents' backyard. We lived in a small house on a recently completed early 1970s development in a village ten miles outside Oxford. The yard was stocked with feeders, shrubs, and a few (ill-fated) elm trees and backed onto wheat fields neatly organized by hedgerows and stands of trees. Inside the house was a copy of the Automobile Association's *Book of British Birds*. I stood at the kitchen window and matched the birds in the book to the real ones outside. I could recognize the Blue Tits, Great Tits, Coal Tits, and Greenfinches on the feeders, the Blackbirds, Song, and Mistle Thrushes prospecting for earthworms on the lawn, and the Great Spotted Woodpeckers and Nuthatches investigating the gnarled bark of the elms looking for grubs. In the summers, unseen cuckoos cuckooed, and a few feet above my bedroom window midnight blue-and-white House Martins reared their chicks in a beehive-like nest of mud and straw. (I often wondered whether they could smell the sickly honeysuckle growing beneath.) By the age of six or seven, I knew the thirty or so species that I could spot in the yard.

It seems odd now that it took such a long time to make the next leap—that different habitats have different birds. I was happy to keep looking at the birds in the yard and never thought about all the other (hundreds) of birds in the field guide. Surely I must have wondered where all the Linnets, Choughs, and Nightingales were? But apparently I didn't; that would have to wait until I started high school. Among all the new discoveries, including the smell of a chemistry lab, taking a bus rather than legs to school, and making new friends, there was one discovery for which I wasn't prepared: I wasn't the only one who enjoyed looking at birds.

My new friends John, Robert, and Matthew were all searching for an excuse to go birding, whether they knew it or not. After school or on weekends we'd explore the woodlands and farmland around Oxford, finding Gray Partridges (the same bird Gerri and I had seen in Calgary), Lapwings, and Yellowhammers. Oxfordshire is a county of agricultural fields and green rolling hills. And it was from one of those hills that John, the tallest of our group, gazed down and suggested we look for birds in the liquid figure of eight below us.

Farmoor Reservoir holds water from the River Thames. The banks and bisecting causeway were built up from material excavated from the two now watery holes. It attracted gulls, shorebirds, migrants, and, when there weren't enough of those to distract you, then you'd notice the legions of evil biting flies. The best part was inside a small brick building ostensibly belonging to the sailing club: a logbook for bird-watchers. I still remember that first time opening the folder and turning the pages. I read through the reports of birds I'd either never heard of, or never imagined seeing: Whinchat, Grey Phalarope, and Smew. I was transfixed, my spine tingling as I hungrily devoured page after page. I read that logbook not like it was a historical record, but as if I were reading the future. And in a way I was. I would come to spend as much free time as I could, finding all those species and more. We'd stumbled, serendipitously, on the birding mecca of Oxfordshire. And although we'd often make the joke "Farmoor Reservoir: Far more birds elsewhere," nothing compared with the excitement of walking up to the bank of that tiny ocean, never knowing what you'd find.

From there it was a short leap to joining the Oxford Ornithological Society (of which I would later become the undergraduate secretary), and the local Royal Society for the Protection of Birds group. There were coach trips around the country, where I met my best friend, Jon, a birder with a car and an insatiable appetite for rare birds. And while my school friends John, Robert, and Matthew had found a comfortable level of birding and were distracted by exams, I found I couldn't stop. Even at seventeen, when I was studying hard to get into Oxford University, and when I was experiencing love for the first time (a blonde-haired fellow violin player called Bryony), I couldn't stop calling Birdline (fifty pence a minute!) to hear about rarities. I was obsessed.

When I moved to the United States, I brought everything in four suitcases—clothes, books, and the life-size, knitted

Mr. Crocodile I'd had since I was a boy. But I didn't bring my binoculars, my telescope, or my bird books. I left the obsession behind. Moving to a new country gives you a chance to reinvent yourself, to start again. It's not that I no longer loved birds—I did. They filled me with joy and life. But chasing birds to add to a country, year, or life list had somehow gotten in the way of life. It was an emotional roller coaster: the awful nervous stomach as you're stuck in agonizing traffic on the M1 motorway, hours away from a bird that you're praying is still going to be there when you arrive. In the UK, chasing birds is called twitching for a reason. Besides, I was thirty-one, and it was probably time for me to focus on my job and on being an adult.

The self-imposed international ban didn't last long, of course. In a place where everything was different, there was something comforting about being with the birds. It was like coming home, finding myself. And while the birds, and even the trees, grasses, and smells were all subtly different, the peace and calming solitude I found among them were still the same.

The birding slump ended on August 19. I was the thirteenth person to see seven hundred species in a year. It was a warm afternoon, and the cottonwood trees were shaking like puppets, their strings pulled by an invisible, yet strong wind. I was in the middle of Lake Patagonia in Arizona, my hands clumsily alternating between camera, binoculars, and paddle. I was suddenly grateful for the life vest that the young boat attendant had thrown at me. Beneath me, the kayak rocked unsteadily and reacted angrily to the wake kicked up by distant motorboats.

Although the New Mexico Blue-footed Booby that I'd chased had gone into rehab and ultimately died, it presaged what would become known as the Year of the Booby. Birds, mostly young ones, began to appear all over California, but not before this one, in southeast Arizona. It's not often in birding that you get such a quick second chance at a bird you've just missed.

This had been a uniquely personal quest, and so perhaps it was appropriate that I was here quietly on my own, back in Arizona, where it had all started. It was a lazy Monday afternoon. I thought of the management team meeting I would have been leading in Boston if I hadn't quit my job. We'd have been reviewing the key performance indicators of the business and worrying about how fast we picked up the phone or how to grow sales in Brazil. I usually tried to push these thoughts out of my head when they invaded. They made me anxious. I could hear in other people's voices how crazy I was to have given all of that up. But now I let them in. Now I had something to offset that craziness: I had some new memories (the Dry Tortugas, Pribilof Islands, Salton Sea, Ruby Mountains, and everywhere in between), and perhaps more important, I could see a future of new exciting memories.

The bird grew steadily as each aching shoulder propelled me closer. Fishermen called them boobies because they were stupid, ridiculously easy to catch when they alit on fishing vessels. But there was nothing docile about the bird drifting in front of me. A large, powerful body, swanlike and brown in color, supported a stiff neck. A massive bill, like a dull, metallic dagger, grew out between a pair of large eyes, giving the bird an odd look somewhere between surprised and malicious. I never saw the feet, which paddled somewhere below, in the dark water, but if I had they wouldn't have been the eponymous blue. This was a young bird, suggested by the darker head and neck. The blue feet are the prize of the adults, the carotenoid-derived coloration being an indicator of good health and nourishment: the more fresh fish they consume, the bluer the feet. The mating dances, where the birds lift their feet, waving them like paddles, rocking back and forth like a slow-motion Charlie Chaplin walk, are choreographed to show off the spectacular cyan of their landing gear.

When I returned to the rental boat shack, I showed the young boat attendant my photos. He was blown away that there was such a mean-looking bird in the middle of the lake. His lake.

"Man, look at that bill!" he said. He studied the pictures for some time, going back and forth before finally committing them to memory. I explained to him that boobies are members of the gannet family—large, gull-like birds that dive from great heights into the ocean for fish, their bills piercing the water like a spear, followed by a streamlined body and folded-back wings. I hoped I'd shown him a spark bird.

"Have you seen one before?" he asked.

"No," I replied, and caught myself before telling him the numerical significance of this particular bird. It was a bird, not a number, and I suspected that if I ever considered them merely ticks on a list, then all the joy would be extinguished from this mad hobby.

I sat on a bench and texted Gerri, then Chris Hitt, then Jay Lehman (who would follow me here a week later for his booby tick), and then Hans de Grys. It was official. I was the newest member of the 700 Club. It was a relief, more than anything. It was a goal I'd never really set myself, just an interesting target in a year of increasingly interesting targets. Besides, I still had more than three months left of my Big Year. It didn't end because I got to seven hundred. As the wind whipped through the trees, giving dance to the twinkling leaves, I leaned back, inhaling a lungful of the refreshing air, and wondered where the wind would take me next.

My bird count at the end of August 2013: 709 (+1 provisional)
John Vanderpoel's bird count at the end of August 2011: 702

Chapter 9

LOSING MY BERINGS

"THIS IS THE PISS bucket," said Dave Porter, placing a large, and thankfully empty, white container a few feet from my bed. "Anything else and you go into the main house."

Since the main house, where the other half of the tour group would stay, contained a modern bathroom, complete with shower and toilet, and, importantly, was only a thirty-second walk away, I assumed that Dave was either incredibly lazy in his toilet habits or he was pulling my proverbial leg. But that first night, as the wind licked the thin wooden membrane of the building, I discovered that a bathroom run, however short, when the cold and wet Alaskan elements were involved, was decidedly less fun than pissing in a bucket.

I was back in Alaska again, this time in a village called Gambell (population 650, mostly native Yupik), which sits on the pea-gravelly northwest promontory of St. Lawrence Island, in the Bering Sea. Its proximity to Asia (Russia is only thirty-six miles away) makes it a favorite haunt for Asian vagrants and desperate birders. I'd flown in earlier, after downsizing planes in Seattle, Anchorage, and most recently Nome, where a retro-looking brown twin-prop made the final hop into the Bering Sea in under an hour. I compared the view out of the window with the printed map of the village on my lap. The two-mile-long north-south rectangle of Troutman Lake barely left enough land for the rest of it: a thin strip of runway was squeezed between the lake and the sea to the west, and the collection of village houses sat loosely on the north shore. To the east, the land rose abruptly to a mesa-like table: Sevuokuk Mountain. I'd read about the eight species of seabirds that breed on its rocky slopes, together with the splintered coffin boxes of ancient native burials, which still spill their ossified contents. (These days there's a cemetery at the top, where the dead are more reliably interred.)

I was here for seven days with Wilderness Birding, during which I hoped to run into some of the spectacular Asian strays that have come to characterize the protracted fall migration here. I'd planned the trip after visiting the Pribilofs in the spring, knowing that the fall brought a different host of rarities—more buntings, warblers, and pipits, as well as a few shorebirds that I still needed (Sharp-tailed Sandpiper and Gray-tailed Tattler). The proximity to the Russian Far East (Chukotka) means that Gambell is less dependent on storms to disorient and whisk up migrants than the more isolated St. Paul, 470 miles to the south. Many of those that reach Gambell breed much farther inland than the rocky coast of Russia I'd spied from the twin-prop. Some harbor a deadly defect to their internal navigational compass, and as the rest of their kind head south and west to their wintering grounds, these birds become misoriented. Incredibly, in some the compass may have flipped 180 degrees, or they have a mirror image of the migratory map. This would explain why birds such as the Dusky Warbler, a small brown bird of the Siberian taiga, which normally heads southwest for the winter, is sometimes found to the northeast at Gambell (and, if you were to continue that line, then all the way to California and to Baja California, Mexico, where, remarkably, Dusky Warblers have also been recorded). These misoriented birds are probably first-year birds. Many will not survive, or refind their breeding population, after their tragic mistake.

Aaron Lang met the plane at the runway (there is no airport, just a strip of tarmac). His infectious enthusiasm was a warm welcome to the bleakness that surrounded us. We loaded our bags onto a modified wooden trailer attached to an ATV (there are no cars on Gambell). This ingenious contraption, with makeshift benches facing outward, would hereafter be referred to as the "bus." And, like the "airport," the "toilet," and the "witty entertainment," would become one of the staples of our existence at the end of the world.

The gravel crunched beneath the bus as we made our way to the two adjacent buildings that we'd call home for the next week. An elevated gravel ridge forms a main road of sorts through the village, organizing the nearest buildings. Most were clad in wood, well overdue for a lick of paint, and looked dark and empty inside. Beyond, the rest of the village was a hodgepodge of kitty-cornered dwellings. The streets, if one could call the negative space that, were empty. ATVs, or carcasses of ATVs, sat outside many of the houses, frequently twinned with the upended jawbones of bowhead whales.

When birders first started coming here in the 1970s, there were huskies tied up outside the buildings, not ATVs. The permafrost had yet to be cracked open for plumbing pipes; water had to be carried down from the mountain springs and then boiled. The toilets were honey buckets, a delightful euphemism for the binary human wastes, and were collected just like the trash. But some things hadn't changed. There were still racks to dry out seal and walrus meat. The old men still carved whalebone and walrus tusks, and the kids still shot at birds for target practice or just for the hell of it.

Our days here soon fell into a routine starting with the morning huddle in the kitchen of the main house while the outside was still a black void. I filled my stomach with as much warm coffee as it could hold, knowing that the heat would dissipate as soon as we ventured outside. A short ride on the bus would bring us to the point, the northwestern tip of Gambell and a couple of hours of sea-watching.

We lined up on the beach like a firing squad, telescopes aimed at the sea. With the sun rising above our shoulders, we watched the morning commute of hundreds of alcids (Horned Puffins, Common Murres, and Crested Auklets were the most common) as they streamed by offshore, heading toward their feeding grounds. They were joined by the occasional shout-out—"Steller's Eider, flying left to right, close to the beach!" and "Yellow-billed Loon, above the horizon going right!"— all in an urgent hurry to be someplace else. The dark, cruci-form Short-tailed Shearwaters (which, incredibly, had been born somewhere around Tasmania, Australia) massed into a haze of hundreds of thousands, like a thick cloud of mosquitoes hanging above their birth puddle. Humpback Whales breached in the distance, and marbled Gray Whales bottom-fed off the beach. When the wind was from the east, the briny sea smell was replaced with that of the raw sewage seeping into the open cesspit behind me.

On a clear day, of which there were precious few, I could see tomorrow: the jagged peaks of the Russian Chukchi Peninsula, like the teeth of some giant leviathan breaching the distant surface on the other side of the invisible international date line. I sat on a discarded piece of cardboard, a surprising luxury against the anesthetically cold gravel ball bearings of the beach, and let my imagination run free. I rewinded to a time (between twenty-two and fifteen thousand years ago) when grassland steppe and shrub tundra stretched out for hundreds of miles in each direction, transiently connecting Asia with the Americas, the angry surf pushed well beyond the limits of my eyesight even with the telescope I now cradled. This was the Bering Land Bridge, across which the ancestors of Native Americans, from Alaska to South America, moved east and south before the temporary land disappeared behind them, Atlantis-like, back into the sea.

After my first morning of sea-watching and geological daydreaming, many of the personalities of the guides had already been stamped indelibly onto the group. James Huntington, a US Postal Service worker from Iowa, was known throughout the birding community as the Mailman. A lithe, athletic figure with a gray mustache and a keen sense of humor, he was an extreme chaser who had paid his birding dues on Attu (fourteen years) and had built up an impressive ABA list of more than 860 species. There was a good chance that if we found anything unusual here, James would already have seen it. He told me that he'd chased the Rufous-necked Wood-Rail in New Mexico a few days after me. He'd flown into Denver and driven eight hours south, only to miss the bird. It wasn't seen during his time there, and he'd assumed the bird had left. It was only when he was dropping off his rental car back in Denver that he heard the bird was being re-seen. He canceled his flight, turned around, and made the 550-mile trip south again. He got the bird. Every year for him seemed to be a big one.

Dave Porter had retired as the chief ranger of Denali. He'd moved to Alaska in 1973, after studying biology in Colorado. His white mustache and receding hairline didn't fool me. He was a big kid who'd never outgrown his cheeky grin. Dave was a human jukebox of witty stories who seemingly had no off button. He was funny enough to potentially cause lasting damage to my diaphragm and intercostal muscles. Many of his personal stories began with him asking permission from "the Warden" to do one stupid thing or another. I later discovered the Warden was his wife and that she had a name (Sondra). Dave sparred with James frequently, each battling the other for the "Most Funny in Gambell" epithet.

Norm Budnitz was a retired history teacher from North Carolina. He was charming, friendly, and interested in finding out about people. In his youth, he'd studied lemurs in Madagascar, and I suspected he brought many of those skills to his people-watching. Time had been unkind to Norm. His once lean and athletic frame seemed twisted in all the wrong directions, and he now had difficulties walking. Norm was our bus driver and his face was our windshield. He wore goggles, like a driver from *Downton Abbey*, but I'm sure that did little to protect his face from being cut by the icy rain.

It was hard to imagine a more entertaining, kind, and professional group with which to bird. And while there were times I longed for quiet, independent birding, I was grateful for this welcome companionship at the end of the world.

After thawing out over breakfast and more coffee, we'd head to the boneyards that would form our study for much of the rest of the day. The boneyards are middens—ancient garbage dumps of slaughtered marine carcasses, mainly seal and walrus. Covered by luxuriously thick green wormwood and arctic sage, they were easy to spot in the otherwise gravel-gray wasteland. They are a vegetative feeding frenzy. The plants, unable to make a living elsewhere, suck out the nutrients from the buried death. There are three boneyards, named with an eye to practicality rather than romance. The near boneyard (at the north end of the runway) was the largest. The other two were to the east of town at the base of Sevuokuk Mountain: the far boneyard and the circular boneyard. At almost a foot in height, the wormwood and sage were the trees, shrubs, and grasses of Gambell, and this is where any lost, hungry bird would seek food and shelter. At least we hoped.

We "swept" the boneyards multiple times each day. We'd line up and slowly walk forward until someone flushed a bird.

It wasn't easy work. You had to divide your attention between looking for birds and looking at your feet to ensure the latter didn't disappear into one of the many, often deep holes which pockmarked the boneyards. (The locals dug the boneyards frequently for buried walrus ivory, the prize of the village carvers.) If I was lucky, I'd get a three-second glimpse of the butt of a tiny bird flying away, its identification invariably coming a split second later as Aaron shouted, "Arctic Warbler!" at the small green blur. Boneyard birding was some of the toughest birding I'd done.

The days soon blended into one another as we searched the same two or three square miles over and over again with the maddening insanity of someone looking through a box of jigsaw pieces in search of that last edge piece (which had long since fallen to the floor). In some ways I was grateful that the Native corporation permitted us only this short leash: around the village and the edges of Troutman Lake. There was more than enough work for us here. Birds could drop in at any time, and so a boneyard that was empty in the morning might not be so empty in the afternoon, though it usually was. But there were times when I longed to see more, to see where the long gravel road led that ran south along the base of Sevuokuk Mountain. We'd occasionally flush Snow Buntings or Lapland Longspurs from the mossy rocks on that road until we reached the improbably placed stop sign and turned right to explore the southern end of the lake and the grassy folds of the revetments. But the road, although closed to us, continued as a cross-tundra trail all the way to Savoonga, the only other village on the island. I followed the gravelly corridor with my eyes until it disappeared over a small rise at the edge of the mountain. The rest was left to my imagination: the sweeping views of mossy tundra and coastal beaches along which it must have passed.

At the end of the day, as we'd slouch, happily distended from a warming meal prepared by one of the guides, and after more than one helping of Norm's excellent cheesecake, Aaron would lead the bird count. This was my favorite part of the day, as we relived the birds we'd seen earlier. Aaron would stand with a giant flip chart divided into seven columns to represent each of our days and an array of colored pens. We'd list all the species we'd seen and provide a daily count for each. Life birds, for any of the group, would receive a Coefficient of Greatness (COG) number. There were nine of us, and so a new bird for one person would receive a COG of 0.11 (one divided by nine). Bruce Stephenson, a banker in his mid-fifties from Connecticut, was the only one who hadn't been to western Alaska before, and many of the 0.11s were proudly his. (Bruce would end up breaking seven hundred on his ABA life list on this trip.) Red-throated Pipit, an annual migrant from northern Russia, was new for both of us and scored 0.22. Life birds were harder to come by for the other three birding clients, all in their sixties or seventies: Tom Condon from Virginia and the very well-traveled husband-and-wife duo of Bob and Laura Payne, both academics in Ann Arbor, Michigan.

At the top of the chart, under a giant sigma sign, Aaron summed the COGs of the individual species. Never before had I seen a pairing of such amateur mathematical genius and birding. It blew my mind, and I'll be forever grateful to Aaron.

Although, I have to say, by the end of the week, we'd improved
on this with a much more theoretical Adjusted Coefficient of
Relative Neediness (ACORN), for which I suspect Gambell
lacked the necessary processing power to compute. That, and
the seemingly arbitrary color of marker pen that Aaron chose
for each species, will have to remain a mystery.

We'd seen all the best birds on the first day within hours of
stepping off the twin-prop. In the corner marsh, an area of
boot-sucking wetland at the northeast corner of Troutman
Lake, Aaron almost stepped on a duck. It sat in the long
grasses of the marsh, trying not to be seen. We gathered
around and watched a small brown bird with a large white
spot at the base of its bill. A pair of large black eyes, framed by
sweeping, pale-brown eyebrows, were placed high on the
head. They gave good binocular vision above, essential for
keeping the ungainly giant beasts nearby under surveillance.
The only colors were in the speculum, a strip of often bril-
liantly iridescent colors in the secondary flight feathers. When
its wings were closed, we could see but a hint of shining green
sandwiched between white and peanut butter. This was a
Baikal Teal, a new bird for me and apparently for Gambell.

Aaron got on the two-way radio, whose crackle always
made my pulse quicken as I anticipated some newfound rarity
a short bus ride away.

"Baikal Teal. Repeat, Baikal Teal. Corner marsh," he said
softly into the receiver, conscious of the duck sitting only a
few feet away.

Within minutes a couple of ATVs sped toward the marsh.
One of the drivers dismounted, and a pair of baggy green

pants marched up to the group. Hidden under the tall, signature, woolen hat, I recognized Paul Lehman, the mapping consultant for almost every major North American field guide and one of the most knowledgeable of US birders. Paul had become a rather common annual fall migrant to Gambell (ABA Code 2), often spending much of August and September documenting the rarities and matching them to weather patterns, his other vice, before returning to his wintering grounds back home in San Diego.

"What do we have here?" Paul asked, like a detective inspector arriving at a crime scene.

The bird had flown a short distance into another patch of wet grass, and I watched as Paul edged closer toward it, unconsciously orchestrating those around him into better viewing positions. This was a new bird for Paul, an occurrence that, after his many years of patrolling the end of the world, was now less than annual. As the bird gently slipped out of the grass, it caught Paul's eye, and I watched as the relief spread across his face. He nodded, partly confirming the identification and partly in recognition of another amazing birding moment. (The bird would later score a stupendous 0.78 COG that evening for our group.)

The remainder of the birds were rarities for the rest of the United States but somewhat expected here: Sharp-tailed Sandpipers, coppery-brown shorebirds, hid in the same grassy marsh, erupting with a sharp whistle if any of us approached too close. These were juveniles, born this year. The adults take a more westerly route to their wintering grounds in Australasia. On the drier areas of the marsh, we found

Red-throated Pipits, long, streaky birds, which flushed from the grass easily, disappearing into the sky and leaving behind a long *tseee* call. And at the village dump, a modern-day bone-yard of slaughtered ovens, ATVs, and household waste, a small group of gulls, including the darker-backed Herring Gulls from Asia and a mean-looking Slaty-backed Gull, picked at the morning's detritus.

After that first day, the three wind turbines from which the native village drew most of its power rotated slowly to the north. The winds brought cold, drizzle, and no new birds. After the excitement of that first day, I experienced the more typical birding of Gambell—long days looking for Asian strays and finding none. I could list the many rarities that had been found there over the years, and I pictured each sitting in the boneyard, waiting for us to find it. Every time we lined up, ready for the boneyard sweep, I felt that same excitement in the pit of my stomach as I did before a pelagic, as we never knew what we might find.

After the evening bird lists, the COG computations, and the often idle discussion, people slowly started slipping away to warm, enticing beds. I ran over to the lodge, where Paul was staying. The doors were usually locked, but there was a protected spot at the back, in the lee of the freezing drizzle, where I could pick up a Wi-Fi signal. Gerri was starting school this week. She had a day of orientation at Boston College and then classes. I was eager to find out how it had gone. I stood there shaking in the cold, my ungloved hands gradually freezing into claws, downloading messages, looking for her name. I spotted it, but not before I'd hungrily digested the news of an Asian Brown Flycatcher on St. Paul and a Sinaloa Wren in Huachuca Canyon, Arizona, only the third ABA record. I ran back to my building as the cogs in my head started to crunch through the chase algorithm. I was careful to avoid spilling the contents of the piss bucket.

Jay arrived two days after me. I watched as his small plane bounced on the runway before slowly pirouetting to a stop in front of the nearby boneyard. Less than thirty minutes later, a heavily burdened Jay (telescope, camera, backpack) strode confidently into the corner marsh, only to discover that it was missing a Baikal Teal (it was last seen the previous day). Jay was here on his own and would stay in the lodge, originally built to house the construction workers of the new school and now a sort of hotel. Neither building existed when Jay had first visited back in 1976. He was planning to stay a week after me, although given the forecast of north winds (which Paul Lehman would have told you were usually the worst for birds), I didn't fancy his chances.

Jay sounded energized, just as I was starting to feel tired and ready to hang up my binoculars for the year. After dealing with his property issues, which had derailed much of his summer, he was in a mad rush to chase down the remaining migrant breeders before they left. Prior to flying here, he'd swung through Arizona (his first visit of the year) and picked up forty-seven new birds, including the Blue-footed Booby that was still sitting on Lake Patagonia. He arrived in Gambell with 630 species and was confident that if he could maintain this pace, he could hit 700. At 710 myself, I couldn't even imagine where my next ten birds would come from.

As I sat on the Wilderness Birding bus, I'd often see Jay walking around in his gray jacket, plowing slowly through the gravel. I marveled at his stamina for a man on the cusp of his seventies. It's a peculiarity of birding that many never have the time nor the funds to pursue their passion until they retire. There are many great birders in their seventies and eighties who are physically strong and can seemingly bird all day in difficult and uncomfortable places. None of them seem to think of their age, except occasionally remembering it in conversation, and then usually with a cocked eyebrow in surprise. Aging for them was a mental battle, and if they didn't acknowledge it, then it didn't exist.

There's a point when you realize it's over. We were down to the last few hours at Gambell, and it reminded me of the end of a pelagic trip, as the boat swings around toward land, and all those future possibilities reluctantly become the ones that got away. It was like the desperation of getting to the last present on Christmas morning, and you already know from the size that it's not going to be the model stegosaurus that you wanted. I'd seen four new birds in Gambell, including the mega-rare Baikal Teal. But compared with other years, it was a poor show. I knew from John Vanderpoel's 2011 Big Year checklist that he had seen nine new birds here, including such mouthwatering rarities as Stonechat, Pallas's Bunting, and one of those 180-degree misoriented Dusky Warblers. Gambell was where my Big Year stalled, and for the first time since the summer, I fell behind John Vanderpoel's pace.

Gerri picked me up from Logan. She was full of stories. Suddenly, her life was rich with school—new friends, classes, professors, and books. I was happy for her. While there was so much I wanted to tell her about Gambell, I let her talk. I knew my year was coming to an end while hers was just starting. It was hard not to feel a pang of jealousy.

I sat in the passenger seat, scratching Khiva Cat's head, listening to Gerri talk about something called psychosocial pathology while I tried to keep my mind from exploding in panic. I always knew there'd be an end to my Big Year, but I never thought in such distances. I was like the baseball manager playing one game at a time. Now, out of nowhere, the season was almost over, and soon there would be no more games to play. It didn't seem fair.

Somewhere on the continent, at some point during the year, I was hoping to find the rarest bird yet—the one that would tell me what to do with my life. But as the miles piled up, filling in the gaps between the cobwebs of my peregrinations, and the unticked checkboxes became ticked, I suspected that this bird probably didn't exist, or at least wasn't in North America. After ever so briefly considering the words *global* and *Big Year*, I knew that I wouldn't find the answer in a single bird or a destination. That left me with the rather trite realization that maybe the journey was everything. Which was jolly nice but didn't particularly solve the more pressing question: what (the hell) do I do next?

I should have known this already. The last time I tried, it hadn't worked. I'd taken a year off after my Ph.D. to travel among the lands of the Silk Road of Central Asia. I'd been looking for the same answers to the same life questions that would still baffle me in middle age. I didn't find them in the turquoise tiles of Samarkand, the baked mud walls of Khiva, or among the camels of the Taklamakan Desert.

When I returned home to England, I took scissors to the unruly beard I'd cultivated and found a job and looked back on the quixotic adventure with a smile. Maybe that year hadn't changed anything—I didn't become a travel writer or an international spy and I wasn't sure what it was, if anything, that I'd learned. Perhaps it was enough to know that at least once in my life I'd left my Hobbit hole and sat and watched the sun set over an alien and unfamiliar land. Maybe that lonely, frightening beauty was the rara avis for which I was still searching.

I got an e-mail from Aaron telling me the news. After staying on at Gambell a couple of extra days to put away the bus for the winter and to clean the houses, Aaron had left James and Norm behind to a miserable forecast of yet more north winds. The pair woke up on the morning of September 8 as they did any other day. The skies were still overcast; the turbines still had their backs turned to the lake. But when they entered the boneyards, they found birds—a Yellow-browed Warbler and a Siberian Accentor (with a second one in the revetments at the south end of the lake). On September 10 they were joined by a Stonechat, found by James in the far boneyard. I was sick of Gambell and wanted my revenge. I flew out of Boston that day. I was headed back to the end of the world.

I paused outside Terminal A, the packed bags lounging at my feet like a pair of obedient dogs. I hugged Gerri and made

LOSING MY BERINGS   231

up my mind that I needed to put an end to this. I'd been
putting it off so long that it was time to say something.

"I love you," I told her.

I'd never said those words to her, not once in the 419 days
that I'd known her. I'd never had that problem before. If
anything, it was the opposite. I was desperate to be accepted
and played that opening gambit early in a relationship just to
hear the (I hoped) comforting response. With Gerri, I'd
missed that natural window.

I suppose the window was draped by those dark, depressed
times of the previous year. I didn't know Gerri at that point,
and I barely felt like I knew myself. I was scared of ending up
in another failed relationship. By the time I came out of that,
and the color came back to my life, through tiny pills and tiny
birds, the window had slammed firmly shut.

"I love you too," she said, after what seemed like an age.

"Good!" I said and smiled. "But you know, you could have
said that too!"

"No," she said. "That's your job."

And I suppose it was my job. Through all the change and
uncertainty of the past year, I'd always known how she'd felt.
It had taken much longer for either of us to know how I felt.

It took me about thirty-five hours to retrace my flights back
to the pea-gravel. Norm Budnitz was waiting on the tarmac.
He was taking my plane to Nome before slowly working his
way to North Carolina. I congratulated him on the new birds,
life birds. He wished me luck in seeing them, although we
both knew they hadn't been refound since yesterday.

I caught a ride to the lodge with Hansen Irrigoo, a gray-haired Yupik native who stared out from behind a pair of thick, black-framed glasses. Hansen looked after the building and the guests with a surprising level of friendliness and efficiency. After passing through a mudroom of sorts, the main door of the lodge opened into a kitchen, hidden behind a communal area of tables and fold-up chairs. This is where I would sit, frequently waiting out bad weather during the day, eating the pathetic amount of food that I'd carried with me from Boston, and chatting with Jay Lehman and Dave Sonneborn, a tall bearded cardiologist from Anchorage. I recognized Dave's beard from field trip photos of Attu, where he'd earned a reputation for birding in the most extreme conditions, stepping outside as the Aleutian weather hurled its worst. His doggedness was rewarded by three ABA firsts that he found by himself. Paul Lehman sat at a desk that seemed to guard the kitchen, working on his laptop, with half an ear open for any juicy bird discussion, which would easily tempt his participation. A pot of coffee spluttered cheerfully nearby.

There was no bus this time, so Jay and I hitched rides on an ATV with Clarence Irrigoo, Hansen's brother. Clarence and Hansen both lived in the old town, overlooking a beach littered with rotting bowhead whale carcasses and the unskinned boats, upturned like skeletal tortoises, that had been used to hunt them. Clarence's hair was short, buzzed around the head, and he wore black-framed spectacles that wouldn't have looked out of place on an architect. Clarence had an unusual interest in birds and snapped photos of them with a small digital camera that he carried with him wherever he went. He was a regular visitor to the lodge, seeking out Paul's opinion on whatever he'd found, which was frequently something good. Earlier in the season, Clarence had found a Little Bunting, a rare bird for Gambell. He had no need for binoculars. As with many of the Yupiks who were lifelong hunters, he had eyes that were as sharp as the icy rain.

With Jay, I revisited the boneyards where the Stonechat, Yellow-browed Warbler, and Siberian Accentor had been found, but of course they weren't there—just a lone arctic ground squirrel angry at our interruption and thumping the ground with its tail. The boneyards were empty of birds, but full of the familiar bitter, pungent smell of wormwood that I would forever associate with this place. If I'd had more experience with Alaskan birding, I'd have known that few things stay in Gambell for long, but with westerly winds from Asia in the forecast, there was hope for something new to blow in. After three long days of cold drizzle and no birds, it did. It was one of those magical moments when the radio, previously a useless, cumbersome appendage, crackled into action.

"Do either of you need Common Snipe?" It was the voice of Paul Lehman, who was working the near boneyard.

"Yes!" we both shouted. This was it. It wasn't a drill.

Jay and I were in the lodge, busy packing away what was left of our heavy clothing. It was an hour before our departure from the island. Paul's news would at least mean that my return here hadn't been a complete waste. I didn't stop to dig out the buried gloves and hat. I ran out the door and into a slow-motion action movie as my feet sunk into the gravel. I moved toward the boneyard as if swimming in treacle.

The Common Snipe is a shorebird with an improbably long bill that it uses to probe deep into mud for tasty crustaceans, snails, and insects. These birds breed across the water in Russia, although they rarely make it to Gambell (they're more common farther south on St. Paul and the Aleutians). Jay and I joined Paul, and we walked over and over the boneyard, trying to find the bird. It was, of course, the worst combination: the largest boneyard with a bird that will only flush if you almost stand on it. It was the proverbial needle in a haystack—and this haystack was about to disappear in less than an hour.

We continued our desperate search until the distant moan resolved into the familiar drone of propellers. Our trip was over. I did consider staying another day, but figured the bird had gone. I got on the plane, and swore that I'd never return. I was fed up with Gambell, the weather, and the constant teasing of good birds that never appeared, at least for me. I felt cheated. And by the time I left Nome that evening, Paul had refound the snipe, like I knew he would.

I watched for the perfect runniness: when the syrupy, translucent albumen is denatured (at sixty-two degrees Celsius), trapping the water into a caged white gel. Three eggs, their bright-orange, sunny faces turned up, spluttered in the pan. Finely chopped scallions, rosy-pink smoked salmon, and sliced, earthy cremini mushrooms rounded out the color palette. I inhaled the welcome smell of home and stood hypnotized by a thought I'd been asking myself ever since leaving Gambell, *How can I see more than seven hundred species, travel to the ends of the continent, and yet fail?* The experiences, the birds, and the new friends I'd made suggested I couldn't, but that didn't stop others from thinking it. I was stupid to think that I could do a Big Year without anyone noticing.

It was usually the Red Sox cap that gave me away or the belabored, plummy accent. There was a time, early on, when I was excited to be recognized, but after hitting seven hundred, it changed, at least for me. Each new goal of five hundred, six hundred, and then seven hundred had been a motivational goal, helping me to organize my plans and push me to keep birding hard every day (not that I needed much encouragement). But after seven hundred there was no obvious target, except to the many birders who had now started to follow my progress. To them, it was all about the record, a fun game of will he or won't he? It was fun for everyone except for me.

I never wanted the Big Year to be about the numbers. It seemed crude, distilling what I'd seen and experienced into a single variable. At best, it measured entirely the wrong thing. Is someone who's seen fifty-six countries more knowledgeable about the world than someone who's seen fifty-two? How do you compare the two, and why would you want to? Besides, I felt like a fraud. I'd never started this to beat any record, and if and when I missed it, I didn't want to be branded a failure.

The *jingle jangles* of the *Seinfeld* theme music pulled me into the double-whammy of the present. Chris Hitt was calling and I'd overdone the eggs. I turned off the gas, wedged the phone against my ear, and rescued a subpar lunch (Coefficient of Greatness: not so good).

"Can you talk?" he asked. I still hadn't met Chris, but his voice, a soft baritone with a rhythmical swing, had become a familiar sound.

"Yes," I said, salting, peppering, and Tabasco-ing the plate. "I can talk."

I'd learned a lot from Chris this year. He'd done it all before, breaking seven hundred in the Lower 48 for his Big Year in 2010. Now he occasionally blogged about other people's Big Year adventures, and he would regularly check in with Jay and me for updates. This time, he called to sympathize about my failed strategy of doubling down on Gambell. He, like any other birder, knew that every year is different. Some are simply better than others. We never spoke of it, not consciously, but we both thought there had been a chance of getting very close to Sandy Komito's record if I had a good Gambell. But I didn't. So that was that.

I told Chris I had a few more pelagics in California the following week to nibble away at the last common seabird gaps on my list. And in October, Jay was planning a trip for Ross's Gull at Barrow, Alaska, the most northerly US city. It was a long way for one bird, but I was thinking of joining him.

"You remember I'll be in Alaska too?" he asked.

I did, although I'd pushed it to the back of my mind. Chris was going to St. Paul on an inaugural ABA Pribilofs trip. Once the north winds take over at Gambell, usually around the second half of September, they'll blow on and off right through the end of the winter. There aren't many birds north of Gambell to be sucked into that. But St. Paul can be good right through October if there are storms. If not, a week can easily slip by without a good bird. I thought it was a shame that we'd decided on different islands for our Alaskan fall migration.

After I hung up on Chris, and fed the remains of the eggy plate to a prowling Khiva Cat, I could hear my words echoing from the past, *I'll do a Big Year, but I'm not going to Alaska.* I'd now been to Alaska four times. The pain of the last trip to Gambell was still fresh. *That's it—I'm never coming back.* But I couldn't seem to ignore those teasing siren calls of future, possible birds. Chris had done it again: he had me thinking about Alaska. Perhaps I hadn't eaten my last Trident fish cannery meal of the year.

I met Jay at the dock in Bodega Bay, Northern California. I'd followed my standard pelagic protocol: arrive late the night before, "sleep" in car, locate morning coffee, and stumble onto boat. Ever since I'd almost missed the ferry to the Dry Tortugas, I didn't trust myself to wake up in time, even with multiple alarms and backup phone calls from Gerri. And while I never felt rested, sleeping in a car did guarantee that I'd be awake every fifteen minutes and be happy to "get out of bed."

Perhaps it was appropriate for us to meet in Bodega Bay, the setting for Hitchcock's movie *The Birds*. While we were grateful that the angry birds were apparently taking a day off, we did step into a mildly scary B movie, Attack of the Killer Kelp Flies. Roughly the size of a housefly, with dark, maroon eyes, these bastards normally live on kelp fields out to sea. But if you get too close, they'll ditch the kelp for the far more interesting prospect of human skin. Debi Shearwater told us not to worry.

"They don't bite. They only tickle," she announced to the twenty or so passengers.

She was right—but they tickled like spiders, and somehow that was much, much worse. At least you know where you are with biting flies, I always say.

Jay looked healthy. He reminded me of myself during the summer, moving from state to state with purpose, tracking down the remaining target birds. After leaving Gambell, he'd birded in Washington State and again in Arizona. He was at 652, and there were at least another fifty birds out there if he could get to them in time. He was guaranteed a race to the finish line.

For me, one of the few redeeming qualities of "other people" is that they usually do an excellent job of reminding you of how sane you are. If ever you think you're doing something even mildly odd, you can bet that there's someone out there doing a whole lot more odd. I met Jay's friend Isaac Sanchez on the boat. Jay and Isaac had been friends in graduate school at the University of Delaware, and now Isaac was a gray-haired, bespectacled professor of chemical engineering at the University of Texas at Austin. This year, when he wasn't studying polymers and nanotechnology, he was doing his own Big Year—a photographic Big Year. Isaac was essentially taking what was already a ridiculous activity and deliberately making it more complicated and unpleasant: he was trying to photograph each of the species he saw. Many of the birds I'd seen this year were but fleeting glimpses in a high forest canopy or whizzing by at sea, or barely visible in the moonlight. I immediately appreciated the difficulty of the task he'd set for himself. (Isaac would end up photographing an astonishing 601 species by the end of the year.)

As a large, batlike Black Storm-Petrel winged by the boat, a happy new tick for all three of us, Jay reminded me of Olaf Danielson. On Jay's boat trip to Attu in the spring, he'd birded with Olaf, who was from South Dakota. Olaf was doing a naked Big Year. He could count a species only if he was naked when it was found. In a bizarre and intricate set of rules, he couldn't strip off after the bird had been found—the bird had to be located while naked. Olaf would go on to write a book, predictably titled *Boobies, Peckers and Tits*.

The next day I was in Orange County for a more typical pelagic where I saw no new birds. But I did meet some more Big Year birders: two young Toms—Tom Ford-Hutchinson and Tom Benson. They were both competing for an Orange County Big Year. I did the math and immediately felt short-changed. At 790 square miles, that was almost 7 million square miles less than I had to cover. They never had to fly anywhere, and I bet they didn't have to sleep in a car either. (I'd just spent the second consecutive night in a car and was feeling less than charitable.) I made a mental note not to tell Gerri that apparently Big Years could be done in a small area around your house.

I didn't get a new bird on that boat, but I did get one back on shore. While I had been wading through wormwood in

Gambell, the ABA Checklist Committee had added a newly introduced bird to the list: Nutmeg Mannikin, a highly social, seed-eating finch native to much of tropical Asia. The ease of breeding them in captivity made them a popular cage bird, and from an initially small population of escaped birds, they've been breeding in the wild in Southern California since the late 1980s. Tom Ford-Hutchinson very kindly gave me directions to a colony in Huntington Beach Central Park and suggested that if I didn't get the bird in twenty seconds (or forty seconds if I parked at the wrong end of the parking lot), then either I was in the wrong park or I was a complete idiot. I was well into the second minute of searching, hoping I was indeed in the wrong park, before I heard the thin, whistling calls of the mannikins. They were stripping a patch of long grass of its seeds and vanished into the overhanging trees once I approached. I picked out a single adult with my binoculars, perched at the edge of the clearing. It had a chocolate-brown back, a dark and pointed bill, and a beautiful black-and-white scaly pattern below. I whispered a word of thanks to the ABA for this unexpected bonus tick (number 713).

My third pelagic in three days was from Half Moon Bay, where I'd first met Jay and Sandy Komito. It was also my third night in a car, and I was in a foul mood. I'd started to resent the frequent recognition: "Are you that Accidental Big Year Birder?" (My blog was called the Accidental Big Year.) Or, more worrying, "Are you the accidental person?" I stopped wearing my signature Red Sox cap. Part of my frustration was having to explain to people that no, I wasn't going to break the record. I guess I didn't realize until then how much I'd wanted that. It was never the original goal, but I had to admit, it was a shame to come so close and miss.

A group of shearwaters lifted off the water near us, and the boat went mental. Debi and Jay started shouting, "Flesh-footed at the bow! Flesh-footed at the bow!" I was already there and with my binoculars easily picked out the chocolate-colored bird that had been sitting, hidden among the common Pink-footed Shearwaters. Jay and I were ecstatic—it was a bird we probably should have seen already but we hadn't. As the rest of the boat exploded in high-fives and laughter, I saw with quiet wonder the relief and excitement in Jay's eyes, and I remembered why we did this. Worrying about the stupid record and the stupid numbers, I'd forgotten the simple joy that comes from seeing the unexpected. I realized I needed this bird now more than ever. I also made a decision.

"Jay," I said, "I'm coming to Barrow. Let's get that Ross's Gull!"

But first, I was going to meet Chris Hitt for dinner in a fish factory in the Bering Sea.

My bird count at the end of September 2013: 718 (+1 provisional)
John Vanderpoel's bird count at the end of September 2011: 719
Sandy Komito's Big Year record, 1998: 748

Chapter 10

THE BIRD THAT LIVES ON TOP
OF THE WORLD

"IN PREPARATION FOR OUR landing in Anchorage, please raise your tray tables, return your seats to the upright position, fasten your seat belts, and raise your binoculars for the Stonechat perched out on the right side of the plane."

Okay, that's not quite how it happened, but in the movie (the one where I'm played by Brad Pitt) I'm sure that's how it'll be rewritten.

There are few remaining joys of air travel. By the end of the year, I'd end up clocking more than 190,000 miles, almost all of which felt like being locked in a tin can full of sharp elbows, smelly feet, and snoring heads. Whatever algorithm they used for seating, it never placed me next to a cute girl, and the view outside was almost always more interesting; the burned red tundra of Alaska, the patchwork quilt of Saskatchewan fields, and the dusty void of the Southwest would all suck my face into the oval window. For the rest of the flight, I'd watch movies I'd never otherwise consider watching, do the crossword in the in-flight magazine, or just stare at the back of the seat in front of me like an idiot while calculating the exact fraction of an inch over which my shared armrest had been violated.

I scrolled through the rare-bird-alert e-mail as the Alaska Airlines Boeing 737 taxied toward its gate, mentally noting how much less snow there was on the mountains now than there had been in the spring. The Stonechat was one of the trifecta of birds for which I'd gone back to Gambell, all of which I'd missed. After that trip I was surprised to be back in the state, but I had to draw the line somewhere on my bird-finding desperation. I wasn't going back to Gambell again, Stonechat or no Stonechat.

"Huh," I said, drawing more than a few pointed stares. The bird wasn't in Gambell. It was seven miles away from where I now sat. The bird had been found a few hours ago, while I was still in the air, and I had the rest of the day free. My flight to St. Paul wasn't leaving until the following morning.

I knew only one person in Anchorage: Dave Sonneborn, the cardiologist I'd met in Gambell. He not only gave me directions for the bird, which he'd seen that morning, but also offered to meet me at my hotel and take me there. I was continually surprised by the kindness of strangers and new acquaintances during my birding adventures. The background check was simple: sharing a love for birds.

Back in March I had stood in Polly Neldner's kitchen, hoping for the yard birds that she'd recently reported on her local Colorado Listserv. She knew nothing about me, except that I was a birder. I received a warm welcome but had to imagine the rest. The flocks of Pinyon Jays and Evening

Grosbeaks and a pair of Harris's Sparrows that apparently visited every day had decided to play hooky. On my way back from Albuquerque, after seeing the rosy-finches at Sandia Crest, Polly told me to stop by again. A huge snowstorm had driven the birds back into her yard. Her husband, Paul, picked me up from outside the only store in town in a vehicle more suitable than mine for the knee-deep snow through which we plowed. Shortly after, I was back again in their kitchen with a cup of coffee and a view of swirling blue and gold birds: Pinyon Jays and Evening Grosbeaks. I hadn't known at the time that I'd end up doing a Big Year, or that those grosbeaks and that pair of shy Harris's Sparrows would be the only sightings of those species I'd see all year.

Dave Sonneborn pulled up outside the Ramada Inn that sits above Ship Creek, in downtown Anchorage. His car was overflowing with the paraphernalia of life that I imagined would fill any Alaskan's car: cross-country skis, boots, and a supply of warm clothing. Dave had grown up outside New York City and moved here in 1978. Many of the birders I'd met in Alaska were transplants attracted by the remote wilderness: Aaron Lang had moved from Minnesota, and Dave Porter had uprooted from Colorado, bought land here, and built his own cabin from which "the Warden" apparently granted him temporary parole. I found heat oppressive and couldn't imagine doing well in the beach resorts to which normal people dream of moving. But moving to Alaska—with its long, cold winters and brief, cool summers—was something else. These people were equally odd, I thought.

The path to Carr-Gottstein Park has an uninspiring start, buried in a modern housing development to the south of the city. But if you follow that muddy trail through a narrow corridor of conifers, it leads to a small domed hill, like a slightly flattened egg. And if you stand on that egg and over-look the boggy, cattail marsh to the south bordering the shore of Cook Inlet, a vast panorama of mountains will likewise look down on you, albeit with less interest.

A group of birders was already there, and they all seemed to know Dave. I'm always torn when I arrive at a chase. Part of me wants to put an end to the nervousness that's churning through the contents of my stomach. "Drive-up birds" are nice, sitting framed within someone else's telescope, but it's more fun to refind the bird yourself. As with solving a crime, you need to interview the witnesses and pick up clues from the surroundings. Of course, I'd rather have a drive-up bird than no bird, and in this case there was no bird. I was left to piece together the story from the overheard conversation: it had been on the hill in the morning and had slowly worked its way down and to the south. I was reminded of Paul Lehman's description of the Stonechat on Gambell, which had similarly slunk away, never to be seen again. I scanned the cattails below in a vain effort to bring it back. After thirty minutes, all I succeeded in seeing was a distant flash of white, like the wisp of a shooting star. It wasn't much, but it was enough to lure me into the marsh.

The mud sucked on my feet like they were Popsicles, as it did on the feet of Dave and the few other birders who followed. We proceeded south as sloppily as the mud would allow, until

we got close to where I'd seen the white flash. Down here it
was easier to scan the tops of the cattails, which is where I
imagined the bird would sit.

"I have it!" I shouted, quietly.

It looked like another cattail head, a plump, sparrow-size top
to one of the many reeds. It perched there, gently swaying,
surveying its surroundings, while Dave and the other two
birders rotated through the scope view. According to the
American Ornithologists' Union I'd already seen this bird—a
Common Stonechat—in the UK. I'd seen many Stonechats as a
kid, and with their black head, red breast, white neck, and rump
(the source of the flash), and with a call that sounds like two
pebbles being knocked together, they'd left a lasting impression.
But the British Ornithologists' Union would tell you that this
was a Siberian Stonechat, previously a subspecies of the Common
Stonechat that was now a full species in its own right. It high-
lighted the ongoing debates about bird taxonomy. Even armed
with powerful new clues from mitochondrial DNA, the barriers
between species are gray and subjective, and there are still things
over which the Americans and the Brits can happily disagree.

I shouldn't have been surprised. Neither of my previous
Pribilof flights had left on time. The list of excuses was piling
up—exploding volcanoes, fog, and now they couldn't find a
plane. My eleven forty-five A.M. departure was now rescheduled for four A.M. I knew these planes didn't work in the fog.
I wasn't excited to see one cope with the dark.

John and Laurie Cairns of New York were at the airport, as
they had been in the spring. They were heading to St. Paul for

the second part of the ABA tour before going on to Barrow for John Puschock's Ross's Gull tour. The canceled flight gave them a chance to try for the Stonechat, although they came up short. The bird was never seen again. The birding gods had indeed smiled on me.

It was still dark when we arrived on the island, but I navigated the runway at the other end like a professional—into the storage hangar, past the chicken wire, dodging the buckets of leaky-roof rainwater, before emerging into the "hotel." It was already bustling with birders. Half the ABA tour was leaving on the plane, to be replaced by new birders. I was back, in the land of the fog, of the Trident fish cannery, and of the twice-weekly chance of escape.

Scott and Doug were overseeing the ebb and flow together with Gavin Bieber, an extra guide to help with the larger group. Gavin had cut his birding teeth on St. Paul, guiding for a cumulative two years (though his prized island list of 216 was about to fall to Scott, who trailed now by only seven birds). Gavin worked for the bird tour company Wings and lived in Tucson, Arizona. Despite his youth, the hair on his head had long since departed south, wintering somewhere in the goatee region. His infectious personality immediately made me feel welcome. He provided the much-needed goofiness to the hard work of finding rare birds.

"Grab your stuff," came a rhythmic voice I associated with the smell of smoked salmon and scallions. "You're rooming with me."

Chris Hitt was taller and more athletic than I'd expected. He was in his early sixties with a head and face covered by an explosion of white hair. His oval, wire-framed glasses gave him an intellectual look. I'd been nervous about meeting Chris. I was the youngest person to join the 700 Club, and I wanted to prove to him that I wasn't a complete birding idiot.

I'm always nervous about meeting new people. I almost never remember their names because I'm too busy remembering mine. I worry that they'll be disappointed, that I won't be entertaining or interesting enough. I don't like small talk, which I know is the glue that holds together these random connections we make, like the ionic bonds in a salt solution. I'm worried that I won't know what to say, that there'll be those awful pauses in the conversation for which I'll feel a failure, like it's my fault the conversation has stalled. I'm almost forty years old and I'm crippled by shyness.

The room was eight by ten with two single beds, a bedside table serving each with a small lamp and a printed copy of the St. Paul Island checklist of birds. A window revealed the maritime tundra beyond and the three wind turbines that powered the town. I didn't have long to unpack before I heard the shouts in the corridor that the bus was about to leave. I changed into my waterproofs and thermal underwear. The group was larger this time (seventeen birders) and so was the vehicle—a blue-and-white bus with double seats on each side and the words ST. PAUL TOUR emblazoned proudly on all sides.

I peered through the dusty windows of the bus and looked upon an island that was barely recognizable to me. It was green, not white. The soft carpet of snow was gone, replaced by a luscious swath of grass spotted with the purples of lupines and monkshood flowers. There were lakes now of a rich Oxford blue. Scott Schuette had been right back in the spring when he'd said that once the snow burned off, this wasteland turned into a kind of paradise.

Dan Sanders and Doreene Linzell, from Columbus, Ohio, leaned over the back of the seat to introduce themselves. Dan joined the 700 Club in 2005, posting a Big Year total of 715. Dan was a retired biology teacher, and no doubt a great one. I enjoyed his gentle, careful explanations about birding and horseshoe pitching (his other passion). Dan matched Chris for height and beardedness; although without his cap, which would come off three times a day for meals, I could see that the frostiness of his beard had yet to reach the youthful hair on his head. Doreene, shorter with a healthy mess of dark hair, had an insatiable appetite for birds that matched Dan's. Every January 1, they'd start a new Ohio State Big Year. This was Dan's nineteenth consecutive Ohio Big Year, and the pair had just come off a spectacular 2012, posting a new record of 320 species. They were here with their friend Laura Keene, a pharmacist from Cincinnati and a talented nature photographer. All three were good friends of Chris's.

Birding legends Paul Sykes and Larry Peavler sat on the other side of the bus. With 883 and 882 species, respectively, they were number two and three on the ABA life list totem pole. Paul was a retired wildlife research biologist who'd worked for the U.S. Fish and Wildlife Service and had guided birders on Attu. He's also one of the few people alive today who'd seen the Bachman's Warbler, a bird of the southeastern swamps that wintered in Cuba, before it quietly slipped into extinction. Paul was built like an ox, albeit a gentle and charming one.

Larry Peavler had worked as a tool and dye maker in a defense plant in Indianapolis. This was his fiftieth trip to Alaska, and he'd seen more birds in the state (358) than anyone else who didn't live there. A few inches shorter than his birding friend Paul, Larry was more reserved, with a soft-spoken voice and a thoughtful manner. The pair were here for a month. If they were extremely lucky, they might add one new bird to their lists.

Chris had already filled me in on the birds I'd missed: a Middendorff's Grasshopper-Warbler (only the second record for the island) and a pair of Gray-tailed Tattlers. A surprise flyover Pacific Swift was a life bird for those who saw it, including the guides, but there were still two Asian vagrants that had been seen as recently as yesterday: a Gray-streaked Flycatcher and a Common Rosefinch. The former fell easily, seen from the bus sheltering on the leeward side of Polovina Hill. It was a bird Jay had seen that spring on Attu, seven hundred miles to the southwest.

By the time we reached the site of the Common Rosefinch that evening, the weather had deteriorated. Gray skies were spitting, and the wind had picked up. The bus disgorged us onto a grassy dune called Black Diamond Hill that sits above the crab pots and gives a panoramic view of the rocky shores to the south. We fanned out along the ridge, scaring up groups of the common Lapland Longspurs, before a fat, brown-and-white finch popped up on a putchkie, or celery plant. If you saw it at the feeder in your yard, you'd probably think it was another female House Finch. Only the brighter white of the breast and a heavier, chunkier build hinted at its rarity value. If it had been a male, it would have looked like a Christmas decoration, dipped headfirst into a vat of scarlet paint.

Common Rosefinches breed from one end of Eurasia to the other, from Western Europe to the Russian Far East. That vast population, probably numbering over a hundred million birds, is highly migratory, which can take them all over the continent and occasionally to this one (in the spring of 1977 a flock of eighteen was recorded at Gambell). Some seven million years ago, an ancestor of this bird made it to Hawaii, the most isolated archipelago in the world. Finding a blank canvas of untapped ecological niches, it would evolve into the spectacularly diverse and unique Hawaiian Honeycreeper family: sixty-odd species of varicolored songbirds, sporting a catalog of bill shapes to fit the bizarre new flowers, snails, and seeds that the birds found there.

I met the rest of the group at dinner that night, over the familiar Formica tables of the fish cannery. The change in the season had brought the welcome addition of halibut, but the Coefficient of Greatness was still about the same (bland). Janis Cadwallader, from San Diego, was tallest of the female birders, and the fiercest, keeping those around her in good order. If there were a murder on the island, which almost happened when the cinnamon rolls started to run out, I could imagine Janis springing into detective action. She reminded me of Miss Marple, and I immediately liked her. The O'Neil sisters, Karen and Ellen, were separated these days by geography, and this far-flung trip was as much a reunion for them as it was an opportunity to add to their bird lists. Both were white-haired, had eyes framed by black glasses, and defied my identification skills all week. I never quite knew who was who. Lucie Bruce and Nick Cooney were from Texas, where they birded and butterflied together. And Bruce Scheible, dwarfing the group in height, hailed from Cedar Rapids, Iowa.

This was the first time the ABA had organized a trip to this remote island, and it was a chance for me to get to know some of the group's staff and volunteers. Susan Jones, from Georgia, was an energetic member of the board with an old-fashioned Southern accent and a modern sense of humor. I regretted not spending more time with her. This would be her last trip to Alaska, before being diagnosed with leukemia, to which she would ultimately succumb. Greg Neise was the web developer of the group. Hidden behind an impressive reddish beard, Greg was a passionate "Big Day" birder (a more rational species than the Big Year variety) in his hometown of Chicago and a willing ear to Chris's discussions of how the ABA could more accurately keep score of birder rankings (there is no peer-reviewed process on posting list numbers—just the honor system). At the center of the group sat Lynne Miller, who worked in the ABA office in Colorado Springs. She'd been following my story all year and was a welcome source of encouragement. Her kindness and quiet calm instantly won me over.

★

"What's a birder wearing red for?" asked Paul Sykes.

It would have been a very good question if the idiot wearing it hadn't been me. Most birders wear cryptic colors like green or brown and try to avoid white, to which there's some evidence that birds have an aversion. Either way, if you're stalking a bird, it's probably not a good idea to be a bright color, and that's exactly what I tried to convey to Gerri when she instructed me to buy it. Apparently the red was a protection from getting lost in the avalanches of snow that she imagined covered the whole state. She thought it would help the rescue teams find me before the polar bears did. I thought about telling her that there were (probably) no polar bears here, but then I might have to also explain that there were (definitely) no rescue teams.

On this particular occasion my red jacket was moving slowly through a grassy marsh, with me inside hoping to flush a Common Snipe. This was the bird I'd left behind in Gambell, which Paul Lehman had found on my departure day. I'd probably seen one on the evening of our first day on St. Paul, but the light was so bad that I couldn't see the diagnostic panel of white on the back of the wings that makes it a Eurasian Common Snipe and not an American Wilson's Snipe. I had seen the bird, yet I couldn't count it.

Birders care about the integrity of their lists like tax accountants bringing order to a pile of receipts. No one wants a birding audit. But while each checkbox on the list invites a simple tick or no tick, there's a nasty gray area around some sightings. The same bird viewed by different birders could be accepted, rejected, or agonized over before a conclusion is reached. Each of us has a slightly different threshold for adding to our life lists, and for some birds we often get only one take.

Dan and Doreene had seen the Pacific Swift the previous week, like most of the others on the tour, but hadn't seen the diagnostic white rump, later shown in Laura Keene's photographs. They didn't count it. They will probably never see another Pacific Swift. Instead, they will agonize over the lost bird, replaying that moment above Webster Lake, wishing they were in a better position to see the bird and the identifying features. James Huntington, the Mailman, told me he'd chased a Sinaloa Wren three times before seeing enough of the bird to feel happy about ticking it.

"Snipe!" shouted Gavin.

I watched as a brown bird, sporting a long Pinocchio nose for a bill, flapped up out of the marsh and hung briefly in the air, as if pondering its options, before urgently making for the distant hills behind which it soon disappeared. The light wasn't great, but it was enough to make out the delicate line of white etched on the back of the wing. I'd seen a Common Snipe, and I'd seen why it was a Common Snipe. I could count it.

I looked forward to the quiet evenings in our room when I could talk to Chris Hitt about birds. Chris talked about Big Years the way proud parents talk about their kids. The Big Year for Chris was an intellectual puzzle for which there was no right answer, only endless permutations, each year posing a different set of challenges. While Chris told me that Sandy

Komito's record of 748 was still, fifteen years later, an incredible achievement, it was Greg Miller's that was perhaps the most remarkable. Greg saw 715 species that same year, but unlike Sandy, and almost every other Big Year birder, he was working a full-time job.

I was still working, or at least I liked to tell myself I was. There were random projects for my new biotechnology consultancy, but it was never full-time, and for some weeks it was no time. As the miles piled up and I became more addicted to the game, I turned down offers for work. On St. Paul I had no work and an uncomfortable feeling that I had more in common with the retirees than I liked to admit. But I knew that my fantasy year was about to end and that I'd have to prepare for my blunt atmospheric reentry into the real world.

I hadn't spoken to many people about quitting my job. I knew there was no going back, and so I avoided any regret by trying not to think about it. Talking about it made me uncomfortable. I felt stupid for giving up a dream job and embarrassed that I could live without it, but mainly I didn't want to deal with the inevitable question of what's next. With Chris, it was easy. He had retired early after spending too much time at work and not enough time with his family. He'd swapped the executive job (he was the president of an organic food chain) for his own sustainable dairy, and although that still took up his time, it never stole it. It hadn't been a straight trajectory for him. It had taken Chris three marriages, and relocating around the country every few years for his job, before he found the happiness he now enjoyed in North Carolina.

I was struck by how Chris and I moved effortlessly in our conversations between birds and life. I had no problem making lists and decisions about the former, while the latter continually stumped me. But what if life was just another Big Year, an intellectual puzzle for which there was no right answer? I didn't know whether I'd been right to quit my job, and I didn't know whether doing a Big Year would help, or whether Gerri was the right answer. But I did know that at the end of it all, there would be only one story to tell. My biggest regret would be not chasing those dreams, feathered or non-feathered. At some point I'd run out of decisions, and I hoped, when all the music stopped, that I'd be in the right place.

"Big storm, dude. Just sayin'," taunted Scott.

It wasn't a big storm. It was a huge storm. It was centered over Asia and moving slowly toward us, although it was still a week away. There weren't many birds still moving in Asia this late in the season, but those that were would probably be very unusual. (Only recently have birders stayed so late in the Bering Sea, finding fewer birds but rarer ones.) Neither the storm nor Scott was making our departure any easier. I was heading back to Anchorage to connect with Jay and our flight to Barrow, and Gavin was heading to Australia to lead a bird tour. Gavin knew that his island list would fall to Scott soon, but it didn't seem to matter. His life was about to change immeasurably. His wife was pregnant with their first child. I didn't think that any bird, however rare, could match the light in his eyes when he talked about being a father, which he did frequently.

St. Paul had been good to me, leapfrogging my Big Year forward by five species. (As well as the flycatcher, rosefinch, and snipe, we flushed an Olive-backed Pipit at Hutchinson Hill and found a late Gray-tailed Tattler in the town harbor.) I'd clawed back some of the lost birds from Gambell, and I was now tied with my pacesetter, John Vanderpoel. Four hundred miles to the north of us, Paul Lehman was boarding a twin-prop plane to Nome and saying goodbye to a season for which he would add a stripy Lanceolated Warbler to the Baikal Teal as his only new island birds. Winter was on its way.

"We'd like to welcome you to Barrow, where the local time is ten A.M. and the temperature is twenty-two degrees. We'd also like to congratulate the local boat crew: they landed a whale yesterday!"

Whales, especially big, blubbery dead ones, apparently generate a lot more clapping and high-fiving than a lost Stonechat.

It was the third and final airport, after stops at Fairbanks and Prudhoe Bay–Deadhorse. I leaned over the back of my seat and spotted Jay in his gray jacket, a few rows back, grabbing his bags. He flashed me a quick smile. Barrow was new for both of us, although it was known to many birders as the only place in the world to see the Arctic migration of the pink-flushed Ross's Gull. We also had a good chance of finding the rarer Ivory Gull, a carnivorous bird of the lonely pack ice that scavenges on polar bear kills. That whale landing wasn't just good news for Barrow; it was also good news for Ivory Gulls.

I walked off the plane into an eerie darkness, like a dogged eclipse that's stuck. The sun is shy this time of year, putting in brief midday appearances above the heat haze of the cold horizon. In another month, it will give up entirely, nervously appearing again sixty-five days later, like a teenager slinking home late after curfew. The tarmac was scorched platinum gray by the frost, and a light dusting of snow hugged the ground. Barrow has a desert-like climate, with only twenty-nine inches of snow per year, most of which would fall this month.

John Puschock was waiting for us at the back of the tiny Wiley Post–Will Rogers terminal, a jumble of brown hair, dark-brown eyes, and a grin and eyebrow permanently set to sarcastic. It was the first time I'd met him in human form. John had invited Jay and me to help scout ahead of his ABA Ross's Gull trip. Next to him stood fellow guide Jess Findlay, a young and talented wildlife photographer. Jess had a mop of straw-blond hair and was friendly in a quiet and genuine way. He lived on the healthier end of the sarcasm spectrum.

We followed John out of the airport double doors, across a busy main street, and to a white van, into which we threw our bags, followed by ourselves. I was the newbie. Jay already knew John and Jess from his trip to Attu in the spring. John Puschock's boat trip was the only way these days for birders to get to this most famous Aleutian Island. It's a fifty-hour trip each way from Adak, an island in the central Aleutians and currently the farthest west you can fly. On the way they'd spotted Short-tailed Albatross (Jay's eight hundredth life bird) while Mottled Petrels streamed by in mind-numbing numbers. They'd arrived in time to survey the result of a strong spring storm, and the pickings were rich: cuckoos, rubythroats, and Smews.

While I'd been birding in the Sax-Zim Bog of Minnesota, Jay had been birding the very edge of the continent, scoring ticks that were more rare and considerably less bitey than mine. He had added eight species that I would miss entirely for the year. I was sitting on the plateau of my Big Year now, where eight birds was almost a month's work. If I'd been to Attu, I reflected, perhaps I could have broken the record. But you can't change one thing without upsetting the rest. Time travel didn't work like that.

Barrow is really three towns. To the south lies the down-town, a confusing maze of curving streets into which the airport somehow fits. The mostly single-story buildings, clad in wood and vinyl, sit on tundra above a 1,300-foot layer of permafrost. There are no people on the streets, just vehicles with block heaters that spout electric cables from their grills, an overnight life-support system for the long Arctic winter. Like many isolated Alaskan communities that aren't connected to the continental road network, the vehicles are brought in by barge.

We headed northeast past the small and frozen Esatkuat Lagoon and into Browerville, a regimented grid of residential houses. We continued, hugging the coast on our left, and past another lagoon on our right, and we were in the Naval Arctic Research Lab and the smallest of Barrow's suburbs. It was just northeast of here that we found the bloody remains of the bowhead whale, or at least what hadn't already been divided up among the kitchen freezers of the native Iñupiat community. Chunks of frozen blubber lay sprinkled across the snowy tundra like giant sugar cubes. A flock of white-winged Glaucous Gulls fed busily on the blood, like a swarm of flies, screeching in eerie delight.

John explained that while the Iñupiat still practiced a traditional subsistence lifestyle, their whale slaughter is regulated: twenty-two strikes, or attempts, per year, whether successful or not. It's a bloody business that doesn't go unnoticed by the local polar bears. I pointed my binoculars through the front windscreen of the van, and at the end of a long spit I could make out a pile of red bones, like a funeral pyre, around which a forklift truck attended. But however hard I squinted, I didn't see any white bears.

We sat in the warm vehicle and scanned through the blubber field looking for the flesh-eating Ivory Gull. If you ask most non-birders what color gulls are, they'd say white, and they'd be entirely wrong. Instead, their backs and wings are shades of gray. There's only one gull that's entirely white, the Ivory Gull. The adult is so white that it looks more like a soft, albino pigeon. The simple lack of color (except for the yellow-blue bill, black legs, and liquid-black eyes) makes it a surprising favorite for those birders who've seen one, and the most-wanted bird for those who haven't. I'd seen only one before, a lost bird in Massachusetts that drew birders from around the continent. (Birders fed it frozen chickens from Star Market to prolong its stay.) It's a bird that's thrown its hat in with the wrong ecological crowd: pack ice and polar bears. By conservative estimates, the population has crashed by 80 percent in the past twenty years. We didn't find one on the blubber.

The beach was a few hundred feet away to our left. It was black, like cooled volcanic lava. The sky was like a watercolor by the English landscape painter J. M. W. Turner in which all of his dizzying reds, blues, and yellows were rendered into a muted kaleidoscope of grays. Angry clouds, sharp enough to cut yourself on, streamed violently across the sky. The ocean was a deep, inky gray and placid. There was something heavy and oppressive about the leaden skies and seas that soon gave me a pounding headache.

The protocol for finding Ross's Gulls is simple: stand around and wait for pink birds to fly by. But there was nothing simple about standing around in subzero temperatures, and I soon discovered that I was woefully underdressed. My nylon overshoes had been fine in St. Paul for keeping my boots dry through the marsh walks, but they did nothing against the windchill here. My feet soon felt like bags of icy blubber cubes around which the remaining tissue screamed like the bloodthirsty cries of the Glaucous Gulls.

To the south of Point Barrow, and to our right, was the vast Elson Lagoon. It was mostly frozen and dotted with gulls standing around or flapping lazily. Our shadows were pulled almost to the breaking point, stretched across the snowy tundra like spindly giants. I swept my scope back and forth across the blinding landscape, like a searchlight, while dancing on my feet to keep them alive. I stopped when I spotted an unusual movement: a large, loping mass of white padding its way across the ice.

"Polar bear!" I shouted, giving up the magnified view to Jay, then Jess and John, who watched its slow progress across the frozen lake.

I'd never seen a polar bear before, and it was not the cute teddy bear that I'd seen abused in countless marketing campaigns. I was struck by how ungainly it was—the long neck oddly articulated, like a fifth leg, alternately swinging from side to side like the other limbs but never hitting the ground. I watched in awe at its fearful beauty. Unlike other bears, which attack you only if they feel threatened, this one will hunt you. I'd seen the teeth and claws before, on a stuffed animal in Anchorage airport, and was immediately grateful for the distance (which I guessed to be about a mile) that now separated us. I watched as the animal reached a patch of open water, where it splayed its legs, jumped, and dived in, like someone belly flopping into a swimming pool.

Ross's Gulls are one of the most mysterious of North American birds. Long thought to breed only on the Arctic coast of Siberia, they were recently discovered in the High Arctic of Canada and in Greenland, suggesting that they are circumpolar breeders. The global population is estimated at some twenty-seven thousand birds, at least two thirds of which have been counted off Barrow in the monthlong migration that starts in the last few days of September. The birds move from the Chukchi Sea west of Point Barrow to the Beaufort Sea in the east. No equivalent spring migration has ever been recorded, and only about two hundred nests have ever been found. Where the rest of them are breeding, and what their movements are for most of the year, remain a mystery.

The gulls passed by singly or in small groups, most staying offshore, flying toward the distant Point Barrow and beyond. The birds were small, but if the light was good, I could make out the pointed, wedge-shaped tail, and the dark undersides to the wings—the same dark gray as the ocean over which they flapped. The upper wings were pale gray and the white body and head were flushed with pink, like cherry blossom. It was one of the most beautiful birds I'd ever seen.

Dinner that night was at the Osaka restaurant, a bright-red beacon of a building in downtown Barrow. The opportunity for defrosting limbs and extremities was better than the actual food, although a beer would probably have cured that. Barrow is a damp town; there's no alcohol for sale, although you can bring it in. (We hadn't brought any in.)

I sat across from John, who told us of his part-time relationship with Alaska. He'd spent six weeks holed up in Barrow in a semi-cylindrical Quonset hut with his young son while his wife was outside researching whales. Another time he'd spent five months in Kotzebue, on the west coast of Alaska, before moving back to Seattle. Somewhere in all those years he'd flirted briefly with rock stardom, worked for a fictional company invented by a character on *Seinfeld*, and, if he ever tired of his Alaska-based bird tour business, he could probably land a job as a stunt double for John Cusack. It was hard to tell when he was joking. His wit was as dry as I imagined Humphrey Bogart's martini to be. He deliberately limited

the number of people on his bird tours by making the name
of his company as unforgettable as it was unpronounceable:
Zugunruhe Birding Tours. As the only person in the country
who could still get birders to Attu, his calm, self-deprecating
demeanor clearly hid a cunning and logical mind.

Jay told us about his recent trip through California. He was
at 672 now and still thought he had a shot at 700, although he
wasn't sure where he was going next. I told him about Scott's
prediction for the massive storm headed for St. Paul. I didn't
have much energy to go back, just a nagging feeling that it
was the right thing to do. I knew that if Jay wanted to go, my
decision would be a lot easier.

Jay and I were sharing a room downtown, not far from the
airport. I had a lot for which to thank Jay. I met John Puschock
through Jay, and I probably wouldn't have come here without
the invite, although I was still shocked to find myself chasing
single birds at the edges of the Alaskan coast. Mostly I was
grateful for his companionship and his birding knowledge. Jay
started to draw birds in the late 1940s as a five-year-old kid.
While his older brother and sister were at school, he'd occupy
his time copying birds from the field guides of the day. It was
easy for me to picture him, hunched over a pad of paper,
awkwardly learning to trace the shapes of bills, tails, and
wings with the same level of attention that would soon help
him find and identify the living versions.

Whenever I saw new birds with Jay, I half-watched him as I
watched the bird. The sight of him filled with wonder and
excitement was an inspiration to me. Jay had spent his life
watching birds. His love of them hasn't waned in the sixty-five

years since he first traced their silhouettes. There's enough joy in birding to fill a lifetime.

When I think back to Barrow, it's not the bright pink Ross's Gull or the galumphing polar bears that I remember most; rather it's sitting up late chatting with Jay in our shared room. I was half in bed, surrounded by my notes, field guides, and checklists. And although there were only ten weeks left of our Big Years, we talked like they were never going to end—where to go next, who still needed what. There would always be one more bird to chase, one new place to see.

It hadn't been like that with the depression. There never was a future, or at least one that was painless enough to imagine. And without a future, without a space to dream of what's next or what could be, I'd become stuck with nowhere to go, condemned to live in the murky past, filled with failure and regrets. Now, it didn't seem to matter what that imagined future was. The next bird was just as good for me as a prospective child, wedding, or vacation was to someone else. Each bird pulled me forward, away from the demons.

John and Jess picked us up the next morning. They were staying at Iḷisaġvik College, which was originally part of the Naval Arctic Research Lab and was now a small town of converted Quonset huts and a few optimistic palm tree sculptures. As we left after breakfast, we spotted a white Snowy Owl sitting on a fence. It was my third of the year. The Iñupiat name for Barrow is Ukpeaġvik, which means "the place where we hunt Snowy Owls." I silently wished the bird well.

We saw more of the cherry-blossomed gulls flap by, each accompanied by an "oh wow!" and our polar bear of the previous day was replaced with a family of three—an adult and two young bears. But we saw no Ivory Gulls, which was a big miss for our Big Years and a reminder that the Arctic is changing faster than the gull. At this speed, there may be no future for the bird that lives on top of the world.

A candle flame danced in the center of the table, releasing a soft aroma of vanilla. The room around me, painted a sprightly apricot and lemon, hummed with subdued conversation, interrupted only by the clinking of silverware and glass. It was a welcome respite from the leaden skies of Barrow. The only excuse now for the dull ache taking root in my head was the parade of drained wine glasses in front of me.

Chris Hitt had just stepped off the plane from St. Paul and was meeting Jay and me for dinner in downtown Anchorage. Chris reminded me that his Big Year in 2010 was as much about finding good food and friends as about finding birds. He'd called it Slow Birding (after the Slow Food movement), although I knew the birding for him was anything but. After the thousands of rare-bird e-mails through which I had been sifting, I was happy to limit my decision-making that night to the handwritten menu (Alaskan rockfish swimming in cara-melized onion puree and a refreshingly tart crème brûlée were the winners). It felt good to be warmed by the company of my newfound friends.

Chris told us that nothing new had turned up on the island after I'd left, except for a Spectacled Eider that was a surprise life bird for him. Paul and Larry were still there, hoping for that one new bird that would make the trip a success, and Scott was still talking about the approaching storm. I told Chris that I was going back. I'd managed to grab the last seat out the next morning, and Jay was on standby. There was nowhere else to go (except home, I suppose), and I couldn't resist the storm warning. I could tell that Chris had wanted to stay, but he'd been on the island for twenty days and seen ninety-two species, nine of which were life birds. He was tired and missed home. I knew how he felt.

By the time the coffee had arrived, the sun had somehow set behind us. There was a tension between Chris and Jay, although they hid it well. Chris didn't believe that Jay (who was now at 671) would make it to 700. He'd followed twelve other Big Years, and none of them were like Jay's. None of the 700 Club had been so far from 700 so late in the year. While Jay's stint on Attu had netted him incredible rarities, he'd had to trade those in for some of the common summer breeders that he'd missed. Some, like the Black Swift, had already left for Central and South America and wouldn't return until next year. The rest included secretive rails and difficult-to-find grouse.

I knew this bothered Jay. He lived alone and didn't have the support back home that Chris and I enjoyed. When a legal dispute broke out with his neighbors, he couldn't tell them that he was doing a Big Year or ask a spouse or girlfriend to settle it. He had to resolve it himself. Meanwhile, the Listserv messages didn't wait, informing him daily of birds that would be seen by everyone but the Ohio birder who'd waited his whole life for this one year. And so Jay was playing catch-up for the rest of the year. I knew Chris didn't doubt Jay's birding ability (although I think that's what Jay thought). We'd both seen enough of his birding to know that if anyone could finish strong, it was Jay.

The coffee arrived, the conversation turned to the Big Year record, and now it was my turn to feel uncomfortable. I was embarrassed to find myself thinking about it and wanting it. I wanted my Big Year to be about the birds and the experiences, not the numbers. But I'd forgotten what it was like to have goals and I was driven now, chasing each new target number: 500, 600, 700, and now, improbably, Sandy's own record. It was impossible not to get caught up in the race. But I knew that goals were dangerous. Having one and failing might somehow be worse than not having one at all.

At 721 species, I found it hard not to feel the pressure and the unspoken thoughts. I was twenty-seven birds away from Sandy Komito's record with twelve weeks to go. Chris knew as well as I did that I was on pace to get very close. We both viewed John Vanderpoel's list as the better comparison (neither of us had been to Attu like Sandy had). I was one bird behind John on this date, and John had ended up five birds short of the record. Chris and Jay knew the pressure I was under and were careful not to speak of the record directly, like superstitious Shakespearian actors talking of "The Scottish Play." But we all knew that my return to St. Paul was a risk. The storm had to produce results. And I had to not get stuck there.

★

It was only a week after my previous visit to St. Paul, but there was a perceptible shift in the season. The cold nibbled, hinting at the larger bites to come. The wormwood burned a deep red, and there were fewer birds. Even the hardy Lapland Longspurs were abandoning the island for the Lower 48 and southern Canada. Time was moving relentlessly forward, and I couldn't stop it.

The approaching winter had thinned out the birder numbers too. There were only seven of us now, including Paul and Larry. Jay was here, his standby ticket upgraded to seated. We were staying in a house in town this time, the duplex, where I shared a room with Bill Frey, who, I discovered, had rafted through the remote Brooks Range of interior Alaska with Chris Hitt back in 2011. I preferred living in the duplex to the hotel/airport. We had a living room, a TV, and a kitchen. The seasoned professionals like Paul and Larry had mailed a box of food here from home and were still eating their way through it. Jay and I survived on visits to the grocery store, which was surprisingly well stocked and unsurprisingly very expensive. At the back of the building was the liquor store. The impressive lineup of beer and wine was almost as long as the handwritten list next to the cash register of those on the island prohibited from buying it.

The storm had missed us. It had veered off to the northwest at the last minute. We were spared the strong winds, which I imagined to be full of colorful lost birds. Just the outer wisps of anti-cyclonic winds lapped our shores. I prayed that any lost waif caught up in that maelstrom had seen our tiny fog-bound island beckoning and leaped aboard.

I fell quickly back into the island routine: checking the windbreaks at Hutchinson and Polovina hills, sweeping through the putchkie patches, walking the marshes at Antone Slough, and zigzagging through the dwindling number of crab pots (it was the start of the king crab season and so the pots were disappearing back into the sea). It was fun acting as tour guide to Jay, although I'm not sure the recent history lessons ("This is where we saw the White-tailed Eagle," "Here's where the Olive-backed Pipit stood") convinced him that he'd made the right decision to come. That would have to wait until the second day, when he flushed a Common Snipe, neutralizing the pain of the bird he'd missed at Gambell.

The long list of rare birds found in western Alaska suggests the trees are dripping with them. They're not (and not just because there aren't any trees). For each bird found, there are days spent searching and miles of habitat carefully scoured and rescoured. That methodical pursuit seemed to suit Scott. His quiet temperament was well matched to life on the island. This was his second year leading the St. Paul tour (he'd first guided here in 2008). His employer was the Tanadgusix Corporation, the native group that owns 95 percent of the island and all the fishing, hotel, and tourist industries.

We were walking the dunes on Black Diamond Hill, above the crab pots, with the rest of the group somewhere behind us. It was our third and penultimate day. All the birders, including Jay and myself, were leaving the next day. Time was running out. It was running out for Scott too. He told me that he typically spends the whole season here, leading birders from May through October. It was a great way to add to his ABA list, although these days he cared as much about his island list. Rarities like last week's Magnolia Warbler from eastern North America were just as prized as a Dusky Warbler from the west. This was his last week of the year, and he was looking forward to wintering in Anchorage.

The dunes fell away from us, rolling down to the breaking sea. I thought back to the previous week, when we'd watched the Common Rosefinch pop up on a stick of putchkie, but it was long gone. Even the flocks of Lapland Longspurs were gone. But that was still the default bird, and so when a single projectile flushed between Scott and me, accompanied by the familiar shout of "bird!" that's initially what I expected it would be. Except longspurs aren't red. The rest of the group caught up while I scanned with my scope, more from habit than with an expectation of seeing anything. But I did see something. A distant bird that looked orange and blue. It most definitely wasn't a Lapland Longspur.

"Red-flanked Bluetail," I shouted to Scott, somewhat disappointedly. It was the bird I'd seen in the park in Vancouver back in January. Of all the birds that the storm could throw at us, I wondered, why did it have to be one I'd already seen?

Scott looked in the scope.

"That's not a bluetail," he said calmly. "It's some kind of redstart. Whatever it is, it's a first for North America. Get a photo!"

That familiar elastic band of time pulled taught again, slowing my competing thoughts. No birder ever expects to find a first, and the pressure was almost crippling. I was the only one with a camera, albeit the one on my phone held up to my telescope to capture the magnified image. The six other birders were hopping around in agony, desperate to look through the scope. Without a view, they couldn't tick it (it was too far to see any detail with their binoculars). I could feel their frustration—Paul and Larry had waited three weeks for this moment. But without a photo, there'd be nothing to tick. The Alaska Checklist Committee will accept a new bird to the state list only if there's a photo or a physical specimen. Meanwhile, Doug was somewhere else on the island. Scott had reached him on the phone and I could hear one half of their excited conversation, although for the most part it sounded like a long string of expletives.

Between getting photos and surrendering the scope to the others, who complained of the brevity of the rationed views, I allowed myself a brief moment to inventory the bird and fix it in my memory. It was about the size of a House Finch but pulled forward into a horizontal posture, with a longer, thinner bill, presumably appropriate for a diet of insects. The back and head were a bluish gray, darker in the wings, and lightening up around the face, into which black beady eyes were set and framed by a pale-white eyebrow. The flanks were a metallic orange and the tail and rump were bright orange-red, like Reese's wrappers. It sat balanced on a putchkie head, surrendering its movement to the light breeze.

Once Doug arrived, we chased the bird around the dunes, sometimes lying flat on the ground before peeking over into the next dune. The bird was flighty and we lost it several times. But it would reappear, sometimes behind us as if by magic, riding the putchkie stalks.

The field guides back in the van told us that it wasn't a Daurian Redstart, the most likely redstart based on geographic range. The lack of white in the wing made it a Common Redstart, a bird from Europe whose breeding range stretches east to Lake Baikal in Russia. It had flown more than three thousand miles in the wrong direction. It should have been heading to a winter in sub-Saharan Africa. I felt like such a fool. It was a bird I'd seen many times in the UK, but I hadn't recognized it out of context.

Storm winds hit the next day, our last day on the island. Horizontal rain battered the windows on our duplex, and the wind screamed around the building. It was Doug's turn to pick us up in the morning.

"Photos still looking good for Common Redstart," he said as he came in the back door, confirming the conclusion of our own late-night study. I wondered if Gavin had heard the news yet. I hoped that Australia, and the excitement of his first child, would dull the pain.

We ran down the back steps of the duplex in double time to limit our drenching and piled into the van. Doug told us that the winds were from the southeast, which, if there's fog, can often slam seabirds against the southern tip of the island. Instead of heading inland to the airport, we drove to the rocky headland above the town.

"Everybody out!" shouted Doug, after taking a quick look through his binoculars.

Even through the steamy windows of the van I could make

out thousands of Short-tailed Shearwaters, streaming from left to right, dark crosses against the angry foaming gray. They were pushed against the island by a wall of fog, which obscured any horizon beyond. With telescopes we could pick out the smaller Mottled Petrels, white underneath. We would lose them whenever they banked and their gray backs and wings disappeared against the sea. It was a life bird for half the group and year bird number 722 for me.

"I'm not going," I said.

It was a hunch, like coming back and finding the Common Redstart. Who knew what else had been blown in on the storm, I wondered. I changed my ticket to a standby for the next departure, two days away, and waited for the plane that would bring one more birder—Norm Budnitz, our bus driver from Gambell—and take everyone else away. I said goodbye to Jay, expecting to see him a week later on a boat in California.

It's hard to imagine birding without the luck. Norm heard the previous evening when he got to Anchorage that we'd hit the birding jackpot. (We would refind the redstart later for him that day before it disappeared for good.) The Big Year had been all about making decisions, some good and others not so good. It was luck that kept pulling at me, rewarding me for being in the right place at the right time, like the Stonechat, the one-day wonder in Anchorage.

Staying on the island, I would discover, was the right decision. Something else had been blown in by the storm—an inquisitive-looking Eye-browed Thrush from the dense coniferous forests of Siberia. It was hiding among the crab pots—the same crab pots that I'd checked and found birdless on each of my nineteen days there that year. But luck was a fickle mistress here. She'd given back to Jay the Common Snipe that she'd withheld in Gambell, but not the White-tailed Eagle that was seen here for three days before our arrival and would be seen again by Norm and me an hour after Jay had disappeared into the Bering sky. When I left for the third and final time, Norm stayed on and found a Gray Wagtail.

Some say that there is no luck or free will, just fate—whatever will be, will be. *Que sera, sera.* I don't believe that. We make our own luck by putting ourselves in the right place at the right time. Luck might not be the reward for the well prepared and the persistent, just the more probable result. Common Redstarts weren't going to fly through my kitchen window, and nor was Gerri. I'd had to look for them both.

I missed her and not a day went by without my thinking of how lucky I was. Not that she'd often know that, since it was hard for me to remember to tell her. She was busy with school now, learning about cognitive behavioral therapy and doing an internship helping college students who had drinking problems. Despite the distractions, I knew she was lonely and missed me.

I wondered if this was the perfect relationship for me—love at a physical distance. The time zones that held us apart gave me space to say all the right things that I couldn't in real time. It was hard to argue and screw things up. But I knew this couldn't last. Those discussions about growing the relationship and moving forward would come once my eyes were back in front of hers. Perhaps that's why I loved the travel so much. I wasn't just running from the past; I was free to dream of a bubble-wrapped future that was safe from my own undoing. I knew that wouldn't work for Gerri. My Big Year was about to end, and I'd be back home staring at my big life and carefully removing the bubble wrap.

My bird count at the end of October 2013: 727 (+2 provisional)
John Vanderpoel's bird count at the end of October 2011: 729
Sandy Komito's Big Year record, 1998: 748

Chapter 11

A WILD GOOSE CHASE

IT HAD BEEN TWENTY-FIVE years since I'd last climbed a tree. It was one of the many fun things, like popping a wheelie, sword fighting with sticks, and licking batteries, that you have to eventually stop doing and trade in for adult responsibility and the wisdom of risk assessment. I'd forgotten what it felt like: that strong, palpable bond with the living world, cradled by the limbs of a tree (an alligator juniper in this case). I remembered not to look down, to avoid the inevitable dizziness that even six feet could induce. Climbing was easier when I was younger, when my hands weren't full of electronic gadgets and my head wasn't full of airport codes.

I was looking for a bird, of course, but the bird wasn't up the tree. Not this tree, at least. The bird was in South Texas, near the Rio Grande, nine hundred miles away from this tree, which was now gently swaying under my weight in southeast Arizona. It was a real bird that had made a virtual presence on my phone. Five minutes earlier, Amazon Kingfisher was just another thumbnail painting in the extreme rarity section at the back of the *National Geographic Field Guide to the Birds of*

North America. That much-read entry had told me that there had been only one previous record in the United States, in South Texas, in 2010. But now, like the other new rarities that had flashed across my phone this year, it jump-started my heart like a double shot of espresso and had suddenly become the most important thing in my life.

If I hadn't been climbing ever higher, trying to get phone reception, then I'd have paused to appreciate the irony—that I was now in a tree, like the birds that I spent so much energy chasing. But that's where the similarity unfortunately ended. My eyesight, for a start, was worse, and not just because my glasses were a prescription behind. I only have three color cones in my eyes, while birds have four. In addition to my red, green, and blue, they also have ultraviolet. Most birds have bigger eyes too, in proportion to their bodies. I'd need to nearly double the size of mine to compare. And my hearing was worse and would continue to fail as the delicate hair cells in my ears became damaged beyond repair by a lifetime of loud noise. At some point I'd join the legion of elderly birders unable to hear the high-pitched calls of the Blackburnian Warbler or the Golden-crowned Kinglet. Birds, in an act of annoying simplicity, just replace those damaged hair cells. And of course I couldn't fly. The 193,758 miles I would fly this year all required at least some kind of mechanical assistance.

The date was November 10. I was in Arizona looking for an Eared Quetzal at the top of Madera Canyon. Laurens Halsey, a local guide, had found the bird the previous day feasting on the strawberry-like fruit of an Arizona madrone tree. I'd arrived this morning to find the tree already staked out by hungry birders, like paparazzi waiting for an A-list star. Before the distraction of the Amazon Kingfisher news, I'd already spent five hours searching for the famously elusive bird. Despite the quetzal's bright red and green plumage, they're remarkably difficult to find in the dense forest canopy. I was happy for the chance to upgrade one celebrity bird for another.

I was now eight feet off the ground, and if I stretched my arm above me, a bar of reception would magically appear on my screen. Except, of course, in this posture I couldn't read the screen, let alone navigate the process of buying a flight to Texas. I inched another couple of feet up the tree, as the dry, scaly limbs bowed under my weight and roughed up my hands like pumice stone. The smell of smoky cedar grew stronger the higher I climbed. Of course, I could have run down the trail to the parking lot, where my phone would work without the need for such arboreal acrobatics. But then I'd definitely miss the quetzal.

A month had passed since I'd left St. Paul. I'd flown to San Diego to meet up with Jay for three days of pelagic boat trips. Jay and I slept a lot on the trips. It was hard not to. The gentle roll of the boat, the blinding strobe light, and the sound of waves breaking against the hull sang to us like soporific sirens. The coffee, served from a small galley kitchen, did little to keep my head off the Formica table. We almost slept through the Craveri's Murrelets. I shook Jay awake as we slowly floated up to a pair of tiny black-and-white birds the size of starlings. Above the sound of the slapping waves, I could hear their insect-like calls, like a pair of rattling cicadas. This Mexican

seabird was a life bird for many on board, and it was the
reason Jay and I had come to San Diego.

We skipped the third day, eager to catch up on sleep in a
bed that didn't roll or make us want to regurgitate our break-
fasts. When the boat returned that night, the birders were still
giddy from the Guadalupe Murrelet they'd all seen. It wasn't
supposed to be there, of course; this cousin of the Craveri's
Murrelet is normally found at least thirty miles offshore.
But then, my whole year was based on birds that weren't
supposed to be where we found them, actively defying the
distribution maps in our field guides. The pain of the missed
murrelet, like a terrestrial form of seasickness, was greater
than the now-forgotten joy of the seen one. I was angry
with myself. New birds were at a premium at this time
of year, and there would be no more pelagics on this side of
the country.

Climbing down the tree proved to be a lot harder than
climbing up. I tried to retrace my steps, but the limbs looked
different, as if they'd deliberately rearranged themselves to
confuse me. A pile of broken branches sat below, like medieval
stakes waiting to impale me. I was so far off the trail I wondered
how long it would take for anyone to find me. I felt clumsy as
my binoculars swung wildly, slamming into the trunk, while
branches of parched, crocodilian skin picked at the stitching of
my backpack. If there was an optimum strategy for scaring off
an Eared Quetzal, I'm sure this was pretty close to it. Not that
I had much hope anyway. After I regained my terrestrial
footing, another three hours patrolling the madrone tree
convinced me I had indeed missed the bird. But I didn't miss

the plane that night to Texas, the first I'd ever booked from
ten feet up a tree.

The Rio Grande Valley Birding Festival was celebrating its
twentieth year. In that time it had become the model for eco-
festivals around the country. Birders came to hear international
speakers, to catch up with friends, and to see the unique birdlife of the Lower Rio Grande Valley. Much like southeastern
Arizona, birds that otherwise might be considered Mexican
trickled across the invisible border. It was the only place to see
birds like the photogenic Green Jay, the yellow-and-black
Audubon's Oriole, and the sweet-natured Olive Sparrow,
although the Tamaulipas Crow had long since receded back
into its Mexico heartland, sparing birders the olfactory abuse
of the Brownsville dump. The Amazon Kingfisher, found
on the penultimate day, had become the star of this year's
festival.

A long line of cars, slowly sinking into the grassy verge of the
road, told me that I'd arrived. I was twelve miles south of the
festival headquarters in Harlingen and guessed that this morning's crowd had missed the bird the previous day. When the
bird was first reported, many of the festivalgoers had been on
buses, bound for birding hot spots around the valley. Given the
limited parking and safety concerns about the busy road, not all
the buses turned around. Some continued on to their original
destinations, full of anxious birders, suddenly wishing they
were somewhere else.

I was so used to seeing Debi Shearwater barking out birds
on a boat that I almost didn't recognize her in non-pelagic

attire. She was smiling. She'd seen the kingfisher before it had disappeared thirty minutes ago. We stood facing a resaca, or oxbow lake, squashed up against the south side of the road and fringed with weeping willows. Dead snags reached up from the stagnant water, like the desperate arms of drowning men. Debi told me that was where the bird was last seen, resting between fishing trips. The bird had even received a police detail, and the officer seemed as genuinely interested in the bird as in the traffic and crowds that he'd been sent to control. There was no shade here, and the sun was baking my head.

When the bird eventually showed, after half an hour with my head stuck under the broiler, it eschewed the photogenic snags, instead burying itself deep in an overhanging willow. I aimed my scope at a plump green-and-white bird. The black, daggerlike bill easily beat the head for length, and looked so heavy I was surprised the bird wasn't pulled forward off its perch headfirst into the water. The light was dappled by the long, thin leaves of the willow and almost blinded me as it reflected off the bright-white belly of the bird. The back, wings, and head were an emerald black, offset by a gleaming collar of white.

I watched the kingfisher, jealous of its shade, and thought about the Greek myth of Alcyone and her husband, Ceyx, a couple so madly in love that no one seemed to notice how annoying this was. Well, no one except Zeus, who was probably at the top of the list of people/gods that you didn't want to annoy. Apparently, the couple had gotten into the habit of giving each other pet names: Zeus and Hera, after the rulers of the Olympian pantheon. When Ceyx decided to take a boat trip alone, the king of the gods saw his opportunity for putting an end to this insubordination. Zeus fired up a thunderbolt and promptly sank the ship. Alcyone discovered her husband's body when it washed ashore. Her grief was so absolute (and perhaps a teeny bit overdramatic) that she decided she couldn't face life alone. She drowned herself. At this point, Zeus realized maybe he'd gone too far (the other gods were giving him the cold shoulder), and so he atoned for his actions by transforming the (dead) couple into a pair of (living) kingfishers. The Greek for kingfisher is *alkyon*, which is where we get Halcyonidae, the family of tree kingfishers common throughout Europe and Australasia.

The story didn't quite end there. Alcyone, reborn as the kingfisher, would lay her eggs each year during the calmest period of winter, when her father, Aeolus, god of the winds, would restrain their gusts. These calm, golden days would come to be known as the halcyon days. As I watched the real-life Amazon Kingfisher drop down in front of me in a failed fish sortie, I thought of my own Big Year. The lack of sleep and the constant exhaustion may not have suggested a period of calm, but the greater mental clarity, free from competing anxieties, felt like Aeolus might have given me a respite too. I wondered if these might perhaps be my own halcyon days.

It was late afternoon and I was daydreaming in Moonbeams—a coffee shop in McAllen, Texas, where the baristas had started to write my name in the foam of my caffe lattes. The Green Parakeets, which would appear like clockwork each evening on the wires outside, squawking at the gloaming, had yet to make an appearance. A report of a Streak-backed Oriole in southeast New Mexico had rattled into my in-box and I was talking myself into the long drive ahead—eleven hours away, on the other side of the desert of West Texas.

I had always been drawn to coffee shops in my travels. I would read (I was currently going through a David Mitchell and Jo Nesbø phase) and plan my next move. I liked being alone in a crowd, able to sit and think without the terror of someone else talking to me.

Apparently, at least half the population is introverted, although that's hard for me to believe. I've always felt that everyone else is louder, more social, and more like the outgoing characters I see on television, popping in on neighbors for mindless gossip and chat. Where are all the quiet people, I often wonder? And why do I feel guilty for letting the friendly opening gambits of conversation die out? On the merry-go-round of flights I was taking, I would meet countless strangers who would remain just that as I hastily reached for my phone, book, or in-flight magazine to ward off their friendly advances.

I was shocked when I first discovered that there were people who liked meeting new people. They not only looked forward to the small talk but also felt revitalized by it. They sought out these experiences like I sought out my next good read in a bookstore. They would phone rather than e-mail or text (and when they did phone, they didn't have a list of agenda items like I had, neatly written on a scrap of envelope). I couldn't get enough time on my own, and wanting more time on your own probably wasn't a great recipe for building or maintaining a relationship.

I suppose that's why my job had seemed to be an uncomfortable fit. The more successful I became, the less I felt like myself. I was always looking for quiet and the space to think, while my job gave me everything but. And trying to be more normal (louder, more outgoing), like other people, only served to make the dichotomy more obvious to me. Whenever I feel regret for leaving my job, I remind myself what it would be like to go back: the endless meetings, listening and talking, my brain bombarded with language with little time to process or reflect.

I'd spent my life unwittingly seeking out places and activities that I could enjoy on my own—like reading in coffee shops. For as long as I can remember, I've carried a book with me everywhere—planes, trains, restaurants—as socially acceptable protection in case someone wanted to talk to me. I never understood why more people didn't do that. Surely, I assumed, you could learn more things from a book than from idle conversation. During the Big Year, I loved going to bars in the evening, enjoying the bitterness of the local beer and the quiet companionship of a book that would transport me somewhere even more exotic and remote.

I wondered if that's why I'd been attracted to birding. The outside world fascinated me, but only if I could process it quietly inside my head, away from the noisy distractions. Birding was the perfect combination of mental stimulation: hunting like a detective for movement, performing a mental Shazam of bird calls, and entering their tiny heads, wondering what they were thinking and dreaming. Wear a pair of binoculars outdoors and it's (almost) okay to be on your own.

I enjoyed birding with other people in the same way that I liked talking during a car ride, as something subordinate and complimentary to the main activity. When being with others got in the way of the birds and I felt like I was losing them, it was as though the two halves of my brain were clashing, like when you try to see both sides of an optical illusion at the same time. I felt the same way about baseball games. Occasionally, I got Red Sox tickets through work, but I enjoyed it best when I could sit on my own and score the game—writing the results of each at bat neatly into a square in a grid of columns ("6-4-3" for a shortstop–second base–first base double play; "BB" for a walk; and "K" for a strike-out, or a backward "K" if the batter didn't bother to take a swing). But if I had to talk as well, and think about what I'd say next, I'd miss the game and resent the conversation. Both were ruined.

I didn't really expect I'd be able to drive through to New Mexico in one go, and I didn't. By the time the tarmac ribbon rolled through Stockton, Texas, I'd hit the rumble strip enough to know to call it quits, so I took an exit promising lodging and food. A storm was starting to blow across the desert. When I awoke early the next morning, the tumbleweed wasn't so much tumbling as flying.

The Streak-backed Oriole had been found by local birder Bob Nieman, at Rattlesnake Springs, an oasis in the Chihuahuan Desert near the considerably more popular Carlsbad Caverns. When I arrived, everything was cold and wet. Cottonwood trees, denuded of their heart-shaped leaves, marched in front of the parking lot, thirstily sitting on the waters of the spring itself. Their grotesque and distorted forms were shaking violently in the wind. It did not seem like a good day to be looking for birds.

A tangle of thickets—mostly silvery Russian-olives—guarded the cottonwoods. It was tighter and thornier than I had expected. It took fifteen minutes to circumnavigate, allowing extra time for crossing the tetanus fence. The grass around the spring was damp, and there were areas where my sneakers disappeared into bone-chilling water. I was starting to shiver, and I'd yet to find any obvious vantage point from which to see into the thicket. Unfortunately, as I'd gleaned from previous reports, that's exactly where the bird had been seen. Or, more accurately, where fleeting glimpses of body parts had been seen.

I eventually found a point of entry, a small opening into the dark interior, and crawled in. As I pushed forward on my elbows the damp grass brushed against my face and smelled of freshly mown lawn. What I hoped might thin out past the boundary wall thickened still more, limiting any further progress. Besides, I thought, if this amount of noise hadn't already scared the bird, I doubted whether I'd be able to twist my neck enough to see it. I crawled back out and continued the circumnavigation.

Ch-ch-ch-ch-ch-ch-ch-ch-ch.

If I hadn't recognized it immediately as the oriole, I might have assumed it was a rattlesnake. It was calling from inside the thicket. Damn it! I thought. I crawled back into the darkness, momentarily wondering whether there was any reason this place was called Rattlesnake Springs, and realizing that if there was, it was probably too late to worry about it now. Inching forward across the damp ground, I was reminded of doing the same thing a month ago over the grassy sand dunes of St. Paul, chasing the Common Redstart. This bird was more common (ABA Code 4: seen less than annually) than the ABA first of the redstart, but they would both count equally on my Big Year list—the same as the House Sparrow or Downy Woodpecker. Rare birds aren't worth more than common birds—every bird is one tick on the list—but as you run out of the common ones, those single ticks become a lot harder to come by.

Ch-ch-ch-ch-ch-ch-ch-ch-ch.

Goddamn it! The bird was now *outside* the thicket. I reversed the earthworm movement and convulsed my way back out. As I wiped off the mud, I noticed that I wasn't alone. Two people were standing twenty feet away. I wondered if they'd watched my embarrassing convulsions, but then realized the persistent swearing would probably have been more embarrassing. They stood perfectly still with their backs to me, telltale elbows sticking out on each side of their heads. They were birders using binoculars. I was about to call out to them when I followed their gaze and spotted a bright orange bird sitting at the top of a leafless shrub. As if on cue, it uttered the familiar rattlesnake call, and flew away.

I caught up with the pair and quickly learned the facts (the proper introductions could wait): they'd just arrived, and the bird had flown in and then flown off. I hadn't missed much. We crept forward in the direction of the bird, looking for the bright-orange beacon in this otherwise monochrome land of gray. It wasn't long before we found it, worming its way through a spiky bush. (I had to admire its technique!) This time I had long enough to inhale the field marks and the beauty of this common Mexican bird that only rarely ventures north: bright orange with a black bib and facemask and a strong, pointed bill like a Red-winged Blackbird (orioles and blackbirds are both members of the Icteridae family). The wings were black, but each feather was delicately edged in ivory, as if someone had taken a white coloring pencil and outlined each feather. The back was flushed with an olive color, down which streaks paraded, giving the bird its name.

The people were later identified as Steven Smith and Jeff Cohen from Roswell. They proudly presented me with a business card, indicating that they were founding members of the UFO Club of Roswell—the United Field Ornithologists. I was happy, after my initial pessimism, that today's flying object had been definitively identified.

"You've known about this for three months now," said Gerri, standing with arms folded in the kitchen.

While that was indeed true, there are a lot of things, to be fair, that I've known about for a lot longer than three months and failed to do anything about—like going to the dentist, buying new underwear, and reading *Moby-Dick*. Given that the air-conditioning had been broken since the beginning of summer, none of this should have been a surprise to her. In this case, the thing I'd known about was the wedding of one of Gerri's best friends, Beth. Beth was getting married in December, and the wedding was in the UK.

"I really don't want to go on my own," she said.

Her words took me back to that conversation we'd had on the drive from Canada, after seeing the owls. That one was about her first trip to the UK—when she visited the then-unengaged Beth alone while I ran away to Sandia Crest to visit the rosy-finches. Except then we hadn't been living together.

Birding had become my escape—a way to move forward from difficult times and to see the future more positively. But somehow it had also become a prison, trumping social engagements, dictating the timing and location of vacations, and becoming the focal point around which any plans were made. I'd tried to explain to Gerri in the many previous iterations of this discussion that there might be birds I still needed in December, although perhaps I let her continue to believe her naïve assumption that the birds would have run out by then. Meanwhile, it had become clear that Beth was rather selfishly unwilling to reschedule her wedding day to a year that wasn't preceded by the word "big." (And I secretly suspected that Gerri might not have even asked her to do this.)

I knew this looked bad. Gerri would be going to the UK—my home country—twice in one year without me. Moreover, I knew that women, especially unmarried ones, don't like going to weddings alone. Yet I doubted whether Gerri's annoyance about going alone was stronger than mine about attending at all. I placed weddings in the same morbid category as funerals. You can live perfectly well, entirely ignorant of death, until a funeral comes along and reminds you of your own mortality. Weddings are worse: they come with a spotlight. Other couples look at you, or hint, that you might be next. It's like some giant hybrid Ponzi-Tupperware pyramid scheme where their marriages are validated only if others follow suit.

I knew at some point the conversation would shift from Beth's wedding to our own. Maybe not for another year or two, but it would come eventually, as predicable as the spring migration after the thaw. I didn't know if I'd handle it any better than the first time. Anna had grown tired with my lack of interest in the subject. Our arguments were replaced with a realization that she needed to move on, and after moving out, finding someone new, and getting married, she'd rather successfully done just that. Would Gerri react the same, I wondered?

It's not that I didn't want to spend my life with Gerri. I did. It's just that I didn't want to promise it all away. I didn't understand how other people could be so certain about their future. Most of them could barely cope with signing a two-year cellphone contract. How could they possibly know they'd stay in the same relationship for the rest of their lives? I didn't even know what I'd be doing in two months, when my Big Year would run out. Looking any further ahead than that scared me. My career had followed a course that was so different from how I'd imagined it (college professor and Nobel Prize winner) before grinding to a halt, and I woke up one day to find that I was approaching forty and spending my life chasing birds (and I'm pretty sure there's no Nobel Prize for that). How could I know that my personal life wouldn't be any less screwed up?

It was easiest for me to talk about Beth's wedding with Gerri in terms of numbers—Big Year numbers. I'd returned from Texas with 732 species. A Sprague's Pipit in a dry lakebed in Austin on the drive back from the oriole had tied me with Bob Ake for third place. Bob was a retired chemistry professor at Old Dominion University, in Virginia, and had done his ABA Big Year in 2010, the same year that Chris Hitt had done his Lower 48 Big Year. I was only 11 birds away from John Vanderpoel's second place and 16 from Sandy Komito's record. The record itself probably wasn't possible, I reasoned, but it was definitely not possible if I went to the UK. And the closer I got, the more I realized I wanted it.

News of the next prospective bird (number 733) left our conversation unresolved and with Gerri wiping away tears of frustration and disappointment.

If I needed proof that I was running out of time and of seasons, then it was the geese, the harbingers of winter. Every year, millions of Canada Geese that breed from Arctic Canada to the northern United States head south to deafen Americans with their honking and carpet bomb the country with their pestilent droppings. (To think, this costs the Canadian military nothing!) The same thing happens in northern Europe, where Pink-footed and Barnacle Geese from Greenland and Iceland appear overnight in the beet fields of England.

That migratory process worked pretty well until recently, when Canada Geese colonized the southwest coast of

Greenland. Their numbers are so large now (well north of forty thousand birds) that occasionally a confused European-bound goose ends up in the wrong flock, joining the Canadas instead on their way to the New World. Apparently, that had just happened on the Atlantic flyway: a Pink-footed Goose had been spotted in Newfoundland, and a Bean Goose (pulled into the crowd from northern Scandinavia or Russia) was mowing the grass of a golf course in Nova Scotia.

It's more expensive to make the four-hundred-mile flight from Boston to Nova Scotia than it is to fly the four thousand miles to Anchorage, Alaska. And so, on a cool, clear Thursday morning, I left home in my own car, depriving Khiva Cat the visual delights of Logan Airport, although Gerri still got a hug and a kiss and a promise to stay in touch. I'd never been to the Canadian Maritimes before, and was excited to fix those "N" provinces on my mental world map.

When you leave the long, forested highways of Maine and unconcertina the maps of Canada (to avoid the international roaming charges), you enter New Brunswick and the western shore of the Bay of Fundy. Saint John isn't the capital (Fredericton is), but it is the largest city and one of the best places to watch the famous tides. The Bay of Fundy has the highest tides in the world—there's more than a fifty-foot difference between low and high tides. But after driving for eight hours, I didn't have the patience to watch the full cycle. I spent five minutes peering down at the murky Saint John River from Bridge Road, whose water flows upstream when the Bay of Fundy tide rises, and imagined the rest.

You can drive to Nova Scotia, a peninsula to the east of New Brunswick, if you continue past Saint John and circle the bay clockwise. I chose the ferry, which would drop me an hour from the Bean Goose and give me a chance for Great Skua from the boat. The *Princess of Acadia*, however, proved to be a better opportunity for sleep (long, plush seats, more crew than passengers) than it was for spotting any piratic, golden-brown Skuas. The rain-speckled windows prevented me from watching from the inside, and the almost-blowing-me-off-the-sides-of-the-boat winds prevented any reasonable attempt from the outside.

Yarmouth was an hour's drive south of the ferry port. The Victorian architecture dissolving in the overcast weather reminded me of Scotland, from which the province takes its Latin name and much of its original immigrant population. I drove south down Main Street, past the Yum Yum Tree gift store and the Nothin' Fancy Furniture warehouse, until the town was in my rearview mirror and the Gulf of Maine opened up on my right. To the left, a golf course climbed on a gentle pitch. There were no geese.

The Canada Geese had apparently been seen all over the golf course with the Bean Goose in tow. They didn't seem to go anywhere else, and there'd even been a report of the Bean Goose this morning while I was on the boat. I left the car and walked up the green. The weight of my telescope and tripod, fulcrumed by my perennially bruised right shoulder, pushed me down into the soggy grass.

"You looking for the goose?" a voice shouted out somewhere behind me.

I shouldn't have been surprised. The goose had made local news, and the golfers were getting used to sharing the links with birders.

"Yes," I replied. "I just arrived but haven't seen it yet."

"Go on up to the clubhouse and look down the other side," he said. He looked to be retirement age, with tufts of gray hair erupting from beneath a dun-colored cloth cap. "They're often in the pond."

I thanked him and made the short drive to the clubhouse. On the other side of the hill, I looked down on the other nine holes, which ran gently downhill to a river valley that bordered the course. I spotted what must have been the pond on the crest of a small hill and I could see the heads of geese—all Canadas—rising above it. I left the car and treated my sneakers to another submersion.

All rarities leave—sometimes just for the day, but their stay, however long, always comes to an end. They migrate, make their way back home, move on to new feeding grounds, or succumb to the local hazards. I'm always worried that the day I choose to go will be the first day of that absence, when the Listservs nervously start reporting, "Bean Goose—NO." I wish I could know the results of each chase. The nervousness of missing (or "dipping" in the birding lingo) is so intense that I'm physically aware of my stomach contents, the wriggling of my bowels, and the accelerated blood pumping loudly through my temples. I like that state of hyper-perception, but I wish I could lose the visceral nervousness that accompanies it. And that sense of heightened awareness is quickly dulled and replaced by relief, as it was when, standing a few hundred yards away, a brown goose with bright orange legs walked out from a bunker following the larger black-and-white Canada Geese.

Bean Goose used to be one species until 2007, when it was split by the American Ornithologists' Union into two: Tundra and Taiga. This was the Tundra species—shorter neck and bill, and a gap between the upper and lower mandibles that gives the bird a distinctive grin, like it's smiling, but in a sarcastic way. I hope it enjoyed the Yarmouth Links public golf course, for it would see no other. After a heavy snowstorm a month later, its remains would be found being ripped apart by a wintering Snowy Owl.

It was short message and to the point: Gerri had booked her flights for Beth's wedding and was going alone. After giving it some more thought, she could see the wisdom in my staying here and chasing any new birds. I suspect she knew how upset I'd be if I missed something while I was away, and she'd realized that she didn't want that responsibility. And so Gerri would go to the UK and to a wedding alone, while I would sit at home checking e-mails in case a bird appeared that I hadn't already seen that year.

I've read enough about relationships to know they're not supposed to be a competition, but, of course, that doesn't mean they aren't or that both of us weren't keeping score. I may have won this battle, but there was no doubt who was winning the war. I knew that at some point this avoidance strategy would have to end. I couldn't spend my life coming up with excuses.

A Big Year is the ultimate deep end into which a new partner has to jump. I knew it wasn't easy for Gerri, and there were many times when I was honestly surprised that she was still with me. I suspected she was dealing with it by counting down the days (forty-six now), knowing that the craziness was finite, and that on January 1 life would go back to normal. But I knew that the shallow end of chasing birds wasn't much shallower than the deep end. There would always be rare birds to chase, new birds to see, and vacations at sewage farms and landfill sites. I just hoped there'd be space in that chaotic world for Gerri to want to make a life.

I landed in Newfoundland the next day. It was a short flight to the northeast from Halifax, the capital of Nova Scotia. Newfoundland (which I soon discovered to be pronounced new-fund-LAND) is roughly the size of Ohio. It's an island shaped like a downward-facing triangle, with the southern point knocked slightly to the left. The Avalon Peninsula, shaped like a capital "H," hangs like a tiny earring off the eastern end of the island. This is where more than half the population lives and is the site of the capital, St. John's.

I left the airport and headed to Bonavista, on the northern part of the island. The Pink-footed Goose had been found in the town duck pond a week ago, but the site was remote enough that no one had been back to check since. If I wasn't so nervous about the seven-hour goose chase and testing my interpretation of the posted speed limits, I'd have taken the time to enjoy the unfolding views: the landscapes burning red, like the autumnal heather moors of Scotland, surrounded by dark forests of black spruce.

For the sake of international relations and to provide a simple-enough story for the tourists, Bonavista is where everyone now agrees that John Cabot landed in 1497 and claimed the new-found-land for King Henry VII of England. But there was an equally good chance that he actually landed somewhere else on the island, or on Nova Scotia, or Maine, or that he was too scared to land anywhere. If he did land here, he would have found a dramatic, rocky coastline with protected coves that made for fine harbors, grassy headlands, and probably would have found as many Pink-footed Geese as I did: zero.

The town pond sat below a gentle slope on which the brightly colored houses of the town perched higgledy-piggledy. The classical revival Memorial United Church sat to one side, dressed in fine white clapboard and outlined in nut-brown trim. One of its twin towers was grotesquely outsized by the inclusion of a clock face.

Apart from a few Mallards (and a definite shortage of Pink-footed Geese), there wasn't much entertainment to be had at the pond. But that didn't seem to prevent a large proportion of Bonavista (population 500) from enjoying an afternoon stroll around the boardwalk. A few stopped to presumably ask what I was doing, although the exact words tumbled out too fast for me to catch. I nodded my head like an idiot, just in case carrying a telescope around a small duck pond wasn't idiotic enough for them. I mumbled something about a goose, whereupon it was their turn to misunderstand and nod their heads. I managed several successful perambulations of the pond adopting this strategy.

I returned from the goose chase in time to see the sun set over St. John's. Brightly painted houses marched down the hill toward the harbor area. Despite heavy losses in the cod fishing industry in the 1990s, the docks were still full of vessels, although most looked to be beneficiaries of the new emerging oil industry. I sat at the bar in the Yellow Belly Brewery with a pint in one hand and a history of Newfoundland in the other.

Newfoundland, I read, was one of the first parts of North America to be settled by the British. Its island geography and isolation from the rest of the world, not least Canada (it would be the last province to join the country in 1949), preserved the accents of the original settlers, most of whom hailed from southwest England and southeast Ireland. That explained my earlier familiarity with the rhythm of the Bonavista accent if not the actual words. As the old brick bar started to fill with thirsty customers, I half listened to the dialogue, most of it a much softer and less rapid brogue than I'd heard earlier in Bonavista. But I could hear the "th" clipped to "t" or "d," as in Ireland, although I failed to hear the pulmonic ingressive that my book talked about—a curious way of saying the word "yeah" or "yes" while breathing in at the same time. After I left the bar, I spent the night practicing my pulmonic ingressive, which, although I failed to make any improvement, did take my mind off the numbing cold. I was sleeping in a car parked in a church parking lot.

I saw more of the historic town the next day as I drove around looking for a Yellow-legged Gull. Yellow-legged

Gulls are, of course, different from Yellow-footed Gulls (which I'd seen in the Salton Sea), although both confusingly have yellow feet and yellow legs. To make matters worse, the Lesser Black-backed Gull, while not named after the color of its feet or legs, also has yellow feet and yellow legs. Yellow-legged Gulls live in and around the Mediterranean Sea, although, for whatever reason, there's been a tradition of a wintering individual or two visiting Newfoundland. A better name for the bird would be Mediterranean Gull, if that weren't already taken.

Jared Clarke, a local birder and guide, had given me a list of local gull spots to check. I spent the day driving between the golf course (empty), the narrow Quidi Vidi Lake at the east end of town (mostly full of creamy-white Iceland Gulls), and the city roofs (packed full of loafing Herring Gulls). With its darker back and whiter head than the Herrings, you'd think my target bird would be easy to find. It wasn't. At best, I could see only half the gulls available. Some were on the other side of the roofs, others were hidden behind other gulls, and many were lazily dozing, their heads tucked into their backs. Depending on the direction of the sun, and the angle at which the birds sat, the gray backs and wings could cover the entire spectrum from white through black. As I began slowly scanning the flocks, some of those I'd scanned would take flight, replaced by others I had yet to scan. I could think of few birding experiences more frustrating. I realized this might take longer than the one day I had allocated to finding it.

I started to become superstitious. There was one apartment building near Quidi Vidi Lake whose roof was covered by about fifty gulls. I couldn't drive past it without being convinced the gull was there, even if I'd just checked it ten minutes before. Each time I would pull over, pull out my scope, and confirm the absence of any Yellow-legged Gulls. I must have known that the roof wasn't flat, as the birds were conveniently arrayed on the pitched surface, but it wasn't until later that day when a gull walked over the top of that same roof that it occurred to me there must be another side to it.

I drove up Kenna's Hill, behind the building, and found a parking lot. As predicted, the other side of the roof was covered in gulls. I raised my binoculars to my eyes, and the first bird I spotted had a bright-white head and a back noticeably darker than that of the surrounding Herring Gulls. And it had yellow legs. This was the bird! I ran back to the car to get my scope, relief flooding through my tired body, and while unfurling the legs of the tripod, I heard the screaming of gulls laughing above my head. I looked back at the roof, which was now empty. I watched the flock circle and waited with a trembling heart for it to return to the roof. It didn't. Instead, they gained altitude and drifted off toward the harbor, where they would presumably spend the night. I was left to reflect on my incredible mix of luck—in finding the bird, and then immediately losing it!

"Sounds like your classic Yellow-legged Gull," said Jared Clarke later that evening.

I was sitting in his kitchen with a beer in my hand. I'd seen enough of the bird to count it, but not enough to feel very happy. I was leaving the next morning, going back to Halifax to start the long drive home, and I would have to live with this one brief snapshot. (Jay would follow in my footsteps two weeks later and enjoy much better views of the gull skinny-dipping in Quidi Vidi Lake.)

The Pink-footed Goose I'd missed in Bonavista turned up in Nova Scotia on my route home. I watched in a light drizzling rain as a flock of Canada Geese alit onto a muddy riverbed in Truro. One of them was smaller and browner and had pink feet. The hours I'd spent perambulating that duck pond had earned me some kind of karma. Whether this was the same lost bird or not, my wildgoose chase for the year was over.

Almost a thousand miles to the west, Jay Lehman was about to see a Little Gull on the shores of Lake Erie, in his home state of Ohio. It would be his 700th species for the year and provide the 700 Club with an even newer member, its fourteenth. Unlike my serendipitous entry into the race, Jay had spent his life planning this one year. I had felt like something of a fraud getting to 700 without him. He'd birded as hard as I had, and had dealt with issues that almost derailed his year. The sense of relief I felt at the news was as palpable as the joy. Now, we'd both done it.

"Okay, now that you got Yellow-legged Gull, I'm getting more interested in your year."

It had taken ten months, two weeks, and 735 species, but funny boy John Puschock was finally interested in my Big Year. He'd even mapped out how it would end.

"You get Rufous-backed Robin, Sagebrush Sparrow, and then Whooping Crane, McKay's Bunting, Great Skua . . . American Flamingo, and Ivory Gull. Whooper Swan, maybe

Whiskered Auklet if you get really crazy. And Hook-billed Kite. Get all those and you're at 746."

It sounded so simple. The first two I would get the following day in Arizona (Sagebrush Sparrow was the result of a recent split of Sage Sparrow into Sagebrush and Bell's). Whooping Crane should, admittedly, be easy in their wintering grounds in coastal Texas in December. But the rest were species that many birders had never seen in their entire lives—McKay's Bunting in coastal western Alaska; Whooper Swan and Whiskered Auklet on the island of Adak in the central Aleutians. Even John, who'd been to Alaska many times, hadn't seen a Whooper Swan, except for an escaped bird in Pennsylvania in 1993 about which he'd correctly noted, "You can't count that shit." Great Skua was in the Atlantic Ocean if I could get out there. I'd already missed the Hook-billed Kite in Texas, and there was an American Flamingo in Florida, but I couldn't find anyone with a boat to take me out there. Even if I could see all that, then I was still two birds short, with only six weeks left. I would end up in second place, ahead of John Vanderpoel, but Sandy's record would end up defying yet another birder.

That was November 20. Three days later I received an e-mail from Dave Sonneborn in Anchorage about a credible report of a Dusky Thrush, an Asian variety of our American Robin. It had wintered in the city the previous two winters and was back for another. And the next day, another e-mail from John: "Four swans seen yesterday at Adak."

I didn't want to go to Adak. I wanted to stay home and try to enjoy a holiday that I still didn't really understand and make amends for missing Gerri's second-ever trip to the UK. Thankfully, Gerri seemed to care about Thanksgiving only marginally more than I did, so if I wanted to go, she said I could. I wasn't sure she'd say the same about Christmas, which, at this rate, I was also expecting to miss, but I wisely decided to keep that expectation to myself.

You'd think I'd be excited about new birds, especially bonus birds like Dusky Thrush, which weren't on mine or John Puschock's expected list. But I wasn't. My heart sank as I heard these reports, imagining first the pain of chasing and missing them. They were rays of hope, moving me closer to the end, but I knew that some of them were false leads, luring me to disappointment and failure. Like many of the boondoggles I'd been on during the year, the fear of future regret of not trying was stronger than the desire to go. It didn't help that they were in Alaska, in winter. But with four possible birds there—Dusky Thrush (Anchorage), McKay's Bunting (Nome), and Whooper Swan and Whiskered Auklet (both on Adak)—none of which I could see anywhere else, I knew I'd regret not making one last trip north to the forty-ninth state.

As with Dave Porter, John had to ask permission for the birding trip, although he had the good sense not to call his wife "the Warden" or anything else quite as incendiary. Over the next few days a plan came together. John advertised an Adak swan trip and got bites from Jay and Bill Sain, a birder from Texas whom I had yet to meet. We would fly out from Anchorage on December 5 on the twice-weekly service to the Aleutian island. Meanwhile, I would go to Alaska a week ahead to look for the Dusky Thrush and the McKay's Buntings.

By the end of the year, I would later calculate, I'd be on a plane every three and a half days, and that's exactly where I spent Thanksgiving. Like Independence Day, it's hard for me to know what to do with these strange new holidays, stripped of meaning by growing up someplace else. I still missed the old, familiar ones—Guy Fawkes Night, Boxing Day, and all those equally confusing bank holidays. I felt like I was in some nether zone, no longer British nor American, despite the dual documentation. Perhaps it was better, then, that I was thirty-five thousand feet above it all, sucking down two Alaska Airlines signature cheese plates.

As it turned out, the next day proved to be the day for giving thanks: I saw the Dusky Thrush with Dave Sonneborn. The bright white eyebrow and rusty red wings made it jump out from the flock of American Robins that were scouring his neighborhood looking for food. The dark breast and flank feathers were edged in white, creating perfect rows of chevrons. It should be wintering with its kin in Japan or southeast Asia. It was probably that first fall migration that went wrong, leaving Siberia on the wrong heading, or getting sucked into the wind tunnel of a storm and spat out here. It was stuck here now. I imagined it spending the summers in the Alaskan wilderness, perhaps impressing the local female robins with its jazzy plumage, before flying to Anchorage for a winter of berry picking with its new friends.

I sat down that evening to a perfect meal of holiday leftovers with Dave and his family. I'd added a surprise new bird

for the year (number 738) and a pair of thick rubber Muck
Boots from a trip to Costco, and enjoyed once more the kindness of new birding friends. The yard outside sparkled with
newly laid snow.

I felt like a private investigator tracking down a missing
person. I handed Mr. Kab (probably not his real name) a
scrunched-up piece of paper on which was penciled the words
"Icy View subdivision." It was the only address I had for the
McKay's Bunting, and I was hoping they hadn't skipped
town yet.

Icy View subdivision turned out to be an appropriate name
for the bleak and isolated suburb of Nome where Mr. Kab
dropped me off. Without a working phone and with no
passing cabs, I knew I'd be walking the two miles back to
town on my own. The landscape that was once springy tundra
was now shrouded in white snow. It was deafeningly quiet.
The gray shards of cloud moved menacingly above me and I
started to shiver.

Most birders are familiar with the Snow Bunting, a white-
and-black bird the size of a sparrow that winters on either side
of the Canadian–Lower 48 border. The McKay's is an even
whiter version of that bird, a ghost in the snow. It breeds on
only two islands: St. Matthew and the neighboring Hall
Island, roughly equidistant between Gambell and St. Paul.
Unless you have a boat to explore the Bering Sea, or have
been lucky enough to catch one on migration at Gambell or
St. Paul, the only chance of seeing this bird is to find it on its
wintering grounds, on the west coast of Alaska.

I walked the streets of the subdivision looking for birds and for the feeders that might attract them. The street signs suggested that someone had taken the time to add a little romance to the place: Out of the Way Road, Teakettle Drive, Round the Clock Road. The houses, most of them two stories and clad in horizontal strips of vinyl, seemed new, well kept, and empty. Only a few lights—beacons, I imagined, from warm, toasty kitchens—suggested that anyone might live here. There were fewer birds than humans. After two circuits of the streets, I came up empty. It started to snow.

Economists like to talk about sunk costs and how that makes people irrational. Was I being irrational, I wondered, coming to this wintry wasteland? McKay's Bunting was one of those birds in the field guide that, for most of us, didn't really exist, because no one goes to Nome in the winter. Was I throwing good money after bad? The uncertainty of the Big Year was starting to eat at me. Would there by some miracle be enough birds to make it to the record? To keep going, I had to pretend there were, like I had to pretend there was a future with Gerri in order to keep cranking open my heart, all the time risking disappointment and failure.

I was into my third hour when I saw them—a few tiny seed husks that littered a front yard. Someone had been feeding the birds, but it looked like the seed had long since run out. I kept vigil across the street in case any curious and forgetful birds might come back. They didn't, but after half an hour a car did. It was the homeowner with his two kids, and judging from their expressions, they were a little surprised to find a telescope pointed at their house.

"Hi! You looking for the snowbirds?" the guy shouted, as he stepped out of the car.

"Yes," I said supposing the snowbirds would be the white birds for which I was looking.

"Well, they were here last week," he said. "The yard was full of them!"

I was too late. I'd rather they hadn't been here than to have my imagination populated with snow-white buntings close enough to almost touch. My disappointment played out across my face. He asked where I'd come from.

"Boston," I said.

"Wait here," he offered. "I think I have some more seed in the garage."

He disappeared into the house, followed by his two young kids. The latter soon reappeared at the front bedroom window, surveying the curious stranger who'd crossed the continent to look at their yard. A few minutes later the guy was dumping a bag of thistle seed over the snow. He wished me luck before disappearing inside.

The birds started to arrive within five minutes. I still have no idea how they did it, how these previously invisible birds knew about the seed. But however the magic worked, I was grateful that it did. The Snow Buntings were the first to appear. And then, through the white curtain of snowflakes, the real snowbirds showed up—McKay's Buntings, ghostly white except for light strokes of black brushed onto the tips of the wings and a pale rusty wash over the head.

I spent an hour watching the birds feed. They'd lift off whenever a car threatened their peace, describing large circles in the frigid air, before returning, dropping in like large snowflakes. They were mesmerizing. From deep within a balaclava and thick woolen hat, I could just make our their high tinkling calls, like the distant ringing of reindeer bells. As with every experience this year, I knew the risk of failure had been worth it. The birds were the bait, pulling me forward to sample one new experience after another.

I walked back into town along the deserted Teller Road, the Costco boots saving me from the frozen-blubber feet I'd endured in Barrow. It was the same road on which I'd driven with Hans and Abe five months before, on which we'd watched parachuting Bluethroats and White Wagtails. I'd had so much fun on that trip. The colors were so rich, the breeding birds were brighter than any I'd ever seen, and the grays of depression were starting to blow away, as if Aeolus himself were in those tiny pills. It was sometime back then that Hans had first joked about the Big Year record. It seemed fitting that I'd come back here to Nome to chase it.

I left Nome on November 30 with 739 birds, fewer than ten birds from Sandy's 1998 record of 748. (I was actually at 741 if both the provisional species—the Rufous-necked Wood-Rail and the Common Redstart—were accepted.) It was a curiously bittersweet feeling; with the intensity and excitement increasing as the finish line approached, so too did the realization that this would be the end. In one month it would all be over. The birds would still be there, of course, as would Gerri, I hoped, if her UK wedding trip didn't help her to put all this into an unfavorable perspective. But the short-term goals would not. Instead, the vast unknown void of the future would open up in front of me. I wondered what that life would be like without chasing snowbirds at the edge of the world.

My bird count at the end of November 2013: 739 (+2 provisional)
John Vanderpoel's bird count at the end of November 2011: 734
Sandy Komito's Big Year record, 1998: 748

Chapter 12

SWAN SONG

I WATCHED THE SHOWER curtain flap lazily in the Aleutian breeze as goose bumps popped up like miniature bubble wrap around my arms. The sides of the house, along with those of many of its neighbors, had been sucked off, exposing boxlike rooms and staircases, as if it were a giant dollhouse. Inside, the furnishings—tables, mirrors, sinks, toilets, and swinging light fixtures—suggested a life before the zombie apocalypse. I'd already seen the emptied municipal buildings that had once housed movie theaters, bowling alleys, and swimming pools. It was a ghost town but one recent enough to feel like there might be survivors. If there were, though, they weren't eating fast food. A McDonald's restaurant stood shuttered behind me, its last Happy Meal long since served.

I'd landed in Adak that afternoon. The flight from Anchorage was one of the most spectacular of the year. After leaving the city on a southwest heading, I watched the mountainous tundra slide below me before it disappeared under Bristol Bay. On my left, to the south, the Alaskan peninsula stepped out alongside me for a few hundred miles, before it, too, gave up, plunging into the cold and frothy water. Beyond that, islands started to claw their way out of the sea, as if gasping for breath. The Aleutian Islands, of which Adak sits in the center, march like stepping stones from the Alaskan mainland to the Russian peninsula of Kamchatka, some 1,200 miles to the west. They are battered on one side by the Bering Sea and on the other by the Pacific Ocean. According to the native Aleuts, this is where the sea breaks its back.

I was on the plane with John Puschock, Jay Lehman, and Bill Sain. I'd met Bill earlier that day in Anchorage when we'd shopped for groceries for our four-day Aleutian trip. With a round and ruddy bespectacled face, covered by a thin white beard, Bill reminded me of Richard Attenborough. I half worried whether Adak might not be some prehistoric cloning site, although an Archaeopteryx would be a major coup for any Big Year. Bill was retired from the Air Force and lived in Alpine, Texas, a small town through which I'd driven this year on my way in and out of Big Bend. The rest of the passenger list was made up of camouflaged men. I'd seen their gun cases at the airport. If Adak has a tourist industry, it's caribou. Dead caribou.

John sat in the row behind me and played tour guide, pointing out each island that slowly passed by: Unalaska, Umnak, Atka, Great Sitka. Volcanoes, covered in snow, reflected the afternoon light like giant golden pyramids. As the plane dipped its nose for the final approach to Adak, I looked down on the abandoned town below and thought of its role in a largely forgotten war. When the Japanese seized the Aleutian islands of Kiska and Attu on June 6 and 7, 1942, an alarmed US Army established a base here on Adak from which to launch bombing raids. The Japanese occupation lasted almost a year, ending with a suicidal banzai attack by the Japanese at Attu. For a pair of small, rocky islands in the middle of nowhere, the casualties were horrific. Many of the men who survived enemy fire succumbed to the brutal frostbite conditions. After the war, Adak was developed as a naval base to counter a new threat: the Soviets. The population, more than six thousand, lived under the blue, crimson, and wine-colored roofs that lined the streets below me. When the cold war petered out, so, too, did the US military commitment. Today, fewer than than one hundred people call Adak home. What the military didn't erase, the brutal Aleutian weather soon will.

I stepped down onto the tarmac after a bumpy landing. A brisk cross breeze bothered my jacket and tugged at the already heavy bags. I closed my eyes and inhaled deeply. It smelled of St. Paul, that same damp, cloying scent of brine, vegetation, and mystery. But here, mountains and volcanoes crammed the horizon. Above, icy clouds raced across a cobalt sky backlit by gold. It was beautiful—the kind of beauty that doesn't give a damn what you think.

There are sixteen miles of road, mostly gravel, radiating north, south, and west from the town of Adak (the east is bordered by the harbor and Kuluk Bay). After picking up the rental car from a local woman named Cynthia, we spent what was left of the golden light bumping over some of those gravel roads hoping to spot our quarry, the Whooper Swans. As we'd flown in, I noticed the island was pockmarked with lakes—some the size of small ponds, others huge lakes of snowmelt. My heart had sunk. I knew then that, despite the size of the birds, there was a good chance we wouldn't find them. As we passed through fields of golden-brown putchkie and dying tundra, we found each pool still and empty.

We spent the evening at the local Mexican restaurant, which, given the lack of street lighting, was almost as hard to find as the elusive swans. We were the only customers. A photograph taken of us, shortly after destroying a meal of enchiladas and burritos, shows us lined up against the grill. We look like rugged explorers conquering a remote part of the world (albeit one that stocked bottles of Alaskan Amber and Dos Equis). Despite coming up short in our cursory search for swans that evening, we look optimistic. As the only birders on the island, we have no idea what our little expedition will find.

"We'll try Haven Lake next," John said the following after-noon, juggling the steering wheel and the optimism. "They've had swans there in the past."

I would have been more excited if John hadn't said the same thing about every other swan-less lake we'd checked. It wasn't just the lakes that were empty of birds. So, too, were the trees. But then maybe the birds hadn't got used to them yet; there weren't supposed to be any trees here. In an attempt to cheer up his troops during World War II, General Simon B. Buckner had planted some pine trees.

We found a tight tangle of Sitka spruces that looked like thirty trees had been compressed into the size of one. The diminutive size of the grove was reflected by the accompanying sign, which proudly proclaimed YOU ARE NOW ENTERING AND LEAVING THE ADAK NATIONAL FOREST! I followed John's instructions and hung another bird feeder, just like I'd done near the (boatless) harbor and in one of those zombie apocalypse culs-de-sac. I wasn't sure how this would attract any swans, but I didn't want to question John's expertise.

There was Big Year history here too, although it had failed to leave any trace on the landscape. John Vanderpoel had never expected to break 700 species either. When he did, he realized that he suddenly had a shot at the record. He spent the summer and fall of 2011 in full chase mode. When the calendar flipped to the final page, he'd seen 734 species, which he suspected (correctly) wasn't going to be enough. He came to Adak, as far west as he could fly, to find more birds before his time ran out. He arrived just before a snowstorm blanketed the island, limiting exploration to an ATV. He never did find any swans, and when the twice-weekly Alaska Airlines flight was canceled, he was stranded for another three days. He added one new species to his Big Year (Whiskered Auklet), but it had cost him over a week.

It's hard to appreciate someone else's insanity until you're faced with the same uncomfortable choices. I hadn't wanted to come here. But like John, I was too close to the record to not come, and too far to rely on anything else showing up closer to home. Apparently there wasn't much left of the slippery slope down which I'd been sliding all year. I felt like I was surrendering to the winds, just like the vagrant birds I was chasing.

We bumped over a small hill, and the tundra was transformed into a large oval mirror, reflecting the busy Aleutian skies above. The vehicle immediately exploded with shouting and swearing as a day of built-up tension was released like a cork from a bottle of champagne. It was lucky the swans couldn't hear us. There were three of them: a gleaming white adult and two gray young birds. Through my binoculars I could make out the large, Roman-nosed black bill, covered almost entirely in psychedelic yellow. The adult looked wary and kept the two young birds close. I remembered that the original sighting included a fourth bird and tried not to imagine its almost certain and tragic end. It was a life bird for all of us, except Jay. He'd seen one in 2004 in the hot springs of Yellowstone after renting a snowmobile to track it down.

We celebrated that night with beer and burgers at the Aleutian Sports Bar and Grill, affectionately known as the ASBAG. As with the Mexican place, it was hidden in the curfew of darkness that descends over the town at night. The bar was half full of what I assumed were locals. I wondered what it must be like to live here, rattling around in an empty city.

The thrill and relief of finding the swans took the pressure off the rest of our trip. Our living quarters—an attached bungalow—were surprisingly comfortable. John used the kitchen to whip up delicious fajitas. I think his domesticity embarrassed him a little; he was more comfortable as the quirky, funny guy, despite being more than capable at all the logistical aspects of running a birding tour.

After dinner we'd chat or read in the comfy chairs of the living room. I could tell Jay was tired. His marathon year had turned into a sprint for the finish line. He'd seen 51 birds since I'd last seen him, and the swans had raised his total to 710. After Adak, I knew he had grouse to flush and buntings to chase before the shock of waking up on January 1 with nothing to do. It was a date that we both quietly feared.

I would sometimes look up from my book (I was reading about Vitus Bering's expedition to the Aleutians) to find Jay asleep, hunched over in his chair with a laptop or book dangling from his fingers. Jay was thirty years older than me, and I almost never noticed the age difference.

When you're young, it's impossible to grasp the magnitude of a human life, so big and yet so finite. My twenties had burned far too quickly, consumed with the wild hopes and aspirations of a generation that thinks itself immortal. I suppose it's like that for everyone, madly rushing around, full of energy but lacking the experience to use it wisely. After that, there would be a lifetime to puzzle over where it had all gone. I was a few weeks away from my fortieth birthday. I was halfway through life and yet still didn't feel much like a responsible adult. But I wondered if that might not be the unspoken secret of life—that none of us ever do feel like adults. Maybe we're all just chasing swans and making up the rest as we go along.

The plane for our return flight never made it to Adak. It turned around because of mechanical issues shortly after leaving Anchorage. But there were worse places to be stuck, I thought. This wasn't the swanless snowstorm in which Vanderpoel had been stranded. We'd seen the Whiskered Auklet, distant specks of black and white diving in the ice-cold waters of Kuluk Bay. And the previous day we found what we thought was a first for North America.

At first I'd thought that the accelerator had broken. I was slammed back into my seat, my stomach left several feet behind my body as the car raced forward. We'd been approaching the old Naval Air Station Administration building, a crumbling edifice outside which we'd hung one of our feeders. I wondered if John had suffered a massive burger-induced coronary, courtesy of the ASBAG. It took less than ten seconds for us to reach the feeder, by which time John, whose cardiovascular system was apparently working fine, had explained the situation with calm, military precision: he'd seen an accipiter (small hawk) fly into the feeder; there were no historical reports of accipiters here; and the most likely possibility would be a Eurasian Sparrowhawk, a bird that wasn't on the ABA list.

We jumped out of the car the minute John stepped on the brakes, and watched as a long-tailed hawk flew out from the building. In its talons wriggled one of the Gray-crowned Rosy-Finches that we'd been feeding over the past two days. The thrill was captured by the violent bursts of camera shutters exploding in both my ears. I tracked the bird in my binoculars until it disappeared behind a warehouse. Despite flushing the hawk again, and losing it high over the quarry, and then flushing it the next day at another feeder, we never got better photos than the backlit silhouettes John and Jay had first captured.

We left Adak the next day. The plane was fixed (or replaced with one that worked) and our flight rescheduled. I half wished we could stay longer and get better looks at the hawk. I was feeling confident in our identification—I'd seen the brown upper parts and the barring underneath that I thought at least ruled out the American accipiters. But I knew we probably didn't have enough to convince the Alaska Checklist Committee. I reflected on our bad luck—it was probably the worst type of bird that we could find. There are hawks on both sides of the Bering Sea that look extremely similar. It reminded me of a bird Bob Ake had found at Gambell in his 2010 Big Year. The dull-looking brown bird, with a broom handle for a bill, was a Blyth's Reed-Warbler—at least, that's what all the experts had said. But it hadn't been accepted by the Alaska Checklist Committee because Ake and other birders hadn't caught and measured the bird, the only definitive way to categorically prove the bird's identification.

I climbed the metal steps to the waiting Boeing 737-400. I paused at the top, turned around, and took a mental snapshot of the horizon. It would be filed with all those other images that would no longer make Adak just an exotic imaginary name. I was glad I'd come to chase the swans and I was sad to leave.

"I don't know. They all look the same to me," I said. We'd spent half an hour here, which was already half an hour more than I'd wanted to.

The Christmas-tree section of Home Depot in Watertown, Massachusetts, marked my return to normal life. Not only did it dwarf the national forest of Adak, but also it had more birds (House Sparrows)—and, as during the rest of the year, I couldn't keep my eyes off them in case one of them might be something else. The tundra and mountains of Alaska already felt ephemeral, the sharply focused memories were fading to a blur. It seemed unreal that a few days before I'd been watching Emperor Geese bathing in the waters of Clam Lagoon with the snowy cap of a volcano as the only high-rise.

"What about the one on the left?" asked Gerri.

"Looks like another House Sparrow to me," I said and then realized she wasn't talking about the birds. "Oh, you mean the tree. Yeah. Looks perfect!"

I drove home, trying my best to avoid decapitation by the green string that held the seven-foot balsam fir to the roof of the car. Gerri was excited about Christmas—choosing the tree, unwrapping last year's decorations, and shopping for new ones. I smiled at the reverence that she placed in arranging the lights, poking in the long glittery firebrands, and hanging each bauble that would soon be pawed and batted by wide-eyed cats. This year there were new decorations. Gerri had bought souvenirs of my Big Year: a Red-headed Woodpecker, a bird we'd seen by the Museum of Fine Arts back in January, a polar bear, and a porcupine (I'd seen one in Minnesota while looking for Golden-winged Warblers), although I'm pretty sure the ornament was supposed to be a hedgehog. I had to admit that the whole ensemble looked magical.

I watched as Gerri pulled various pieces of clothing from the closet, held them up to the light, and mentally graded them. If they passed, they were bundled up into her small suitcase, along with a dress that she'd bought for the wedding and a few gifts for Georgina and her kids, whom she would also visit.

It was an odd moment of panic for me, as I saw her bags sitting by the front door. I could feel my chest pounding, as it had in Adak when John had stamped on the accelerator. I knew she'd be back in four days, but I felt helpless and alone. We'd been separated so often this year, and I'd thought nothing of leaving for days or weeks at a time. It was only now that I could see there was a difference between going and staying behind.

For the whole year I'd known what to do next, guided by the empty boxes on the ABA Checklist. Now, I had nowhere to go. There was nothing in the ABA Area that I hadn't seen, and I was reliant on something new turning up. After returning from Adak, nothing had. I was five birds behind the record, but it might as well have been fifty. I knew that I'd run out of not only birds, but also time.

Part of me wanted the whole thing to be over. While the New Year scared me, I couldn't seem to make any plans while my head was full of Big Year numbers and rare birds. And I was still blinded by hope. Perhaps after the unknown was known, it would be easier to think of the future, although I had no idea what those future plans could possibly be.

I drove Gerri to the airport, kissed and hugged her as usual, but then I got back into the car. I watched long after she'd disappeared behind those familiar sliding glass doors. I wondered how she'd coped with all my trips—hearing me talk about the next bird that suddenly trumped everything else in our lives. It must have seemed like I always wanted to be somewhere else. I didn't—I just wanted both. I drove home while Khiva Cat sat and stared out the back window.

The house was quiet and lonely. I wondered if I'd made the right decision. What if there were no more birds out there? What if my Big Year was already over and I didn't know it? Maybe I should have gone with her, I thought. But I didn't have to wait long before I knew the answer, courtesy of John Puschock.

"Little Bunting. Northern California."

The news felt like a drug. The calmness of the planning—checking flights and juggling airport codes—kicked in immediately as the sense of purpose returned. The tension and restlessness were gone. I was back in the race, and it helped me not to think about Gerri and how I missed her in a way I never had before.

I landed in Oakland at midnight the next day. I skirted over the bay on the Richmond–San Rafael Bridge, whose dips and climbs make it feel like a gentle roller coaster. I was headed north toward McKinleyville, a small town on the coast just beyond Eureka. I passed through Marin, Sonoma, and Mendocino counties, which all looked the same in the dark, until I crossed into Humboldt County, and the redwoods sucked whatever light was reflected off the moon. The trunks stood on the very edge of the road, as if in defiance of the thin strip of tarmac that had recently divided this ancient forest. I weaved through the tight bends and was thankful to emerge safely back into the waxing gibbous moonlight.

The pastures of Northern California reminded me of those in England, although the morning fog was perhaps a little heavier. I watched the cows as they methodically converted the greenery into milk or meat, assiduously avoiding the armor-clad spikes of the giant thistles. But my mind was already elsewhere—in Florida. A quick fifteen-minute rest stop at three A.M. had turned into a two-and-a-half-hour miserable slumber, and an early-morning coffee was prolonged by exciting news from the Sunshine State: a La Sagra's Flycatcher had been found south of Miami, and the White-cheeked Pintail, which I'd missed twice in the spring, had been reported again at Pelican Island National Wildlife Refuge. Suddenly, the record wasn't looking so remote.

By the time I arrived in McKinleyville, the farm road was jammed with cars and birders. A strong whiff of manure hit me as I stepped out of the car, and above the chatter of the birders I could hear the distant honking of geese. The ground was hopping with sparrows, but there was only one bird on which a line of twenty or so birders was focused. I followed their collective gaze to a small bird that at first glance looked like just another sparrow. But this one had a face the color of burned toffee. Small black eyes, like the tiniest of beads, were encircled by a pair of bright-white monocles. Like many Eurasian buntings, the tail was edged in white, which it would flash each time it flitted between thistles and fences, accompanied by an explosive tsik! I followed the bird in my binoculars as my heart thudded in delight like a galloping horse.

I wanted to stay longer. The bird somehow knew it was the center of attention and was putting on a show, flirting with the birders and photographers. I felt guilty for coming so far and spending only a few minutes. It felt like a lack of respect to the bird, like walking out halfway through a concert or a movie. But I also wanted to catch the last flight out to Florida, where I hoped two birds were waiting for me. I retraced my route back to Oakland. The daylight replaced the mystery of the night with the mundane, except for the redwoods. I could see perhaps fifty feet into the woods before the trunks dissolved into a black hole of darkness.

Driving gives you lots of time to think, which sometimes isn't a good thing. None of the radio stations, nor the smiling photos that Gerri was sending back from the wedding, could distract me from the awkwardness of the situation in which I'd suddenly found myself. The Little Bunting had tied me with John Vanderpoel (and that didn't include the recent Sparrowhawk and the other two provisional species). I was now exactly where I did and did not want to be: with only one target left—the Big Year record. Only four birds now separated Sandy Komito and me.

It would have been better to miss by ten birds, I thought, than by one or two. I knew where I could have made up that deficit of a few species if I'd been paying attention earlier in the year—the Spotted Redshank in Indiana or the Citrine Wagtail in Vancouver. And like John, I'd made mistakes. I should have spent longer in the lonely outposts of western Alaska. And I discovered too late that birders were now boarding cruise ships in the Pacific, where the cheesy entertainment was in the form of deepwater gadfly petrels seldom seen on coastal pelagics. I knew these thoughts would haunt me. The closer I got to the record, the greater the regret would be.

It's dangerous to dream. Perhaps it's my British defense mechanism of always expecting the worst so that you'll never be disappointed. When other people started thinking I had a shot at the record, I forced myself not to listen. I was scared of wanting something so badly and then missing it. Besides, I didn't need a record to tell me whether the year had been a success.

But now, I could barely contain my antsy excitement. There were just over two weeks left in the year, and four birds didn't seem so impossible now. And so I rather reluctantly joined the Big Year–record bandwagon. If you never think anything good will happen, it might mean you'll never be disappointed, but it also means you never dream. And if you never dream, those dreams (however stupid, insignificant, and embarrassing) won't come true.

The next morning I stood at a mangrove-fringed pool at Matheson Hammock Park, a few miles south of Miami. A light breeze flicked at the tops of the distant Australian pines. I was hidden on a side trail, in a tunnel of dark trees, the type of place, public yet not public, where I imagined drug deals went down. But the only illicit activity this morning was a scruffy-looking guy in a trench coat sprinkling handfuls of Friskies for the population of feral cats. Somewhere behind me, in the open spaces of the park, I could hear the soft, methodical thudding of the normals out jogging.

The secretive La Sagra's Flycatcher appeared shortly after me, calling—*wink! wink!*—before nervously emerging from the mangroves. It reminded me of my first rarity of the year, the Nutting's Flycatcher. They're both members of the Myiarchus family—large flycatchers with long tails, brown backs rising to a crest at the rear of the head, and grayish breasts. The faded yellow of the Nutting's belly is replaced by a fine gray on the La Sagra's, and the rising *wheep!* of the Nutting's by an explosive and high-pitched *wink!* Otherwise they were near-identical bookends to my year. Both had been out of their normal range (the Nutting's from Mexico and the La Sagra's from Cuba or the Bahamas), and both were either lost or pioneering new territory.

I'd come to find these lost birds to feel less lost myself. Knowing that they existed, seeing something else navigate the confusion of being someplace new, somehow made me feel better about being lost myself. Perhaps I was pioneering new territory too, or feeling more at ease in the new world of middle age and second chances.

The White-cheeked Pintail predictably broke my streak of good luck. I walked around the trails at Pelican Island National Wildlife Refuge as the sun slowly crossed the sky, seeing every other type of duck except for the one from the Bahamas that I wanted. The sun eventually set with a fanfare, and the sky filled with colors, as if it had been refracted through a prism. The duck had beaten me again and reminded me that somewhere out there I still had a nemesis.

A text message came through at three A.M. My heart immediately started to thump violently as I imagined all sorts of bad news: My parents? The cats? A European Hoopoe in my yard?

But it wasn't bad news. It was Aaron Lang and it was an emergency of the Rustic Bunting kind.

I turned on the light and greedily read about a streaky rusty-chestnut bird that was visiting a yard in Homer, Alaska, Aaron's hometown. Alaska, I thought. Would I really be going back again before the end of the year? But I already knew the answer. The flight was booked before I could talk myself out of it. I would be going back to Alaska for the eighth time this year. During Gerri's four days in the UK, I would have touched the four corners of the United States— from Massachusetts to California, Florida, and then Alaska. It wasn't just Jay, I realized. We were both sprinting to the finish line.

I wondered whether it was too early to take one of the small white pills that I was still swallowing every morning. The pills made me drowsy, and I couldn't sleep. The trip to Alaska was keeping me awake like a child on Christmas Eve.

I was surprised how such a routine procedure could be so difficult to follow. It wasn't just the travel this year, waking up in new places every few days, and the forever-shifting time zones throwing me off the schedule. Taking pills was so mundane that I could never tell whether my most recent pill was that morning or the previous morning or even last week. They all fused into the same memory. I came up with bizarre rituals—like jumping around on one foot or doing different bird noises (Mangrove Cuckoo was a favorite—*mwaaaaah, mwaaaaah, mwaaaaah* . . .) to make the memory stick. It was ironic that the medication regimen was as monotonous and unvarying as the symptoms it was supposed to be abating.

The pills hadn't changed me. That had been my biggest fear when handed that first prescription, that I'd be happy but different. But I still felt like the same person. I realized now, lying awake in bed, how that was almost worse. How was it that I could be the same person and experience extremes, sliding between depression and optimism, and yet not really be able to tell the difference? I suppose that's the problem with the brain: it might be the most amazing computational organ, interpreting a huge set of data and innumerable stimulations, but it's not very good at knowing when it's broken (or when, for example, to apologize and be the bigger person). It's like never knowing whether the color green that you see is the same as the green that everyone else sees.

Whatever my color of green is, there's certainly a lot more of it now than there was a year ago. It still shocks me that it took so long for me to see that my colorful world had faded to gray. The mood and the mood-o-meter lobes of my brain were both broken. I'd guessed that there was something wrong, but for a long time I didn't believe it. It was true only when I was forced to listen to my own words describing it to the psychiatrist: I'd messed up my one chance for happiness and success. There was nothing to look forward to, and there was no joy. I was going through the motions of living a life where the only goal was scratching another day from the calendar.

I didn't feel like that anymore, although I still worried about the future, and I wasn't cured of dwelling on the past. But time had slowed down somehow, and reduced the panic that went with it, either because I was creating complicated memories or because I wasn't letting it slip away while I lived in the past. And somehow, I was being given a second chance at a relationship—to do all the things I should have done the first time. I'd seen both sides now, and however daunting making a commitment was, I knew that the alternative was worse.

I'd read somewhere that one of the secrets to happiness is setting goals for yourself. Chasing birds might be one of the best happiness projects around. I wondered what would happen at the end of the year, when those goals would disappear. Would the pills keep me going, I wondered? I didn't know, and to be honest, it did scare me. But I knew that I'd found something in the birds that had helped, some quiet place that would be there long after the manic chases.

Left at Chili's. Down the escalator. Down the next escalator. No time to look at the dead polar bear. Past the musk ox (the one with the Santa hat). Into the tunnel.

I didn't have to read the signs to know where to run before the rental car desk closed for the night. I'd spent more than two months in Alaska this year, and Anchorage airport had become a familiar portal. As we'd pulled into the gate, the pilot had told us that it was snowing outside and the temperature was minus six degrees Fahrenheit.

It takes four hours to drive from Anchorage to Homer, but you can safely double that when you can barely see through the curtains of snow and the bends are lubricated with ice. It reminded me of the trip to Ottawa in March, when I'd sat hunched behind the steering wheel, peering through a tiny hole in the frosted windshield. Gerri had sat next to me then. She'd been asleep but her presence was enough to keep me awake and focused. This time I felt alone and scared. I passed cars buried in the verges of the road, reminders of the danger of letting your concentration slip. Fear, I discovered, is even better than caffeine at keeping me awake.

Occasionally, the snowfall would lighten enough to reveal the two moons: the celestial flashlight above and its twin, dancing in the icy waters of Turnagain Arm. It was impossible not to pull over and stare. I was reminded of something that Janis Cadwallader had said to me in St. Paul: some views can be so beautiful that it hurts to look. She was right. In beauty there is pain, an almost crushing eternal arrogance that reminds you of your own ephemeral mortality.

It was still dark when I pulled into Two Sisters Bakery in Homer. I slumped into a comfy chair with a warm cup of coffee and wrapped my hands around a bowl of steaming oatmeal. The smell of homemade bread and ground coffee beans together with the electric wall colors were intoxicating after my minimalist and lonely drive. The place purred with steaming espresso machines and the quiet hum of conversation. Hipsters sat behind laptops, reading or quietly growing mustaches. I leaned against the pane of a window through which I could see the sky still shimmering a midnight blue.

Aaron Lang arrived with the whitening of the dawn. A coffee container was stuck in one palm, the steering wheel of his truck in the other. A characteristic happy-to-be-alive grin was plastered across his face, which was immediately mirrored on my own. I was happy to see him. As we drove through

town, it was hard to believe it was the same place I'd visited in
June, waiting then for the volcano to stop spewing into the
Bering Sea.

Aaron reminded me that this year had been a Big Year for
him too. After guiding in Alaska (and Bhutan) with Wilderness
Birding Adventures for thirteen years, he'd taken over the
business. I hadn't yet met Bob Dittrick, who founded the
company with his wife, Lisa, but I could see why he trusted
Aaron with his baby. Bob had pioneered one of the most
rugged of birding trips: being dropped by plane into the remote
Brooks Range of northern Alaska, rafting through the thawing
tundra, and then getting picked up by plane downriver. It was
the only reliable way to see the Gray-headed Chickadee, whose
nesting site Bob had found. It was a bird I'd never seen, and the
eight-day trip was too long to fit into this Big Year.

We pulled up outside an attractive teal-colored house. A
wooden deck and railing ran around the second floor, which,
I could see, was where the bird activity seemed to be focused.

"It's here!" shouted a couple of tightly bundled birders
standing on a snowbank that overlooked the yard.

I followed Aaron up the snow and joined the crowd. At first
I could see only Dark-eyed Juncos, which I could also hear *zit-
zitting* around the deck and the nearby trees. And then, out
popped a fatter and slower-moving bird. It seemed comfortable
with the juncos, although it would never have known them
back home in the wide coniferous belt that runs from northern
Scandinavia to the Russian Far East. It leaned forward like the
juncos, hunching over the seed that covered the deck. A slight
crest gave the peak of the head a jagged look, and a dark

triangle filled the area around the ears. Chestnut stripes were painted down the flanks and across the breast. It seemed nervous and a little embarrassed as it hopped from one pile of seed to another. Occasionally, it would follow the juncos into the trees that bordered the yard.

Someone in the crowd asked me what number it was. Number? I thought I'd misheard, until I realized, of course, that they were talking about my Big Year. I'd been so mesmerized by this Asian wonder (a life bird for me) to remember that it was also something else (number 746). And I was happy with that. I was happy that the birds hadn't become commoditized into just numbers, and that in seeing so many I'd never lost the simple joy of watching each one.

There are endless variations of birds. Some, like the toucans, have huge bills, which are packed full of blood vessels and used for heat regulation (by pumping blood in or out of the bill). Others, like the cave-dwelling Oilbirds of South America, use echolocation like bats to "see" in the dark; and yet others, like the Kakapo of New Zealand, a flightless, nocturnal parrot, mate only two or three times a decade. When I think of that explosion of evolutionary invention, I think of Plato's idea of a perfect form. The Greek philosopher thought that all the horses that we see, for example, are imperfect copies of one perfect form, which exists somewhere else (he never did explain where that was, which, arguably, would have made his idea a lot more interesting). We can recognize the concept of "horseness" and know that one horse is superior to another—one with a mane is horsier than one without, and one with four legs trumps one with three legs. I suppose it's like that for birds too. We all have an image of a perfect bird lodged somewhere in our heads. It's a template that allows us to see a copy, however different, and recognize it as a bird.

I still don't know why I'm obsessed with birds. I wonder whether I'm searching for that perfect bird form, or just continually surprised by all the myriad copies that are perfect in their own way, adapted for their own specialized lives. I'd like to think that I get closer to the essence and the mystery of birds the more time I spend with them. But I suspect I'll never really know what I'm looking for and will never know it even if I find it. Perhaps it's like that good book that you read for the journey and not for the ending.

I spent the early hours of my fortieth birthday passing in and out of sleep on a bench in the airport in Portland, Oregon. It wasn't how I'd ever imagined it, but I was happy for the lack of fanfare. After sleeping on so many objects that were never designed for the purpose, it was a comfortable slumber. The padded seats allowed me to fully recline, and the concourse was gloriously free of blasting TVs or cleaning crews.

When you stop counting down the days in excitement, birthdays have a habit of creeping up on you, even the big ones. After years of worrying about the impending doom of a milestone age, this one happened quietly while I was searching for sleep. And as with most things in life, the reality of a difficult transition is often not as great as the fear. In an odd way, I was happy for the chance of a new decade. It could be no more cruel than the previous one. My thirties had developed into some kind of stunted, evolutionary dead end.

Like many people, I suppose, the naïveté and optimism of my youth had been extinguished by the new reality of work and adulthood. When you worry about financial independence, that's when you're most vulnerable. I greedily accepted the salary and the responsibility of a new career, and when I could see that both were markers for success, I wanted more. It didn't seem to matter that the more I accepted, the unhappier I became. As old friends married and moved away (and I moved away too), I realized that the days of making good friends were behind me. I looked to replace that lost happiness with relationships, but found only disappointment and failure.

This year had been the last of my thirties, and it was a big year. I'd seen more of my new homeland than many people who are born here. And so far, I'd seen more species of birds in one year than anyone else except Sandy Komito. But I wondered how much of an outlier the other parts of this year would be. I'd found that you can make friends again, and I'd discovered that just because you've made memories with one person, that doesn't stop you from making new (and better) memories with someone else. I'd also found that there is hope for the second half of a life.

My bags sat packed, as they had been for most of the year, ready for an emergency trip. But the week before Christmas came and went and the bags stayed put. The only birds of interest were those that Gerri was adding to the Christmas tree. I watched as each new decoration (the latest was a Cedar Waxwing) pirouetted clockwise and counterclockwise, as if restlessly trying to escape the twine. I felt like I'd been left dangling too. Because of the provisional species—the three birds that could be new for the ABA Area—I still didn't know whether I'd seen enough birds.

If all three were accepted (a process that could take several years), then I'd end up on 749, one bird ahead of Sandy Komito. The Common Redstart I'd found on St. Paul seemed a slam-dunk, with no questions over the identification or the provenance. But the other two were keeping me awake at night. The Eurasian Sparrowhawk on Adak was a nightmare of identification, which wasn't helped by the quality of our photographs. And while the Rufous-necked Wood-Rail in New Mexico was obviously a Rufous-necked Wood-Rail, was there a chance it might have escaped from captivity? After seeing the freakish bird, I had to wonder why anyone would want such a beast in their collection. New Mexico had hosted another ABA first, at the very same refuge back in 2008: a Sungrebe. It was eight hundred miles from its home, and when the rarities committee accepted it, some birders were skeptical. I hoped the committee hadn't felt burned and wouldn't be more cautious with this bird.

And so unless I could add to my list of 746 species, I could expect to spend the next few years in limbo, waiting for the rulings before discovering whether I'd set a new record, tied one, or just missed one. With only a week left, things weren't looking good on the new-bird front. The White-cheeked Pintail hadn't been reported from Florida again, and there were no reports of Hook-billed Kites. I was hoping the annual Christmas Bird Counts would turn up something. But the century-old holiday pastime, in which Audubon Society clubs across the country simultaneously survey the birds in count circles (with a diameter of fifteen miles), so far had not.

My best chance was looking like another trip offshore. There was still one bird out there—the Great Skua. This European bird, like a giant brown gull, winters in the Atlantic. Some of them reach our offshore waters, where they eke out their living harassing gulls and terns for food. Jay and I had been in touch with Brian Patteson in Hatteras, North Carolina, and were getting closer to planning a trip—one more pelagic for the year.

Christmas Day was a quiet affair, spent playing games, throwing balls of wrapping paper for the cats to fetch, eating caramelized Brussels sprouts, and checking for bird reports every fifteen minutes as if they were life-and-death messages from a loved one. Two thousand miles away, Jay was spending his holiday chasing Gray Partridges near Spokane, Washington. I wished him luck and hoped that they'd be easier to find in the snow-white fields than they had been in the alleyways of Calgary. I remembered how, even ten feet away, these cryptic birds could vanish into their surroundings.

The motel room came with cable TV, a fridge, and complimentary banging on the door in the middle of the night. I reached for my phone to check the time—two thirty A.M.!— and pulled myself out of bed. On the other side of the door was a creature that looked as bedraggled as I imagined I did myself. Jay had just driven the five hours nonstop from Raleigh–Durham International Airport. We exchanged critical information—which was his bed (the one currently with my bags on it), what time we needed to get up (five A.M.), and whether he'd seen Gray Partridges or not (he hadn't). I said goodnight and fell asleep somewhere in the middle of all the unpacking. But one thought registered before I made it there: this would probably be the last time the two of us Big Year birded together. I remembered now that when Gerri had asked me what I wanted for Christmas, I'd more than half wished that the birds and the year would never end.

Brian and Kate were hosing down the boat when we arrived. It was a smaller vessel than they used for the more distant pelagics. The boat was called *Skua*. I hoped that was a good sign. It was the name of the bird we were chasing today as well as the license plate of Sandy Komito, whose record I was also chasing.

The other birders stood nearby, brightly illuminated under a pool of light from the single store on the dock that was open. I already knew Lynne Miller from St. Paul. She'd flown in from Colorado Springs. Great Skua was a life bird for her, but I suspected she was equally excited to see the end of the Big Year. R. Bruce Richardson was a singer-songwriter, artist, philosopher, birder, and seemingly all-round good guy. When he wasn't at home in nearby Manns Harbor, he was probably in Australia, drawn by family, exotic birds, and wanderlust. He wore a pair of oval-framed glasses and a sand-colored cap, out of which snaked a long, gray ponytail. Nate Swick also lived in North Carolina, and, apart from Kate, was the only one of us holding on to his original hair color. Nate had been one of those precocious child birders, seemingly born with an innate ability to identify birds, and I was very happy for the addition of his sharp eyes to the boat.

The sun climbed above the horizon as we turned east around the barrier island and headed for the wintry Atlantic. It was a pelagic desert, barely a bird to be seen. But not for long. As soon as Kate started scooping out the noxious chum, the air started to fill with the raucous calls of gulls. Clearly, the ocean must not be particularly well provisioned for gulls, as the slightest whiff of beef fat not only lured the birds in but also caused fights to break out.

Great Skua is, I think, the only bird named after a Faroese word (the islands, not the misspelled Egyptian). They nest there, on the Faroe Islands, a rocky archipelago belonging to Denmark but closer to Scotland, where they're known as bonxies. But whatever they're called, they're bullies. They are the pirates of the high seas—chasing gulls and terns until they drop or regurgitate their food. I looked at the chum Kate was busy shoveling into the sea and imagined how it must appear after a bit of regurgitation. Maybe that's why skuas look so grumpy. It's a hard life being a gull pirate.

Looking less grumpy was R. Bruce Richardson. While the pit in my stomach grew, as each passing minute meant one less minute in which to find a skua, he provided the lighthearted entertainment. But I could tell that he was nervous too. A Great Skua would be a life bird for him, and each life bird was celebrated with pie. (Given the number of birds the guy had seen, I had to wonder at the sheer volume of pie consumed.) I chatted to him and Lynne as Nate kept scanning the horizon and Jay dozed in the cabin. The anxious wait was periodically broken by sightings of a hammerhead shark and a pair of logger-head turtles, weighed down by a shell stuck with barnacles.

"Skua."

It was so soft that I thought it was my own voice, which I was mentally practicing for when I spotted the bird. Or perhaps it was the one that I was mentally willing someone else to say.

"Skua!" shouted Nate. This time it was real. "Six o'clock, on the horizon."

The horizon was a mess of gulls, and after several seconds of panic I still couldn't find the bird in my binoculars.

"Going left, below the horizon," shouted Kate. "Going away from the boat."

Away from the boat? That didn't sound good, I thought. I knew Great Skuas weren't curious about boats in the way many pelagic species were. They came in low and then beat a hasty retreat. Maybe I'd missed the window, my one chance . . . and then I spotted it. Even at this distance I could see how heavy the bird was, laboring over each flap.

"I've got it," I said. "Jay?"

Jay didn't have the bird. I could see his binoculars racing through the distant flock.

That's why we chase birds, because of the unpredictability and the frustrating uncertainty. To know and feel that we don't control the world, that there are still realms in which we haven't imposed order, and we have to let nature decide for us. Birds are perhaps one of the easiest ways to be reminded of the mysteries of life. But this one time, I wished this bird would cooperate.

It must have heard me. It turned and started to fly right toward the boat. Kate was shouting directions as the bird circled, and Brian was following it, expertly maneuvering the boat. I could hear the oohs and ahs of appreciation as we saw the bold white flashes of white in the brown wings, and the golden-brown flecking on the back. And I could hear that one of those oohs was Jay's.

It was the last bird I saw that year. After 250,000 miles, fifty-five rental cars, twenty-eight states, six provinces, fifty-six airports, and 195 days away from home (fifteen of which were spent on a boat, one in a kayak, and one up a tree), I'd seen 747 species. I'd missed the record by one bird.

My bird count at the end of December 2013: 747 (+3 provisional)
John Vanderpoel's bird count at the end of December 2011: 743
Sandy Komito's Big Year record, 1998: 748

EPILOGUE

"SURPRISE!"

Gerri is terrible at keeping secrets. For the past few days she had been baking a surprisingly large number of cakes for some nebulous other party as well as sneaking around the house, cleaning and furtively texting. By the time I returned home with my friend Bill from an evening drink at the Cambridge Common and saw the mountain of shoes that sat piled behind the front door, I wasn't too surprised at the surprise.

The biggest surprise was some of the guests who had been hiding in the darkness. I'd never met Jeff Gordon, the president of the ABA, but I instantly recognized his friendly, hirsute face from the pages of the ABA magazine, *Birding*. His wife, Liz, came bearing gifts: a Rufous-necked Wood-Rail and a Great Skua painted onto a pair of Christmas tree baubles. Seeing Jim McCoy reminded me of that first pelagic trip of the year out of Westport, Washington, shortly after I'd seen the "poo-tail" under that dark, aromatic canopy of cedar. And Jay Lehman had driven thirteen hours from Cincinnati (arriving only fifteen minutes before I did). I felt like one of those rare birds that I'd been chasing all year, inexplicably becoming the center of attention. But unlike a rare bird, I didn't feel lost. Not this time, at least.

It wasn't the first celebration. After seeing the Great Skua, Jay and I had swapped our sea legs for car legs and arrived late that night at Chris Hitt's home in Chapel Hill, North Carolina. Chris and his wife were ready with a chilled bottle of champagne and a simple toast: to the Big Year! It wasn't obvious then, or now, what exactly we were celebrating. Each of our Big Years had given us a bounty of birds, but had also given us something less tangible and less countable: a journey.

As I moved through the mixed flock of friends, sneaking bites of Gerri's bird-on-a-wire cookies and Jackie's owl cupcakes, I spied the photos that Gerri had tacked up on the walls: the birds I'd seen the previous year. To everyone else I'm sure they were just mediocre shots of unusual birds. But to me they were like a family photo album, memories to a secret narrative. I spotted the out-of-focus Fieldfare and remembered how lost I'd felt back then as I'd watched it jab at the frosted bloodred bittersweet berries. The image of the Swainson's Warbler stung, as I thought of the argument with Gerri about her moving in, and then the photo of the Mountain Quail (footprints in the gravel road) reminded me of how happy I was when she did. Many of the snapshots were reminders that I hadn't been alone, and I thought of the new friends the birds had introduced me to: Bristle-thighed Curlew (Hans), Buller's Shearwater (Jay), and Common Rosefinch (Chris).

The surprise party was like a birthday where no one quite knew how many candles should be on the cake. I still didn't know how many birds I'd seen. I'd ended the year at 747, one bird behind the record. Once again I felt like I was in a Jules Verne novel, this time like Phileas Fogg arriving home after circling the world in eighty-one days only to lose his bet by one day. Fogg forgets that he has crossed the international date line, which rather conveniently gives him that one day back. I remembered sitting on the cold, pea-gravel beach at Gambell the previous fall, looking for that invisible line, hovering somewhere in front of the Chukchi Mountains of Russia and imaging then my own race back to the oak-paneled rooms of the 700 Club. In the end I couldn't manufacture an extra day, but I did have my own plot device: three provisional species—potential first records awaiting a checkbox on my ABA Checklist. Unlike Fogg, though, I would have to wait considerably longer to calculate the discrepancy.

The Common Redstart from St. Paul Island was accepted by the Alaska Checklist Committee in December 2013 and then by the ABA in August 2014. It tied my record with Sandy Komito's record of 748 species. Shortly afterward, the same Alaska committee rejected the Eurasian Sparrowhawk we'd seen on Adak. Our photographs and descriptions weren't conclusive enough to eliminate similar-looking hawks. Meanwhile, the New Mexico Bird Records Committee accepted the Rufous-necked Wood-Rail in October 2014. The ABA sat on the decision for the rest of the year and into 2015. *Was there a problem?* I wondered.

While I was waiting for the results, I had time to reflect on the Big Year and what it had meant to me. It was easier to understand what it wasn't—a competition or an exercise in checking off birds. I was reminded how vast this continent is and how many birds are scattered across it, seldom seen without such a special effort. I imagine a Big Year is what many birders might do with only a year left to live, a final chance to say goodbye to the feathered friends that have brought joy throughout their lives. I suppose that's how I'd felt. I had been trapped under the ruins of a collapsed relationship, I'd quit my job, and depression had prematurely aged me, making me feel that the best years of my life were behind me. I'd always known about the magic of the birds, but until my Big Year I'd never guessed at the full power of their healing.

I made new friends that year, long after I thought that was possible. It's easy to make friends when you're young, when the world is new and shiny and when you need help to explore it. As you get older, the world shrinks as boundaries snap into position, hugging the new familiars of work, family, mortgage, and routine. The Big Year was the sledgehammer I needed to break out of that box, to see the world again with innocent eyes, to fill the memory card in my head, and to meet fellow explorers. The birds may have been the reason for my Big Year, and they kept me on the move, gave me a future to imagine, and filled me with wonder again and again. But they were also the surprising glue that formed human bonds in a way that no amount of thumbing through my field guide ever could have prepared me for.

As the colors came back to my world through Golden-winged Warblers, Red-flanked Bluetails, and Flame-colored Tanagers, so too did the discovery that maybe the real prize wasn't in the Bering Sea or in a tick-infested bog but rather at home. Gerri was also doing a Big Year, albeit one with less glamor and fewer birds. The biggest and best surprise at the end of my Big Year was returning home to discover that she'd survived and hadn't abandoned me for a normal life.

The Big Year somehow managed to thwart my fear of commitment. The distractions of the birds, travel, and rare-bird alerts allowed me to get to know Gerri at the right speed: slow enough to fall in love with her but not fast enough to erect permanent boundaries around the future and to be scared off by the familiar horror of commitment and adult decisions. I still worry about where we're heading. But it's the kind of fear I've learned to sit with, like waiting for a Tundra Bean-Goose to appear: discomfort from never knowing the outcome, but happy to accept the risk.

Gerri deserved a lot for putting up with the craziness of the Big Year and my slow thaw. Her Christmas present from me that year was a vacation to Hawaii the following summer. She accepted it gratefully, knowing that, unlike normal vacations to Hawaii, this one would involve long hours gazing out to sea and slogging through red mountain mud in search of new birds.

I'm still taking the tiny pills. I'll never know what role they played, or whether the real medication was feathered. But I do know the best prescription, at least for me, for a tired and spent life, was to leave my Hobbit hole and experience life in all its bigness. I'd left home with a list of questions: What do I do next with my life? How will I know the next relation-ship won't fail? Could mankind really lose the recipe for almond croissants? None of them had answers by the time I returned, and I suspect that if I'd looked in more places, I still wouldn't have found them. Maybe that was the biggest discovery of the Big Year: that there are no simple answers in life, no guarantees, no right paths, and that that's okay.

In June of 2015 the American Birding Association Checklist Committee accepted the Rufous-necked Wood-Rail and created a new checkbox on its list. Long after the end-of-year celebrations had ended, the shoes had been returned to the correct feet, the owl cupcakes had been consumed, and a pair of cats had emerged from their hidey holes, I added the last bird to my 2013 year list: number 749. It was, I had to admit, rather a big year.

ACKNOWLEDGMENTS

Watching birds and writing a book share a surprising number of similarities. Both involve long periods of time hoping for something interesting to happen, although in my experience the birds were almost always more obliging than the cursor. As I traded in the long hours of travel behind a windshield for the equally slow periods of inertia in front of a laptop screen, I found myself chasing ideas and memories that would disappear as fleetingly and maddeningly as many of the avian targets of the year before. Finding the birds and the words both involved a surprisingly large checklist of very talented and generous people. Without them none of this would have happened. It also wouldn't have been half as much fun.

My special thanks go to my wonderful agent, Laurie Abkemeier, for her sharp eyes in spotting a story among the overgrown foliage of a Big Year bird race and for her patience in waiting for it to finally reveal itself. Laurie's professionalism and ease of navigating the literary world made my job a lot easier. I couldn't have asked for a more encouraging publisher than Bloomsbury, or a more enthusiastic editor than

Jacqueline Johnson. Jackie's excitement in the project kept me going long after the frustrating discovery that there's a lot more involved in writing a book than making it to the final sentence. I'd also like to thank Sara Kitchen, my production editor at Bloomsbury, for her expert scrutiny of the tertial patterns, primary projections, and plumage molts of the English language. I suspect she'd make a fine birder herself. Special thanks also to Paul Lehman, whose authority on birding is matched by his editorial eagle-eyed attention to detail. I'd like to think that proofreading my text in the lodge at Gambell, St. Lawrence Island, saved him from the wind that howled and screamed through the boneyards outside, but I know that's where he'd rather have been. Paul saved me from any number of ornithological mistakes. All of which means I have no excuses: any errors in the text are most definitively and deliberately mine.

As for the Big Year itself, I left home looking for birds, and returned with a long list of new friends. In Chris Hitt I found not only a good friend but also a mentor. Chris taught me the Big Year histories, shared his own experience of a Big Year, and helped pick me up whenever I was flagging. He told me to go west to Alaska, a state hitherto unknown to me, and whose stark, raw beauty continues to draw me back. My time exploring the tundra of Nome with Hans de Grys was the happiest and most carefree of my Big Year. I quickly forgave him for his lack of a cape, a fluffy cat, or any of the other imagined paraphernalia of a Big Year arch-nemesis. And while his Big Year ended shortly thereafter, I'm happy to report that we've been able to pick up the friendship from where we left off (as long as he continues to leave the fluffy cat at home). I spent more of my Big Year with Jay Lehman than with anyone else. Despite wanting to lose myself among the birds, it was Jay who showed me that I could do both—experience the quiet of solitude and the camaraderie of a shared goal. Jay was one of the rare finds of the year, and I'm grateful for his kindness, generosity, and enthusiasm. I'm also grateful for his sense of humor, not least on our first day in Adak in the Alaskan Aleutians, when I totally and irrecoverably destroyed the bathroom plumbing.

Big Years can't be done alone. I'm grateful to the expert eyes of Aaron Lang, Alan Schmierer, Bob Barnes, Brian Patteson, Cameron Cox, Chris Traynor, Dave Lambeth, Dave Porter, Dave Sonneborn, David Sarkozi, Debi Shearwater, Doug Gochfeld, Gavin Bieber, James Huntington, John Drury, John Puschock, Jon Dunn, Kate Sutherland, Laurens Halsey, Melody Kehl, Nate Swick, Norm Budnitz, Paul Lehman, Scott Schuette, Terry Poulton, Tom Johnson, and others who helped me find rare and secretive birds on land and sea. I'd like to thank the many birders who shared their sightings of unusual birds, who invited me into their kitchens to spy a rare visitor to their yard, and who shared their refrigerator contents and spare bedrooms. The checklist of help is too great to thank each personally. You know who you are. Thank you.

Gerri was left to deal with the unglamorous side of the Big Year: airport pickups, canceled plans, and rearing Sally Cat and Khiva Cat single-handedly. She never made fun of the Big Year or tried to talk me out of the ridiculousness, somehow (rightly) sensing its importance to me. Her patience, support, and encouragement were unwavering at a time when I needed it most. I hope Gerri liked her Christmas present—the trip to Hawai'i the following summer. As predicted, there were a lot of birds for us to see—O'ahu 'Elepaio, Parrotbill, and 'Akohekohe. But I'm glad that we made time one day to watch the sunrise on Haleakala Crater. That's when I discovered that a Big Year doesn't necessarily need to involve birds: I asked Gerri to marry me and she said yes. But that, I suspect, is another story.

APPENDIX

The following is a chronological list of species recorded during Neil Hayward's 2013 Big Year. The American Birding Association (ABA) defines the territory as the US (excluding Hawaii) and Canada plus up to two hundred miles of gut-wrenching sea that form the sidelines. For a species to count, it must be alive, unrestrained, appear on the ABA Checklist for that year, and be conclusively identified by sight and/or call. Any species recorded during the year that is new to the territory can only be counted if retroactively approved by the ABA Checklist Committee. The clock starts ticking on Jan 1 and ends 365 days later. The only referee is the honor system.

Neil Hayward's Big Year Bird List

#	Species	Date first seen	Location	State/ province	Country
1	Canada Goose	1/3/13	Honey Pot Road, Hadley	MA	US
2	Common Merganser	1/3/13	Honey Pot Road, Hadley	MA	US
3	Bald Eagle	1/3/13	Honey Pot Road, Hadley	MA	US
4	Red-tailed Hawk	1/3/13	Honey Pot Road, Hadley	MA	US
5	Mourning Dove	1/3/13	Honey Pot Road, Hadley	MA	US
6	Belted Kingfisher	1/3/13	Honey Pot Road, Hadley	MA	US
7	Hairy Woodpecker	1/3/13	Honey Pot Road, Hadley	MA	US
8	Peregrine Falcon	1/3/13	Honey Pot Road, Hadley	MA	US
9	American Crow	1/3/13	Honey Pot Road, Hadley	MA	US
10	Horned Lark	1/3/13	Honey Pot Road, Hadley	MA	US
11	European Starling	1/3/13	Honey Pot Road, Hadley	MA	US
12	Snow Bunting	1/3/13	Honey Pot Road, Hadley	MA	US
13	American Tree Sparrow	1/3/13	Honey Pot Road, Hadley	MA	US
14	Clay-colored Sparrow	1/3/13	Honey Pot Road, Hadley	MA	US
15	Savannah Sparrow	1/3/13	Honey Pot Road, Hadley	MA	US
16	Song Sparrow	1/3/13	Honey Pot Road, Hadley	MA	US
17	Dark-eyed Junco	1/3/13	Honey Pot Road, Hadley	MA	US
18	Northern Cardinal	1/3/13	Honey Pot Road, Hadley	MA	US
19	Cooper's Hawk	1/4/13	Honey Pot Road, Hadley	MA	US
20	Common Raven	1/4/13	Honey Pot Road, Hadley	MA	US

21	Vesper Sparrow	1/4/13	Honey Pot Road, Hadley	MA	US
22	Rock Pigeon	1/5/13	Parc du Mont-Royal, Montreal	QC	CA
23	Black-capped Chickadee	1/5/13	Parc du Mont-Royal, Montreal	QC	CA
24	Lapland Longspur	1/5/13	Route 12, Bridport	VT	US
25	Barred Owl	1/5/13	Route 125, Cornwall	VT	US
26	Downy Woodpecker	1/6/13	Bob and Dana Fox's yard, North Andover	MA	US
27	White-breasted Nuthatch	1/6/13	Bob and Dana Fox's yard, North Andover	MA	US
28	Cape May Warbler	1/6/13	Bob and Dana Fox's yard, North Andover	MA	US
29	House Finch	1/6/13	Bob and Dana Fox's yard, North Andover	MA	US
30	American Goldfinch	1/6/13	Bob and Dana Fox's yard, North Andover	MA	US
31	Pine Grosbeak	1/6/13	North Wilmington Commercial Park	MA	US
32	American Robin	1/6/13	Behind Kohl's, Burlington Mall	MA	US
33	Yellow-breasted Chat	1/6/13	Behind Kohl's, Burlington Mall	MA	US
34	Northern Harrier	1/6/13	Honey Pot Road, Hadley	MA	US
35	Red-headed Woodpecker	1/10/13	Museum of Fine Arts, Boston	MA	US
36	Common Eider	1/10/13	Deer Island, Boston	MA	US
37	Common Goldeneye	1/10/13	Deer Island, Boston	MA	US
38	Barrow's Goldeneye	1/10/13	Deer Island, Boston	MA	US
39	Red-breasted Merganser	1/10/13	Deer Island, Boston	MA	US
40	Ring-billed Gull	1/10/13	Deer Island, Boston	MA	US
41	Herring Gull	1/10/13	Deer Island, Boston	MA	US
42	Iceland Gull	1/10/13	Deer Island, Boston	MA	US
43	Great Black-backed Gull	1/10/13	Deer Island, Boston	MA	US

(Continued)

#	Species	Date first seen	Location	State/ province	Country
44	Red-throated Loon	1/11/13	Salisbury Beach State Reservation	MA	US
45	Common Loon	1/11/13	Salisbury Beach State Reservation	MA	US
46	Horned Grebe	1/11/13	Salisbury Beach State Reservation	MA	US
47	Great Cormorant	1/11/13	Salisbury Beach State Reservation	MA	US
48	Red-breasted Nuthatch	1/11/13	Salisbury Beach State Reservation	MA	US
49	Red Crossbill	1/11/13	Salisbury Beach State Reservation	MA	US
50	White-winged Crossbill	1/11/13	Salisbury Beach State Reservation	MA	US
51	Common Redpoll	1/11/13	Salisbury Beach State Reservation	MA	US
52	White-winged Scoter	1/11/13	Parker River NWR, Plum Island	MA	US
53	Black Scoter	1/11/13	Parker River NWR, Plum Island	MA	US
54	Long-tailed Duck	1/11/13	Parker River NWR, Plum Island	MA	US
55	Red-necked Grebe	1/11/13	Parker River NWR, Plum Island	MA	US
56	Black-legged Kittiwake	1/11/13	Parker River NWR, Plum Island	MA	US
57	Razorbill	1/11/13	Parker River NWR, Plum Island	MA	US
58	American Black Duck	1/11/13	Parker River NWR, Plum Island	MA	US
59	Northern Pintail	1/11/13	Parker River NWR, Plum Island	MA	US
60	Double-crested Cormorant	1/12/13	JFK Bridge, Cambridge	MA	US

61	Bufflehead	1/12/13	Somerset St, Winthrop	MA	US
62	Mallard	1/12/13	King's Beach, Lynn/ Swampscott	MA	US
63	Bonaparte's Gull	1/12/13	King's Beach, Lynn/ Swampscott	MA	US
64	Black-headed Gull	1/12/13	King's Beach, Lynn/ Swampscott	MA	US
65	Western Grebe	1/12/13	Parker River NWR, Plum Island	MA	US
66	Tufted Titmouse	1/12/13	Bob and Bonnie Buxton's yard, Merrimac	MA	US
67	Brown Creeper	1/12/13	Bob and Bonnie Buxton's yard, Merrimac	MA	US
68	Carolina Wren	1/12/13	Bob and Bonnie Buxton's yard, Merrimac	MA	US
69	White-throated Sparrow	1/12/13	Bob and Bonnie Buxton's yard, Merrimac	MA	US
70	Blue Grosbeak	1/12/13	Bob and Bonnie Buxton's yard, Merrimac	MA	US
71	House Sparrow	1/12/13	Bob and Bonnie Buxton's yard, Merrimac	MA	US
72	Dovekie	1/13/13	Jodrey State Fish Pier, Gloucester	MA	US
73	Canvasback	1/14/13	Jamaica Pond, Boston	MA	US
74	Redhead	1/14/13	Jamaica Pond, Boston	MA	US
75	Hooded Merganser	1/14/13	Jamaica Pond, Boston	MA	US
76	Ruddy Duck	1/14/13	Jamaica Pond, Boston	MA	US
77	Pied-billed Grebe	1/14/13	Jamaica Pond, Boston	MA	US
78	American Coot	1/14/13	Jamaica Pond, Boston	MA	US
79	Sanderling	1/15/13	King's Beach, Lynn/ Swampscott	MA	US

(Continued)

#	Species	Date first seen	Location	State/ province	Country
80	Ring-necked Duck	1/16/13	Encanto Park, Phoenix	AZ	US
81	Neotropic Cormorant	1/16/13	Encanto Park, Phoenix	AZ	US
82	Eurasian Collared-Dove	1/16/13	Encanto Park, Phoenix	AZ	US
83	Gila Woodpecker	1/16/13	Encanto Park, Phoenix	AZ	US
84	American Kestrel	1/16/13	Encanto Park, Phoenix	AZ	US
85	Rosy-faced Lovebird	1/16/13	Encanto Park, Phoenix	AZ	US
86	Northern Mockingbird	1/16/13	Encanto Park, Phoenix	AZ	US
87	Curve-billed Thrasher	1/16/13	Encanto Park, Phoenix	AZ	US
88	Great-tailed Grackle	1/16/13	Encanto Park, Phoenix	AZ	US
89	Great Blue Heron	1/17/13	Salt River, Blue Point Recreation Area	AZ	US
90	Red-breasted Sapsucker	1/17/13	Salt River, Blue Point Recreation Area	AZ	US
91	Ladder-backed Woodpecker	1/17/13	Salt River, Blue Point Recreation Area	AZ	US
92	Hutton's Vireo	1/17/13	Salt River, Blue Point Recreation Area	AZ	US
93	Northern Rough-winged Swallow	1/17/13	Salt River, Blue Point Recreation Area	AZ	US
94	Verdin	1/17/13	Salt River, Blue Point Recreation Area	AZ	US
95	Phainopepla	1/17/13	Salt River, Blue Point Recreation Area	AZ	US
96	Yellow-rumped Warbler	1/17/13	Salt River, Blue Point Recreation Area	AZ	US

97	Lark Sparrow	1/17/13	Salt River, Blue Point Recreation Area	AZ	US
98	Loggerhead Shrike	1/17/13	Salt River, Blue Point Recreation Area	AZ	US
99	White-crowned Sparrow	1/17/13	Salt River, Blue Point Recreation Area	AZ	US
100	Cinnamon Teal	1/17/13	Riparian Preserve at Water Ranch, Gilbert	AZ	US
101	Northern Shoveler	1/17/13	Riparian Preserve at Water Ranch, Gilbert	AZ	US
102	Green-winged Teal	1/17/13	Riparian Preserve at Water Ranch, Gilbert	AZ	US
103	Gambel's Quail	1/17/13	Riparian Preserve at Water Ranch, Gilbert	AZ	US
104	Great Egret	1/17/13	Riparian Preserve at Water Ranch, Gilbert	AZ	US
105	Snowy Egret	1/17/13	Riparian Preserve at Water Ranch, Gilbert	AZ	US
106	Green Heron	1/17/13	Riparian Preserve at Water Ranch, Gilbert	AZ	US
107	Common Gallinule	1/17/13	Riparian Preserve at Water Ranch, Gilbert	AZ	US
108	Killdeer	1/17/13	Riparian Preserve at Water Ranch, Gilbert	AZ	US
109	Black-necked Stilt	1/17/13	Riparian Preserve at Water Ranch, Gilbert	AZ	US
110	American Avocet	1/17/13	Riparian Preserve at Water Ranch, Gilbert	AZ	US
111	Least Sandpiper	1/17/13	Riparian Preserve at Water Ranch, Gilbert	AZ	US

(Continued)

#	Species	Date first seen	Location	State/ province	Country
112	Dunlin	1/17/13	Riparian Preserve at Water Ranch, Gilbert	AZ	US
113	Long-billed Dowitcher	1/17/13	Riparian Preserve at Water Ranch, Gilbert	AZ	US
114	Wilson's Snipe	1/17/13	Riparian Preserve at Water Ranch, Gilbert	AZ	US
115	Inca Dove	1/17/13	Riparian Preserve at Water Ranch, Gilbert	AZ	US
116	Anna's Hummingbird	1/17/13	Riparian Preserve at Water Ranch, Gilbert	AZ	US
117	Black Phoebe	1/17/13	Riparian Preserve at Water Ranch, Gilbert	AZ	US
118	Marsh Wren	1/17/13	Riparian Preserve at Water Ranch, Gilbert	AZ	US
119	Blue-gray Gnatcatcher	1/17/13	Riparian Preserve at Water Ranch, Gilbert	AZ	US
120	American Pipit	1/17/13	Riparian Preserve at Water Ranch, Gilbert	AZ	US
121	Orange-crowned Warbler	1/17/13	Riparian Preserve at Water Ranch, Gilbert	AZ	US
122	Abert's Towhee	1/17/13	Riparian Preserve at Water Ranch, Gilbert	AZ	US
123	Red-winged Blackbird	1/17/13	Riparian Preserve at Water Ranch, Gilbert	AZ	US
124	Black-bellied Whistling-Duck	1/17/13	91st Avenue and Broadway, Tolleson	AZ	US
125	American White Pelican	1/17/13	91st Avenue and Broadway, Tolleson	AZ	US

126	White-faced Ibis	1/17/13	91st Avenue and Broadway, Tolleson	AZ	US
127	Turkey Vulture	1/17/13	91st Avenue and Broadway, Tolleson	AZ	US
128	Osprey	1/17/13	91st Avenue and Broadway, Tolleson	AZ	US
129	Burrowing Owl	1/17/13	91st Avenue and Broadway, Tolleson	AZ	US
130	Lincoln's Sparrow	1/17/13	91st Avenue and Broadway, Tolleson	AZ	US
131	Western Meadowlark	1/17/13	91st Avenue and Broadway, Tolleson	AZ	US
132	Yellow-headed Blackbird	1/17/13	91st Avenue and Broadway, Tolleson	AZ	US
133	Red-naped Sapsucker	1/18/13	Bill Williams NWR	AZ	US
134	Say's Phoebe	1/18/13	Bill Williams NWR	AZ	US
135	Nutting's Flycatcher	1/18/13	Bill Williams NWR	AZ	US
136	Bewick's Wren	1/18/13	Bill Williams NWR	AZ	US
137	Black-tailed Gnatcatcher	1/18/13	Bill Williams NWR	AZ	US
138	Ruby-crowned Kinglet	1/18/13	Bill Williams NWR	AZ	US
139	Crissal Thrasher	1/18/13	Bill Williams NWR	AZ	US
140	Pacific Loon	1/18/13	Havasu Springs Resort	AZ	US
141	Greater Scaup	1/18/13	Lake Havasu	AZ	US
142	Clark's Grebe	1/18/13	Bill Williams NWR, Headquarters	AZ	US
143	Costa's Hummingbird	1/18/13	Bill Williams NWR, Headquarters	AZ	US
144	Tree Swallow	1/18/13	Bill Williams NWR, Headquarters	AZ	US

(Continued)

#	Species	Date first seen	Location	State/ province	Country
145	Sandhill Crane	1/18/13	Mohave Road, Parker Fields	AZ	US
146	Mountain Plover	1/18/13	Mohave Road, Parker Fields	AZ	US
147	Greater Roadrunner	1/18/13	Mohave Road, Parker Fields	AZ	US
148	Prairie Falcon	1/18/13	Mohave Road, Parker Fields	AZ	US
149	Bendire's Thrasher	1/19/13	Baseline Road/ Salome Highway, near Buckeye	AZ	US
150	Le Conte's Thrasher	1/19/13	Baseline Road/ Salome Highway, near Buckeye	AZ	US
151	Green-tailed Towhee	1/19/13	Baseline Road/ Salome Highway, near Buckeye	AZ	US
152	Canyon Towhee	1/19/13	Baseline Road/ Salome Highway, near Buckeye	AZ	US
153	Brewer's Sparrow	1/19/13	Baseline Road/ Salome Highway, near Buckeye	AZ	US
154	Ferruginous Hawk	1/19/13	Santa Cruz Flats	AZ	US
155	Long-billed Curlew	1/19/13	Santa Cruz Flats	AZ	US
156	White-throated Swift	1/19/13	Santa Cruz Flats	AZ	US
157	Crested Caracara	1/19/13	Santa Cruz Flats	AZ	US
158	Merlin	1/19/13	Santa Cruz Flats	AZ	US
159	Vermilion Flycatcher	1/19/13	Santa Cruz Flats	AZ	US
160	Brewer's Blackbird	1/19/13	Santa Cruz Flats	AZ	US
161	Black-crowned Night-Heron	1/19/13	Christopher Columbus Park, Tucson	AZ	US
162	Pyrrhuloxia	1/19/13	Christopher Columbus Park, Tucson	AZ	US
163	American Wigeon	1/19/13	Roger Road WRF, Tucson	AZ	US

164	Harris's Hawk	1/19/13	Roger Road WRF, Tucson	AZ	US
165	White-winged Dove	1/20/13	Green Valley	AZ	US
166	Mexican Jay	1/20/13	Madera Canyon	AZ	US
167	Fox Sparrow	1/20/13	Madera Canyon	AZ	US
168	Golden Eagle	1/20/13	Florida Canyon	AZ	US
169	Canyon Wren	1/20/13	Florida Canyon	AZ	US
170	Cactus Wren	1/20/13	Florida Canyon	AZ	US
171	Hermit Thrush	1/20/13	Florida Canyon	AZ	US
172	Rufous-capped Warbler	1/20/13	Florida Canyon	AZ	US
173	Chipping Sparrow	1/20/13	Florida Canyon	AZ	US
174	Black-chinned Sparrow	1/20/13	Florida Canyon	AZ	US
175	Black-throated Sparrow	1/20/13	Florida Canyon	AZ	US
176	Lesser Goldfinch	1/20/13	Florida Canyon	AZ	US
177	Gadwall	1/20/13	Tubac Golf Course	AZ	US
178	Eared Grebe	1/20/13	Patagonia Lake SP	AZ	US
179	Botteri's Sparrow	1/20/13	Patagonia Lake SP	AZ	US
180	Lazuli Bunting	1/20/13	Patons' yard, Patagonia	AZ	US
181	White-tailed Kite	1/21/13	San Rafael Grasslands	AZ	US
182	Rough-legged Hawk	1/21/13	San Rafael Grasslands	AZ	US
183	Chestnut-collared Longspur	1/21/13	San Rafael Grasslands	AZ	US
184	Baird's Sparrow	1/21/13	San Rafael Grasslands	AZ	US
185	Eastern Meadowlark	1/21/13	San Rafael Grasslands	AZ	US
186	Brown-headed Cowbird	1/21/13	San Rafael Grasslands	AZ	US
187	Rufous-crowned Sparrow	1/21/13	Harshaw Canyon	AZ	US
188	Northern Flicker	1/21/13	Kino Springs	AZ	US
189	Gilded Flicker	1/21/13	Kino Springs	AZ	US
190	Gray Flycatcher	1/21/13	Kino Springs	AZ	US
191	Lawrence's Goldfinch	1/21/13	Kino Springs	AZ	US
192	Plumbeous Vireo	1/21/13	Patagonia Lake SP	AZ	US

(Continued)

#	Species	Date first seen	Location	State/ province	Country
193	Acorn Woodpecker	1/21/13	Sonoita Creek Preserve, Patagonia	AZ	US
194	Bridled Titmouse	1/21/13	Sonoita Creek Preserve, Patagonia	AZ	US
195	Rock Wren	1/21/13	Sonoita Creek Preserve, Patagonia	AZ	US
196	Pine Siskin	1/21/13	Sonoita Creek Preserve, Patagonia	AZ	US
197	Cassin's Sparrow	1/21/13	Patagonia Lake SP	AZ	US
198	Black Vulture	1/22/13	De Anza Trail, Rio Rico	AZ	US
199	Rufous-winged Sparrow	1/22/13	De Anza Trail, Rio Rico	AZ	US
200	Sharp-shinned Hawk	1/22/13	Montosa Canyon	AZ	US
201	Spotted Towhee	1/22/13	Montosa Canyon	AZ	US
202	Magnificent Hummingbird	1/22/13	Madera Canyon, Kubo B&B	AZ	US
203	Painted Redstart	1/22/13	Madera Canyon, Kubo B&B	AZ	US
204	Yellow-eyed Junco	1/22/13	Madera Canyon, Kubo B&B	AZ	US
205	Hepatic Tanager	1/22/13	Madera Canyon, Kubo B&B	AZ	US
206	Wild Turkey	1/22/13	Madera Canyon, Santa Rita Lodge	AZ	US
207	Arizona Woodpecker	1/22/13	Madera Canyon, Santa Rita Lodge	AZ	US
208	Wood Duck	1/22/13	Amado Wastewater Treatment Plant	AZ	US
209	Bronzed Cowbird	1/22/13	Amado Wastewater Treatment Plant	AZ	US
210	Lewis's Woodpecker	1/22/13	Tubac Golf Course	AZ	US
211	Western Screech-Owl	1/22/13	Patagonia Lake SP	AZ	US
212	House Wren	1/22/13	Patagonia Lake SP	AZ	US

213	Scaled Quail	1/23/13	Lake Cochise and Twin Lakes Golf Course, Willcox	AZ	US
214	Chihuahuan Raven	1/23/13	Lake Cochise and Twin Lakes Golf Course, Willcox	AZ	US
215	Snow Goose	1/23/13	Whitewater Draw	AZ	US
216	Ross's Goose	1/23/13	Whitewater Draw	AZ	US
217	American Bittern	1/23/13	Whitewater Draw	AZ	US
218	Greater Yellowlegs	1/23/13	Whitewater Draw	AZ	US
219	Ruddy Ground-Dove	1/23/13	Whitewater Draw	AZ	US
220	Common Yellowthroat	1/23/13	Whitewater Draw	AZ	US
221	Lark Bunting	1/23/13	Whitewater Draw	AZ	US
222	Western Bluebird	1/24/13	Catalina SP, Tucson	AZ	US
223	Golden-crowned Sparrow	1/24/13	Catalina SP, Tucson	AZ	US
224	Lesser Scaup	1/24/13	Roger Road WRF, Tucson	AZ	US
225	Black-throated Gray Warbler	1/24/13	Roger Road WRF, Tucson	AZ	US
226	Virginia Rail	1/24/13	Sweetwater Wetlands, Tucson	AZ	US
227	Sora	1/24/13	Sweetwater Wetlands, Tucson	AZ	US
228	Least Grebe	1/24/13	Sun Lakes	AZ	US
229	Brown Pelican	1/24/13	Tempe Town Lake	AZ	US
230	Harlequin Duck	1/26/13	Andrew's Point, Rockport	MA	US
231	Brant	1/27/13	Short Beach, Nahant	MA	US
232	Surf Scoter	1/27/13	Short Beach, Nahant	MA	US
233	Blue Jay	1/28/13	River Road, Stratham	NH	US
234	Hoary Redpoll	1/28/13	River Road, Stratham	NH	US
235	Black Guillemot	1/29/13	Bass Rocks, Gloucester	MA	US
236	Glaucous Gull	1/29/13	Jodrey State Fish Pier, Gloucester	MA	US
237	King Eider	1/29/13	Salt Island, Gloucester	MA	US
238	Northwestern Crow	1/31/13	868 W. 17th Street Vancouver	BC	CA

(Continued)

#	Species	Date first seen	Location	State/ province	Country
239	Brambling	1/31/13	868 W. 17th Street Vancouver	BC	CA
240	Golden-crowned Kinglet	1/31/13	Queen's Park, New Westminster	BC	CA
241	Red-flanked Bluetail	1/31/13	Queen's Park, New Westminster	BC	CA
242	Varied Thrush	1/31/13	Queen's Park, New Westminster	BC	CA
243	Cackling Goose	1/31/13	104th Street and Ladner, Delta	BC	CA
244	Trumpeter Swan	1/31/13	105th Street and Ladner, Delta	BC	CA
245	Eurasian Wigeon	1/31/13	106th Street and Ladner, Delta	BC	CA
246	Snowy Owl	1/31/13	Boundary Bay–72nd Street access	BC	CA
247	Short-eared Owl	1/31/13	Boundary Bay–72nd Street access	BC	CA
248	Tundra Swan	1/31/13	Dry Slough Road, Mount Vernon	WA	US
249	Mew Gull	1/31/13	Dry Slough Road, Mount Vernon	WA	US
250	Gyrfalcon	1/31/13	Dry Slough Road, Mount Vernon	WA	US
251	Northern Shrike	1/31/13	Dry Slough Road, Mount Vernon	WA	US
252	Rusty Blackbird	1/31/13	7th Avenue NE, Arlington	WA	US
253	Bushtit	2/1/13	Magnuson Park, Seattle	WA	US
254	Pacific Wren	2/1/13	Magnuson Park, Seattle	WA	US
255	Brandt's Cormorant	2/1/13	Alki Beach, Seattle	WA	US
256	Rhinoceros Auklet	2/1/13	Alki Beach, Seattle	WA	US
257	Black Turnstone	2/1/13	Alki Beach, Seattle	WA	US
258	Surfbird	2/1/13	Alki Beach, Seattle	WA	US
259	Glaucous-winged Gull	2/1/13	Alki Beach, Seattle	WA	US
260	Pelagic Cormorant	2/1/13	Point Brown Jetty, Ocean Shores	WA	US

261	Rock Sandpiper	2/1/13	Point Brown Jetty, Ocean Shores	WA	US
262	Laysan Albatross	2/2/13	Westport, offshore waters	WA	US
263	Black-footed Albatross	2/2/13	Westport, offshore waters	WA	US
264	Northern Fulmar	2/2/13	Westport, offshore waters	WA	US
265	Short-tailed Shearwater	2/2/13	Westport, offshore waters	WA	US
266	Western Gull	2/2/13	Westport, offshore waters	WA	US
267	Thayer's Gull	2/2/13	Westport, offshore waters	WA	US
268	Common Murre	2/2/13	Westport, offshore waters	WA	US
269	Ancient Murrelet	2/2/13	Westport, offshore waters	WA	US
270	Cassin's Auklet	2/2/13	Westport, offshore waters	WA	US
271	Great Horned Owl	2/3/13	Dungeness	WA	US
272	Thick-billed Murre	2/3/13	Ediz Hook, Port Angeles	WA	US
273	Pigeon Guillemot	2/3/13	Ediz Hook, Port Angeles	WA	US
274	Greater White-fronted Goose	2/3/13	Schmuck Road, Sequim	WA	US
275	Black Oystercatcher	2/3/13	John Wayne Marina, Sequim Bay	WA	US
276	Marbled Murrelet	2/3/13	John Wayne Marina, Sequim Bay	WA	US
277	Chestnut-backed Chickadee	2/3/13	Marymoor Park, Redmond	WA	US
278	Eastern Screech-Owl	2/4/13	Fresh Pond, Cambridge	MA	US
279	Mute Swan	2/4/13	Jamaica Pond, Boston	MA	US
280	Bohemian Waxwing	2/5/13	High Street, Plymouth	NH	US
281	Cedar Waxwing	2/5/13	High Street, Plymouth	NH	US
282	Lesser Black-backed Gull	2/6/13	Christopher Columbus Park, Boston	MA	US

(Continued)

#	Species	Date first seen	Location	State/ province	Country
283	Red-bellied Woodpecker	2/6/13	Boston Nature Center Wildlife Sanctuary, Boston	MA	US
284	Le Conte's Sparrow	2/13/13	Concord	MA	US
285	Purple Sandpiper	2/13/13	Eastern Point, Gloucester	MA	US
286	Monk Parakeet	2/15/13	Shakespeare Theatre, Stratford	CT	US
287	Black-billed Magpie	2/17/13	Waiparous Village	AB	CA
288	Gray Jay	2/18/13	Banff NP	AB	CA
289	Clark's Nutcracker	2/18/13	Banff NP	AB	CA
290	Mountain Chickadee	2/19/13	Johnson Lake, Banff	AB	CA
291	American Three-toed Woodpecker	2/20/13	Banff NP	AB	CA
292	Boreal Chickadee	2/20/13	Banff NP	AB	CA
293	Townsend's Solitaire	2/20/13	Johnson Lake, Banff	AB	CA
294	Gray Partridge	2/20/13	Nose Hill Park neighborhood, Calgary	AB	CA
295	Great Gray Owl	3/2/13	Green's Creek, Ottawa	ON	CA
296	Northern Hawk Owl	3/2/13	Old Quarry Trail, Ottawa	ON	CA
297	Black-backed Woodpecker	3/2/13	Stoney Swamp, Ottawa	ON	CA
298	Boreal Owl	3/2/13	Ottawa	ON	CA
299	Northern Lapwing	3/5/13	New Egypt– Brynmore	NJ	US
300	Common Grackle	3/5/13	Wrightstown	NJ	US
301	Barnacle Goose	3/5/13	Lincoln Park West, Jersey City	NJ	US
302	Tufted Duck	3/5/13	Heckscher Park, Huntington	NY	US
303	Fish Crow	3/5/13	Heckscher Park, Huntington	NY	US
304	Steller's Jay	3/7/13	La Veta	CO	US

305	Mountain Bluebird	3/7/13	La Veta	CO	US
306	Pygmy Nuthatch	3/8/13	Sandia Crest Road	NM	US
307	Cassin's Finch	3/8/13	Sandia Crest Road	NM	US
308	Gray-crowned Rosy-Finch	3/8/13	Sandia Crest, Cibola NF	NM	US
309	Black Rosy-Finch	3/8/13	Sandia Crest, Cibola NF	NM	US
310	Brown-capped Rosy-Finch	3/8/13	Sandia Crest, Cibola NF	NM	US
311	Western Scrub-Jay	3/8/13	Tijeras Ranger Station	NM	US
312	Williamson's Sapsucker	3/9/13	Coalmine Campground, Cibola NF	NM	US
313	Juniper Titmouse	3/9/13	Coalmine Campground, Cibola NF	NM	US
314	Sage Thrasher	3/9/13	Acomita Lake	NM	US
315	Pinyon Jay	3/10/13	Paul and Polly Neldner's yard, La Veta	CO	US
316	Harris's Sparrow	3/10/13	Paul and Polly Neldner's yard, La Veta	CO	US
317	Evening Grosbeak	3/10/13	Paul and Polly Neldner's yard, La Veta	CO	US
318	California Gull	3/10/13	Cherry Creek State Park	CO	US
319	American Dipper	3/10/13	Morrison Park	CO	US
320	Fieldfare	3/18/13	Carlisle	MA	US
321	American Woodcock	3/20/13	Parker River NWR, Plum Island	MA	US
322	Northern Gannet	3/23/13	Chincoteague NWR	VA	US
323	Tricolored Heron	3/23/13	Chincoteague NWR	VA	US
324	Red-shouldered Hawk	3/23/13	Chincoteague NWR	VA	US
325	Black-bellied Plover	3/23/13	Chincoteague NWR	VA	US
326	Piping Plover	3/23/13	Chincoteague NWR	VA	US

(Continued)

#	Species	Date first seen	Location	State/ province	Country
327	Willet	3/23/13	Chincoteague NWR	VA	US
328	Lesser Yellowlegs	3/23/13	Chincoteague NWR	VA	US
329	Black-tailed Godwit	3/23/13	Chincoteague NWR	VA	US
330	Marbled Godwit	3/23/13	Chincoteague NWR	VA	US
331	Laughing Gull	3/23/13	Chincoteague NWR	VA	US
332	Forster's Tern	3/23/13	Chincoteague NWR	VA	US
333	Eastern Phoebe	3/23/13	Chincoteague NWR	VA	US
334	Carolina Chickadee	3/23/13	Chincoteague NWR	VA	US
335	Brown-headed Nuthatch	3/23/13	Chincoteague NWR	VA	US
336	Eastern Towhee	3/23/13	Chincoteague NWR	VA	US
337	Boat-tailed Grackle	3/23/13	Chincoteague NWR	VA	US
338	Yellow-crowned Night-Heron	3/27/13	Scusset Beach State Reservation	MA	US
339	Winter Wren	3/28/13	Cold Spring Park, Newton	MA	US
340	Muscovy Duck	3/29/13	Southern Florida, birding by car	FL	US
341	Anhinga	3/29/13	Southern Florida, birding by car	FL	US
342	Cattle Egret	3/29/13	Southern Florida, birding by car	FL	US
343	Glossy Ibis	3/29/13	Southern Florida, birding by car	FL	US
344	Swallow-tailed Kite	3/29/13	Southern Florida, birding by car	FL	US
345	Pileated Woodpecker	3/29/13	Southern Florida, birding by car	FL	US
346	Mottled Duck	3/29/13	Pelican Island NWR	FL	US
347	Blue-winged Teal	3/29/13	Pelican Island NWR	FL	US

348	Wood Stork	3/29/13	Pelican Island NWR	FL	US
349	Little Blue Heron	3/29/13	Pelican Island NWR	FL	US
350	White Ibis	3/29/13	Pelican Island NWR	FL	US
351	Caspian Tern	3/29/13	Pelican Island NWR	FL	US
352	Northern Parula	3/29/13	Pelican Island NWR	FL	US
353	Palm Warbler	3/29/13	Pelican Island NWR	FL	US
354	Florida Scrub-Jay	3/29/13	Martha Wininger Reflection Park	FL	US
355	Common Ground-Dove	3/29/13	Bill Baggs Cape Florida SP	FL	US
356	Thick-billed Vireo	3/29/13	Bill Baggs Cape Florida SP	FL	US
357	Prairie Warbler	3/29/13	Bill Baggs Cape Florida SP	FL	US
358	Royal Tern	3/29/13	Crandon Marina Flats	FL	US
359	Common Myna	3/29/13	Crandon Marina Flats	FL	US
360	Ruddy Turnstone	3/29/13	Rickenbacher Causeway	FL	US
361	Purple Martin	3/30/13	Homestead	FL	US
362	White-eyed Vireo	3/30/13	Lucky Hammock	FL	US
363	Sedge Wren	3/30/13	Lucky Hammock	FL	US
364	Gray Catbird	3/30/13	Lucky Hammock	FL	US
365	Roseate Spoonbill	3/30/13	Everglades NP	FL	US
366	Stilt Sandpiper	3/30/13	Everglades NP	FL	US
367	Great Crested Flycatcher	3/30/13	Everglades NP	FL	US
368	Northern Waterthrush	3/30/13	Everglades NP	FL	US
369	Yellow-throated Warbler	3/30/13	Everglades NP	FL	US
370	Black Skimmer	3/30/13	Everglades NP	FL	US
371	Shiny Cowbird	3/30/13	Everglades NP	FL	US
372	Red-whiskered Bulbul	3/30/13	82nd Street, Miami	FL	US
373	Magnificent Frigatebird	3/31/13	Key West Botanical Gardens	FL	US

(Continued)

#	Species	Date first seen	Location	State/ province	Country
374	Short-tailed Hawk	3/31/13	Key West Botanical Gardens	FL	US
375	Ovenbird	3/31/13	Key West Botanical Gardens	FL	US
376	Black-throated Green Warbler	3/31/13	Key West Botanical Gardens	FL	US
377	White-winged Parakeet	4/1/13	University of Miami	FL	US
378	Spot-breasted Oriole	4/1/13	SW 23rd Avenue, Miami	FL	US
379	Least Bittern	4/1/13	Green Cay Wetlands	FL	US
380	Purple Gallinule	4/1/13	Green Cay Wetlands	FL	US
381	Limpkin	4/1/13	Green Cay Wetlands	FL	US
382	Painted Bunting	4/1/13	Green Cay Wetlands	FL	US
383	Snail Kite	4/1/13	Loxahatchee NWR	FL	US
384	White-crowned Pigeon	4/2/13	Saddlebunch Key	FL	US
385	Mangrove Cuckoo	4/2/13	Saddlebunch Key	FL	US
386	Black-whiskered Vireo	4/2/13	Key West Botanical Gardens	FL	US
387	Western Spindalis	4/2/13	Key West Botanical Gardens	FL	US
388	Baltimore Oriole	4/2/13	Key West Botanical Gardens	FL	US
389	Grasshopper Sparrow	4/2/13	Sparrow Fields, Miami	FL	US
390	Tropical Kingbird	4/2/13	Homestead	FL	US
391	Reddish Egret	4/2/13	Everglades NP	FL	US
392	Spotted Sandpiper	4/2/13	Everglades NP	FL	US
393	Chuck-will's-widow	4/2/13	Everglades NP	FL	US
394	White-tailed Ptarmigan	4/3/13	Loveland Pass	CO	US
395	Greater Sage-Grouse	4/4/13	Craig	CO	US
396	Dusky Grouse	4/4/13	Black Canyon of the Gunnison NP	CO	US
397	Gunnison Sage-Grouse	4/5/13	Waunita Hot Springs Lek	CO	US

398	Ring-necked Pheasant	4/5/13	Wray	CO	US
399	Greater Prairie-Chicken	4/6/13	Wray	CO	US
400	McCown's Longspur	4/6/13	Pawnee National Grassland	CO	US
401	Franklin's Gull	4/6/13	Neegronda Reservoir	CO	US
402	Lesser Prairie-Chicken	4/7/13	Holly	CO	US
403	Swainson's Hawk	4/7/13	Holly	CO	US
404	Cliff Swallow	4/7/13	Santa Fe Trail, Holly	CO	US
405	Snowy Plover	4/7/13	Neegronda Reservoir	CO	US
406	Baird's Sandpiper	4/7/13	Neegronda Reservoir	CO	US
407	Long-eared Owl	4/7/13	Loveland	CO	US
408	Plain Chachalaca	4/11/13	Sabal Palm Sanctuary	TX	US
409	White-tipped Dove	4/11/13	Sabal Palm Sanctuary	TX	US
410	Buff-bellied Hummingbird	4/11/13	Sabal Palm Sanctuary	TX	US
411	Golden-fronted Woodpecker	4/11/13	Sabal Palm Sanctuary	TX	US
412	Green Jay	4/11/13	Sabal Palm Sanctuary	TX	US
413	Black-crested Titmouse	4/11/13	Sabal Palm Sanctuary	TX	US
414	Clay-colored Thrush	4/11/13	Sabal Palm Sanctuary	TX	US
415	Long-billed Thrasher	4/11/13	Sabal Palm Sanctuary	TX	US
416	Black-and-white Warbler	4/11/13	Sabal Palm Sanctuary	TX	US
417	Nashville Warbler	4/11/13	Sabal Palm Sanctuary	TX	US
418	Olive Sparrow	4/11/13	Sabal Palm Sanctuary	TX	US
419	Crimson-collared Grosbeak	4/11/13	Sabal Palm Sanctuary	TX	US
420	Hooded Oriole	4/11/13	Sabal Palm Sanctuary	TX	US
421	Solitary Sandpiper	4/11/13	Brownsville, FM Road 3068	TX	US

(Continued)

#	Species	Date first seen	Location	State/ province	Country
422	White-tailed Hawk	4/11/13	Old Port Isabel Road, Port Isabel	TX	US
423	Barn Swallow	4/11/13	Old Port Isabel Road, Port Isabel	TX	US
424	Aplomado Falcon	4/11/13	Laguna Atascosa NWR	TX	US
425	Scissor-tailed Flycatcher	4/11/13	Laguna Atascosa NWR	TX	US
426	Altamira Oriole	4/11/13	Laguna Atascosa NWR	TX	US
427	Fulvous Whistling-Duck	4/11/13	Estero Llano Grande SP	TX	US
428	Short-billed Dowitcher	4/11/13	Estero Llano Grande SP	TX	US
429	Least Tern	4/11/13	Estero Llano Grande SP	TX	US
430	Common Pauraque	4/11/13	Estero Llano Grande SP	TX	US
431	Great Kiskadee	4/11/13	Estero Llano Grande SP	TX	US
432	Bank Swallow	4/11/13	Estero Llano Grande SP	TX	US
433	Cave Swallow	4/11/13	Weslaco	TX	US
434	Green Kingfisher	4/11/13	Edinburg Scenic Wetlands	TX	US
435	Chimney Swift	4/11/13	10th Street, McAllen	TX	US
436	Broad-winged Hawk	4/11/13	10th Street, McAllen	TX	US
437	Western Kingbird	4/11/13	11th Street, McAllen	TX	US
438	Red-billed Pigeon	4/12/13	Salineño	TX	US
439	Couch's Kingbird	4/12/13	Salineño	TX	US
440	Audubon's Oriole	4/12/13	Salineño	TX	US
441	White-collared Seedeater	4/12/13	Las Palmas Trail and Zacate Creek, Laredo	TX	US
442	Black-chinned Hummingbird	4/12/13	Neal's Lodges area, Concan	TX	US
443	Ash-throated Flycatcher	4/12/13	Neal's Lodges area, Concan	TX	US
444	Bell's Vireo	4/12/13	Neal's Lodges area, Concan	TX	US

445	Tropical Parula	4/12/13	Neal's Lodges area, Concan	TX	US
446	Yellow Rail	4/13/13	Anahuac NWR	TX	US
447	Seaside Sparrow	4/13/13	Anahuac NWR	TX	US
448	Eastern Kingbird	4/13/13	Anahuac NWR	TX	US
449	Rufous Hummingbird	4/13/13	High Island, Boy Scout Woods	TX	US
450	Blue-headed Vireo	4/13/13	High Island, Boy Scout Woods	TX	US
451	Red-eyed Vireo	4/13/13	High Island, Boy Scout Woods	TX	US
452	Brown Thrasher	4/13/13	High Island, Boy Scout Woods	TX	US
453	Prothonotary Warbler	4/13/13	High Island, Boy Scout Woods	TX	US
454	Tennessee Warbler	4/13/13	High Island, Boy Scout Woods	TX	US
455	Summer Tanager	4/13/13	High Island, Boy Scout Woods	TX	US
456	Scarlet Tanager	4/13/13	High Island, Boy Scout Woods	TX	US
457	Orchard Oriole	4/13/13	High Island, Boy Scout Woods	TX	US
458	American Golden-Plover	4/13/13	Rollover Pass, Bolivar Peninsula	TX	US
459	Wilson's Plover	4/13/13	Rollover Pass, Bolivar Peninsula	TX	US
460	Semipalmated Plover	4/13/13	Rollover Pass, Bolivar Peninsula	TX	US
461	American Oystercatcher	4/13/13	Rollover Pass, Bolivar Peninsula	TX	US
462	Red Knot	4/13/13	Rollover Pass, Bolivar Peninsula	TX	US
463	Western Sandpiper	4/13/13	Rollover Pass, Bolivar Peninsula	TX	US
464	Sandwich Tern	4/13/13	Rollover Pass, Bolivar Peninsula	TX	US
465	King Rail	4/13/13	Anahuac National Wildlife Refuge	TX	US
466	Pectoral Sandpiper	4/13/13	Anahuac National Wildlife Refuge	TX	US
467	Wilson's Phalarope	4/13/13	Anahuac National Wildlife Refuge	TX	US
468	Black Rail	4/14/13	Anahuac National Wildlife Refuge	TX	US

(Continued)

#	Species	Date first seen	Location	State/ province	Country
469	Common Tern	4/14/13	Anahuac National Wildlife Refuge	TX	US
470	Swamp Sparrow	4/14/13	Anahuac National Wildlife Refuge	TX	US
471	Upland Sandpiper	4/14/13	Anahuac National Wildlife Refuge	TX	US
472	Whimbrel	4/14/13	Anahuac National Wildlife Refuge	TX	US
473	Swainson's Thrush	4/14/13	High Island, Boy Scout Woods	TX	US
474	Hooded Warbler	4/14/13	High Island, Boy Scout Woods	TX	US
475	Rose-breasted Grosbeak	4/14/13	High Island, Boy Scout Woods	TX	US
476	Indigo Bunting	4/14/13	High Island, Boy Scout Woods	TX	US
477	Black Tern	4/14/13	Rollover Pass, Bolivar Peninsula	TX	US
478	Ruff	4/14/13	Anahuac National Wildlife Refuge, Skillern Tract	TX	US
479	Clapper Rail	4/14/13	Bolivar, Yacht Basin Road	TX	US
480	Buff-breasted Sandpiper	4/14/13	Bolivar, Fort Travis	TX	US
481	Yellow-billed Cuckoo	4/14/13	Lafitte's Cove, Galveston	TX	US
482	Eastern Wood-Pewee	4/14/13	Lafitte's Cove, Galveston	TX	US
483	Yellow-throated Vireo	4/14/13	Lafitte's Cove, Galveston	TX	US
484	Warbling Vireo	4/14/13	Lafitte's Cove, Galveston	TX	US
485	Wood Thrush	4/14/13	Lafitte's Cove, Galveston	TX	US
486	Worm-eating Warbler	4/14/13	Lafitte's Cove, Galveston	TX	US
487	Blackburnian Warbler	4/14/13	Lafitte's Cove, Galveston	TX	US
488	Yellow Warbler	4/14/13	Lafitte's Cove, Galveston	TX	US

489	Louisiana Waterthrush	4/18/13	Chestnut Hill Reservoir, Boston	MA	US
490	Northern Goshawk	4/21/13	Crane Pond WMA	MA	US
491	Pine Warbler	4/21/13	Crane Pond WMA	MA	US
492	Purple Finch	4/25/13	Bahama Woodstar stakeout, Denver	PA	US
493	Red-cockaded Woodpecker	4/27/13	St. Sebastian River Preserve SP	FL	US
494	Bachman's Sparrow	4/27/13	St. Sebastian River Preserve SP	FL	US
495	American Redstart	4/27/13	Fort De Soto County Park	FL	US
496	Blackpoll Warbler	4/27/13	Fort De Soto County Park	FL	US
497	Black-throated Blue Warbler	4/27/13	Fort De Soto County Park	FL	US
498	Nanday Parakeet	4/27/13	30th Avenue N, St. Petersburg	FL	US
499	Eastern Bluebird	4/27/13	Hernando Beach	FL	US
500	Gray Kingbird	4/28/13	Honeymoon Island SP	FL	US
501	Purple Swamphen	4/28/13	Chapel Trail	FL	US
502	Gray Vireo	4/30/13	Beeline Highway, Sunflower	AZ	US
503	Common Black-Hawk	4/30/13	Beeline Highway, Sunflower	AZ	US
504	Cassin's Kingbird	4/30/13	Beeline Highway, Sunflower	AZ	US
505	Western Tanager	4/30/13	Beeline Highway, Sunflower	AZ	US
506	Lesser Nighthawk	4/30/13	Sweetwater Wetlands	AZ	US
507	Dusky-capped Flycatcher	5/1/13	Madera Canyon	AZ	US
508	Lucy's Warbler	5/1/13	Madera Canyon	AZ	US
509	Hermit Warbler	5/1/13	Madera Canyon	AZ	US
510	Wilson's Warbler	5/1/13	Madera Canyon	AZ	US
511	Black-headed Grosbeak	5/1/13	Madera Canyon	AZ	US
512	Brown-crested Flycatcher	5/1/13	Madera Canyon	AZ	US
513	Gray Hawk	5/1/13	Madera Canyon	AZ	US
514	Broad-billed Hummingbird	5/1/13	Madera Canyon	AZ	US

(Continued)

#	Species	Date first seen	Location	State/ province	Country
515	Townsend's Warbler	5/1/13	Madera Canyon	AZ	US
516	Elegant Trogon	5/1/13	Madera Canyon	AZ	US
517	Greater Pewee	5/1/13	Madera Canyon	AZ	US
518	Red-faced Warbler	5/1/13	Madera Canyon	AZ	US
519	Northern Beardless-Tyrannulet	5/1/13	Florida Canyon	AZ	US
520	Five-striped Sparrow	5/1/13	California Gulch	AZ	US
521	Spotted Owl	5/2/13	Miller Canyon	AZ	US
522	Broad-tailed Hummingbird	5/2/13	Miller Canyon	AZ	US
523	Calliope Hummingbird	5/2/13	Miller Canyon	AZ	US
524	Cassin's Vireo	5/2/13	Miller Canyon	AZ	US
525	Grace's Warbler	5/2/13	Miller Canyon	AZ	US
526	Scott's Oriole	5/2/13	Ash Canyon	AZ	US
527	Buff-breasted Flycatcher	5/2/13	Huachuca Canyon	AZ	US
528	MacGillivray's Warbler	5/2/13	San Pedro House	AZ	US
529	Bullock's Oriole	5/2/13	San Pedro House	AZ	US
530	Violet-green Swallow	5/2/13	Madera Canyon	AZ	US
531	Whiskered Screech-Owl	5/2/13	Madera Canyon	AZ	US
532	Elf Owl	5/2/13	Madera Canyon	AZ	US
533	Mexican Whip-poor-will	5/2/13	Madera Canyon	AZ	US
534	Hammond's Flycatcher	5/2/13	Madera Canyon	AZ	US
535	Zone-tailed Hawk	5/3/13	Mt. Lemmon	AZ	US
536	Olive Warbler	5/3/13	Mt. Lemmon	AZ	US
537	Virginia's Warbler	5/3/13	Mt. Lemmon	AZ	US
538	Violet-crowned Hummingbird	5/3/13	Patons' yard, Patagonia	AZ	US
539	Band-tailed Pigeon	5/4/13	Portal	AZ	US

540	Western Wood-Pewee	5/4/13	Portal	AZ	US
541	Blue-throated Hummingbird	5/4/13	Cave Creek Canyon	AZ	US
542	Dusky Flycatcher	5/4/13	Cave Creek Canyon	AZ	US
543	Heermann's Gull	5/4/13	Kennedy Park, Tucson	AZ	US
544	Flammulated Owl	5/4/13	Mt. Lemmon	AZ	US
545	Montezuma Quail	5/5/13	Madera Canyon	AZ	US
546	Pacific-slope Flycatcher	5/5/13	Madera Canyon	AZ	US
547	White-eared Hummingbird	5/5/13	Miller Canyon	AZ	US
548	Bobolink	5/9/13	Bill Baggs Cape Florida SP	FL	US
549	Gray-cheeked Thrush	5/9/13	A. D. Barnes Park	FL	US
550	Common Nighthawk	5/9/13	Marathon Airport	FL	US
551	Antillean Nighthawk	5/9/13	Marathon Airport	FL	US
552	Masked Booby	5/10/13	Fort Jefferson, Dry Tortugas	FL	US
553	Brown Booby	5/10/13	Fort Jefferson, Dry Tortugas	FL	US
554	Semipalmated Sandpiper	5/10/13	Fort Jefferson, Dry Tortugas	FL	US
555	White-rumped Sandpiper	5/10/13	Fort Jefferson, Dry Tortugas	FL	US
556	Brown Noddy	5/10/13	Fort Jefferson, Dry Tortugas	FL	US
557	Black Noddy	5/10/13	Fort Jefferson, Dry Tortugas	FL	US
558	Sooty Tern	5/10/13	Fort Jefferson, Dry Tortugas	FL	US
559	Roseate Tern	5/10/13	Fort Jefferson, Dry Tortugas	FL	US
560	Veery	5/10/13	Fort Jefferson, Dry Tortugas	FL	US
561	Magnolia Warbler	5/10/13	Fort Jefferson, Dry Tortugas	FL	US
562	Bay-breasted Warbler	5/10/13	Fort Jefferson, Dry Tortugas	FL	US

(Continued)

#	Species	Date first seen	Location	State/ province	Country
563	Black-capped Vireo	5/11/13	Kerr WMA	TX	US
564	Field Sparrow	5/11/13	Kerr WMA	TX	US
565	Acadian Flycatcher	5/11/13	Lost Maples State Natural Area	TX	US
566	Golden-cheeked Warbler	5/11/13	Lost Maples State Natural Area	TX	US
567	Cordilleran Flycatcher	5/12/13	Big Bend National Park–Pinnacles Trail	TX	US
568	Colima Warbler	5/12/13	Big Bend National Park–Pinnacles Trail	TX	US
569	Lucifer Hummingbird	5/12/13	Christmas Mountain Oasis	TX	US
570	Varied Bunting	5/12/13	Christmas Mountain Oasis	TX	US
571	Ruby-throated Hummingbird	5/13/13	Warbler Woods, Cibolo	TX	US
572	Chestnut-sided Warbler	5/13/13	Warbler Woods, Cibolo	TX	US
573	Groove-billed Ani	5/13/13	Resaca de la Palma SP, Brownsville	TX	US
574	Philadelphia Vireo	5/13/13	Resaca de la Palma SP, Brownsville	TX	US
575	Red-crowned Parrot	5/13/13	Oliveira Park, Brownsville	TX	US
576	Alder Flycatcher	5/14/13	Bentsen–Rio Grande Valley SP	TX	US
577	Yellow-bellied Flycatcher	5/14/13	Santa Ana NWR	TX	US
578	Willow Flycatcher	5/14/13	Santa Ana NWR	TX	US
579	Green Parakeet	5/14/13	10th Street, McAllen	TX	US
580	Northern Bobwhite	5/15/13	King Ranch, Norias Division	TX	US
581	Mississippi Kite	5/15/13	King Ranch, Norias Division	TX	US
582	Hudsonian Godwit	5/15/13	King Ranch, Norias Division	TX	US

583	Gull-billed Tern	5/15/13	King Ranch, Norias Division	TX	US
584	Ferruginous Pygmy-Owl	5/15/13	King Ranch, Norias Division	TX	US
585	Dickcissel	5/15/13	King Ranch, Norias Division	TX	US
586	Ringed Kingfisher	5/15/13	Chalk Bluff Park, Uvalde	TX	US
587	Little Gull	5/17/13	Joppa Park, Newburyport	MA	US
588	Black-billed Cuckoo	5/17/13	Pike's Bridge Road, West Newbury	MA	US
589	Blue-winged Warbler	5/17/13	Pike's Bridge Road, West Newbury	MA	US
590	Eastern Whip-poor-will	5/18/13	Parker River NWR, Plum Island	MA	US
591	Wandering Tattler	5/21/13	Girdwood	AK	US
592	Red-necked Phalarope	5/21/13	Girdwood	AK	US
593	Arctic Tern	5/21/13	Girdwood	AK	US
594	Bristle-thighed Curlew	5/21/13	Anchor Point	AK	US
595	Aleutian Tern	5/22/13	Kachemak Bay, Homer	AK	US
596	Kittlitz's Murrelet	5/22/13	Kachemak Bay, Homer	AK	US
597	Tufted Puffin	5/22/13	Kachemak Bay, Homer	AK	US
598	Horned Puffin	5/23/13	Kachemak Bay, Homer	AK	US
599	Red-faced Cormorant	5/24/13	St. Paul Island, Pribilof Islands	AK	US
600	White-tailed Eagle	5/24/13	St. Paul Island, Pribilof Islands	AK	US
601	Red-legged Kittiwake	5/24/13	St. Paul Island, Pribilof Islands	AK	US
602	Least Auklet	5/24/13	St. Paul Island, Pribilof Islands	AK	US
603	Crested Auklet	5/24/13	St. Paul Island, Pribilof Islands	AK	US
604	Parakeet Auklet	5/25/13	St. Paul Island, Pribilof Islands	AK	US
605	Pacific Golden-Plover	5/25/13	St. Paul Island, Pribilof Islands	AK	US

(Continued)

#	Species	Date first seen	Location	State/ province	Country
606	Bar-tailed Godwit	5/25/13	St. Paul Island, Pribilof Islands	AK	US
607	Parasitic Jaeger	5/26/13	St. Paul Island, Pribilof Islands	AK	US
608	Wood Sandpiper	5/27/13	St. Paul Island, Pribilof Islands	AK	US
609	Pomarine Jaeger	5/27/13	St. Paul Island, Pribilof Islands	AK	US
610	Thick-billed Kingbird	5/28/13	Patagonia, roadside rest area	AZ	US
611	Sulphur-bellied Flycatcher	5/28/13	Madera Canyon	AZ	US
612	Common Poorwill	5/28/13	Madera Canyon	AZ	US
613	Buff-collared Nightjar	5/28/13	Madera Canyon	AZ	US
614	Northern Pygmy-Owl	5/29/13	Huachuca Canyon	AZ	US
615	Mexican Chickadee	5/30/13	East Turkey Creek, Chiricahua Mountains	AZ	US
616	Ruffed Grouse	5/31/13	Rice Lake NWR	MN	US
617	Yellow-bellied Sapsucker	5/31/13	Rice Lake NWR	MN	US
618	Golden-winged Warbler	5/31/13	Rice Lake NWR	MN	US
619	Canada Warbler	5/31/13	Rice Lake NWR	MN	US
620	Least Flycatcher	6/1/13	Sax-Zim Bog	MN	US
621	Connecticut Warbler	6/1/13	Sax-Zim Bog	MN	US
622	Mourning Warbler	6/1/13	Sax-Zim Bog	MN	US
623	Henslow's Sparrow	6/2/13	Murphy-Hanrehan Park Reserve	MN	US
624	Cerulean Warbler	6/2/13	Murphy-Hanrehan Park Reserve	MN	US
625	Olive-sided Flycatcher	6/2/13	Murphy-Hanrehan Park Reserve	MN	US
626	Kentucky Warbler	6/3/13	Kettle Moraine State Forest	WI	US
627	Emperor Goose	6/5/13	Nome	AK	US

628	Willow Ptarmigan	6/5/13	Nome	AK	US
629	Arctic Loon	6/5/13	Nome	AK	US
630	Red Phalarope	6/5/13	Nome	AK	US
631	Slaty-backed Gull	6/5/13	Nome	AK	US
632	Long-tailed Jaeger	6/5/13	Nome	AK	US
633	Eastern Yellow Wagtail	6/5/13	Nome	AK	US
634	Rock Ptarmigan	6/6/13	Nome	AK	US
635	Northern Wheatear	6/6/13	Nome	AK	US
636	Steller's Eider	6/6/13	Nome	AK	US
637	Bluethroat	6/7/13	Nome	AK	US
638	White Wagtail	6/7/13	Nome	AK	US
639	Sabine's Gull	6/7/13	Nome	AK	US
640	Arctic Warbler	6/8/13	Nome	AK	US
641	Yellow-billed Loon	6/8/13	Nome	AK	US
642	Kirtland's Warbler	6/10/13	Grayling	MI	US
643	Bicknell's Thrush	6/13/13	Cannon Mountain, Franconia	NH	US
644	Nelson's Sparrow	6/13/13	Scarborough Marsh	ME	US
645	Swainson's Warbler	6/14/13	Great Dismal Swamp NWR	VA	US
646	Manx Shearwater	6/19/13	Revere Beach	MA	US
647	Saltmarsh Sparrow	6/19/13	Parker River NWR, Plum Island	MA	US
648	Spruce Grouse	6/21/13	Moose Bog, Wenlock WMA	VT	US
649	Atlantic Puffin	6/23/13	Seal Island NWR	ME	US
650	Red-billed Tropicbird	6/23/13	Seal Island NWR	ME	US
651	Yellow-green Vireo	6/25/13	Resaca de la Palma State Park, Brownsville	TX	US
652	Flame-colored Tanager	6/26/13	Big Bend National Park, Boot Spring	TX	US
653	Red-necked Stint	6/28/13	Sandy Point State Reservation	MA	US
654	Black-capped Petrel	7/6/13	Hatteras, offshore waters	NC	US
655	Cory's Shearwater	7/6/13	Hatteras, offshore waters	NC	US

(Continued)

#	Species	Date first seen	Location	State/ province	Country
656	Great Shearwater	7/6/13	Hatteras, offshore waters	NC	US
657	Audubon's Shearwater	7/6/13	Hatteras, offshore waters	NC	US
658	Wilson's Storm-Petrel	7/6/13	Hatteras, offshore waters	NC	US
659	Leach's Storm-Petrel	7/6/13	Hatteras, offshore waters	NC	US
660	Band-rumped Storm-Petrel	7/6/13	Hatteras, offshore waters	NC	US
661	Bridled Tern	7/6/13	Hatteras, offshore waters	NC	US
662	South Polar Skua	7/6/13	Hatteras, offshore waters	NC	US
663	Oak Titmouse	7/10/13	Los Alamos County Park	CA	US
664	California Towhee	7/10/13	Los Alamos County Park	CA	US
665	Elegant Tern	7/11/13	Hollywood Beach	CA	US
666	Pink-footed Shearwater	7/11/13	Santa Barbara Channel, boat to Santa Cruz Island	CA	US
667	Sooty Shearwater	7/11/13	Santa Barbara Channel, boat to Santa Cruz Island	CA	US
668	Scripps's Murrelet	7/11/13	Santa Barbara Channel, boat to Santa Cruz Island	CA	US
669	Island Scrub-Jay	7/11/13	Santa Cruz Island, Prisoners Harbor	CA	US
670	Yellow-billed Magpie	7/11/13	Happy Canyon Road, Santa Ynez	CA	US
671	California Quail	7/11/13	Pine St, Santa Ynez	CA	US
672	Tricolored Blackbird	7/12/13	Arnold Road, Oxnard	CA	US
673	Allen's Hummingbird	7/12/13	Ocean Trails Reserve, Rancho Palos Verdes	CA	US
674	California Gnatcatcher	7/12/13	Ocean Trails Reserve, Rancho Palos Verdes	CA	US

675	Spotted Dove	7/12/13	Salt Lake Park, Los Angeles	CA	US
676	Nuttall's Woodpecker	7/12/13	Eaton Canyon Nature Center, Pasadena	CA	US
677	Wrentit	7/12/13	Eaton Canyon Nature Center, Pasadena	CA	US
678	White-headed Woodpecker	7/13/13	Buckhorn Campground	CA	US
679	Black Swift	7/13/13	Monkeyface Falls	CA	US
680	Barn Owl	7/13/13	Sonny Bono Salton Sea NWR	CA	US
681	Yellow-footed Gull	7/13/13	Sonny Bono Salton Sea NWR	CA	US
682	Northern Saw-whet Owl	7/13/13	Wildhorse Meadows	CA	US
683	Chukar	7/15/13	Galileo Hill, Silver Saddle Ranch and Club	CA	US
684	Sooty Grouse	7/16/13	Mt. Whitney Portal	CA	US
685	Budgerigar	7/22/13	Hernando Beach	FL	US
686	Fork-tailed Flycatcher	7/22/13	Lake Apopka	FL	US
687	Lesser Sand-Plover	7/23/13	Bayshore Bikeway, 7th St. San Diego	CA	US
688	Black-vented Shearwater	7/23/13	La Jolla seawatch	CA	US
689	Slate-throated Redstart	7/27/13	Huachuca Canyon	AZ	US
690	Black-capped Gnatcatcher	7/27/13	Montosa Canyon	AZ	US
691	Buller's Shearwater	7/28/13	Half Moon Bay, offshore waters	CA	US
692	Fork-tailed Storm-Petrel	7/28/13	Half Moon Bay, offshore waters	CA	US
693	Ashy Storm-Petrel	7/28/13	Half Moon Bay, offshore waters	CA	US
694	Little Stint	7/29/13	Central Valley	CA	US
695	California Thrasher	7/30/13	Kelso Valley Road, Kern County	CA	US
696	Berylline Hummingbird	7/31/13	Madera Canyon	AZ	US
697	Himalayan Snowcock	8/3/13	Lamoille Canyon	NV	US

(Continued)

#	Species	Date first seen	Location	State/ province	Country
698	Plain-capped Starthroat	8/4/13	LeMay/Behrstock yard, Hereford	AZ	US
699	Mountain Quail	8/9/13	Tassajara Road, Los Padres NF	CA	US
700	Blue-footed Booby	8/19/13	Patagonia Lake SP	AZ	US
701	Curlew Sandpiper	8/20/13	Mecox Bay	NY	US
702	Herald Petrel	8/25/13	Hatteras, offshore waters	NC	US
703	Vaux's Swift	8/27/13	Frank Wagner Elementary School, Monroe	WA	US
704	Sky Lark	8/28/13	Saanichton	BC	CA
705	Smith's Longspur	8/30/13	Ocean Shores	WA	US
706	Baikal Teal	8/31/13	Gambell, St. Lawrence Island	AK	US
707	Spectacled Eider	8/31/13	Gambell, St. Lawrence Island	AK	US
708	Sharp-tailed Sandpiper	8/31/13	Gambell, St. Lawrence Island	AK	US
709	Red-throated Pipit	8/31/13	Gambell, St. Lawrence Island	AK	US
710	Sinaloa Wren	9/7/13	Huachuca Canyon	AZ	US
711	Black Storm-Petrel	9/20/13	Bodega Bay, offshore waters	CA	US
712	Nutmeg Mannikin	9/21/13	Huntington Central Park	CA	US
713	Flesh-footed Shearwater	9/22/13	Dana Point, offshore waters	CA	US
714	Common Stonechat	9/24/13	Carr-Gottstein Park, Anchorage	AK	US
715	Common Rosefinch	9/26/13	St. Paul Island, Pribilof Islands	AK	US
716	Gray-streaked Flycatcher	9/27/13	St. Paul Island, Pribilof Islands	AK	US
717	Common Snipe	9/28/13	St. Paul Island, Pribilof Islands	AK	US
718	Olive-backed Pipit	9/29/13	St. Paul Island, Pribilof Islands	AK	US
719	Gray-tailed Tattler	10/1/13	St. Paul Island, Pribilof Islands	AK	US
720	Ross's Gull	10/3/13	Barrow	AK	US

721	Mottled Petrel	10/9/13	St. Paul Island, Pribilof Islands	AK	US
722	Eyebrowed Thrush	10/10/13	St. Paul Island, Pribilof Islands	AK	US
723	Least Storm-petrel	10/13/13	San Diego, offshore waters	CA	US
724	Bell's Sparrow	10/14/13	Upper Otay Reservoir	CA	US
725	Craveri's Murrelet	10/15/13	San Diego, offshore waters	CA	US
726	Golden-crowned Warbler	10/23/13	Frontera Audubon Center	TX	US
727	Eurasian Tree Sparrow	10/24/13	St. Louis, Dogtown	MO	US
728	Sharp-tailed Grouse	11/6/13	Grand Forks, western plains	ND	US
729	Amazon Kingfisher	11/10/13	Route 100, south of Harlingen	TX	US
730	Rose-throated Becard	11/11/13	Santa Ana NWR	TX	US
731	Streak-backed Oriole	11/12/13	Rattlesnake Springs, Carlsbad Caverns NP	NM	US
732	Sprague's Pipit	11/13/13	Bob Wentz Windy Point Park, Lake Travis	TX	US
733	Tundra Bean-Goose	11/15/13	Yarmouth Golf Club	NS	CA
734	Yellow-legged Gull	11/17/13	St. John's	NL	CA
735	Pink-footed Goose	11/18/13	Tidal Bore Road, Truro	NS	CA
736	Rufous-backed Robin	11/20/13	Cameron Trading Post	AZ	US
737	Sagebrush Sparrow	11/21/13	Baseline Road/ Salome Highway, near Buckeye	AZ	US
738	Dusky Thrush	11/29/13	Anchorage	AK	US
739	McKay's Bunting	11/30/13	Nome	AK	US
740	American Flamingo	12/3/13	Cox Bay	TX	US
741	Whooping Crane	12/3/13	Aransas NWR	TX	US
742	Whooper Swan	12/6/13	Adak Island	AK	US
743	Whiskered Auklet	12/7/13	Adak Island	AK	US

(Continued)

#	Species	Date first seen	Location	State/ province	Country
744	Little Bunting	12/14/13	McKinleyville Bottoms	CA	US
745	La Sagra's Flycatcher	12/16/13	Matheson Hammock	FL	US
746	Rustic Bunting	12/18/13	Homer	AK	US
747	Great Skua	12/28/13	Hatteras, offshore waters	NC	US
	Provisional species				
Rejected	Eurasian Sparrowhawk	12/7/13	Adak Island	AK	US
748	Common Redstart	10/8/13	St. Paul Island, Pribilof Islands	AK	US
749	Rufous-necked Wood-Rail	7/8/13	Bosque del Apache NWR	NM	US

LIST OF ILLUSTRATIONS

All images created by the author.

INDEX

Note: The abbreviation NH refers to Neil Hayward

A NOTE ON THE AUTHOR

Neil Hayward is a lifelong birder with a passion for science and travel. He grew up in the UK, where birding ranks high among soccer, tea, and sarcasm as national pastimes. After gaining a Ph.D. in genetics at Cambridge University, he joined a start-up biotech company and moved to Cambridge, Massachusetts, as the managing director for the US business. He also brought his binoculars and quickly started using them. In 2011, he left his job to set up his own biotechnology consulting company.

Neil is the field trip coordinator and board director for the Brookline Bird Club, the most active birding club in the country, for which he leads free birding walks. He is also a council member of the Nuttall Ornithological Club, and teaches birding classes at the Cambridge Center for Adult Education. Neil has spoken at birding festivals, ornithological clubs and associations, bird clubs, and Audubon Society chapters throughout the United States. He lives with his wife, Gerri, in Cambridge, Massachusetts. This is his first book.